L'Amour Actually

L'AMOUR ACTUALLY

Summersdale Publishers Ltd
46 West Street
Chichester
West Sussex
PO19 1RP
UK

www.summersdale.com

Printed and bound by CPI Group (UK) Ltd, Croydon, CR0 4YY

ISBN: 978-1-84953-419-2

Substantial discounts on bulk quantities of Summersdale books are available to corporations, professional associations and other organisations. For details contact Nicky Douglas by telephone: +44 (0) 1243 756902, fax: +44 (0) 1243 786300 or email: nicky@summersdale.com.

L'Amour Actually

Falling in love
in the heart of France

Melanie Jones

summersdale

*For Ciaran and Emily,
still my greatest achievements*

Chapter One

'Ladies and gentlemen, as the captain has now illuminated the "Fasten Seatbelts" sign, would you please return to your seats...'

The gentle Irish lilt of the stewardess roused me from my daydreams and as the plane started its descent into South West France, I took a deep breath. I knew that the slightly sick feeling in the pit of my stomach had more to do with the reality of starting a new life in another country than the change in altitude. What on earth had I been thinking? Was it really only three months since that awful day at work when I had decided to leave everything I knew and loved in London, and move to deepest rural France? It had seemed such a good plan at the time. Well, at least to me. Now, as the reality began to sink in, I had to admit that the whole thing seemed like a rubbish idea.

I had secretly hoped my boyfriend of the past year would want to share my dream of living the good life, but Alex had just laughed and told me to let him know when I came to my senses. He had said it in that particularly patronising way of his that made me want to squeeze his neck. Tight. Although he wasn't Mr Right – more Mr Right Now – a friendly face beside me and a bit of moral support would have made all the difference.

'Ahhhh, I always breathe a sigh of relief when I get home,' commented the woman in the next seat, leaning across me and absorbing the view from the tiny window as if she was a Russian dissident being allowed back to her homeland for the first time in decades.

And I'll breathe a blooming sigh of relief when you get home too, I thought. She was one of those irritating expat types and clearly felt she owed it to the world to impart every ounce of her superior knowledge about life in France.

'You speak the language of course, don't you?' had been her first question when I told her I was moving to France. We had barely taken off when the interrogation started.

'Well, not exactly. I did French GCSE but, it wasn't exactly my greatest moment.'

'But you did do a refresher course before you left, at least?'

'Er, not exactly.' Leafing through the pages of French *Vogue* at work probably didn't count.

'Oh!' she exclaimed. 'How on earth will you manage?'

'I'll be fine. I have a French dictionary, a phrase book and some language tapes, and I'm sure I can find some lessons when I get there. I mean, how difficult can it be?'

'Ah,' said the woman, wagging her finger in my face, 'many a person has said just that until they got to the subjunctive.' She was, as it turned out, a retired French teacher.

'Oh well,' she continued, 'I suppose you'll manage the same way as all the others who couldn't be bothered to learn the language. You'll just rely on those of us, like me,' she said pointedly, 'who do.'

I smiled politely and went back to the book I was reading, determined not to spend the rest of the flight being talked at by this woman. If I avoided engaging with her, I might just stand a chance.

'And then there's integration...'

I smiled and carried on reading. The woman was clearly on a roll and had no intention of stopping.

'Integration is the key. You have to find yourself a few nice French friends. Get to know them and their way of life; join their clubs, not the expat ones. Learn how to play *boules*. Have people round for *apéros* or hold a few *soirées*. Watch out for the Brits, most of them are on the run from the taxman or their ex-wife.'

Or her, I thought before saying aloud, 'Oh, I'm sure that's not true. It's France, not the Costa del Crime.'

Damn. I'd broken the rules and engaged her in conversation. That was definitely A Bad Move.

'They're all builders from Birmingham...'

'What? All of them?' I was starting to get a bit irritated.

'Well, those that haven't re-invented themselves. Everyone's apparently had some fantastic job and a marvellous life with a huge house in the country. No one ever comes from a council estate in Bradford. Which, of course, begs the question, why are they here? So what did you do?'

'Celebrity PR, films, that sort of thing.'

The woman looked at me disbelievingly.

'Of course you did. Well Trevor, that's my husband...'

Poor bugger, I thought.

'... and I never mix with the English. What's the point of moving to a foreign country then building your own Little England?'

I realised that if I didn't stop her right then, she'd be bending my ear all the way to France.

'Actually,' I said, leaning in towards the woman, 'I'm planning to integrate my way into the boxers of the first good-looking Frenchman I see. Can't think of any better way to learn the language myself. You wouldn't happen to know the French for "Fancy a shag?" would you? *Voulez-vous coucher avec moi* just seems a bit 1970s these days.'

The woman recoiled as if she'd been slapped. I winked at her and went back to my book. Shock and bore, I thought. It works every time. I shock you because you bore me.

Still, at least the woman had given me a whole new vocabulary to look up in my ridiculously outsized English/French dictionary, a present from my former boss, office Lothario and all-round buffoon.

As the plane touched down, I craned my neck to catch a glimpse of my newly adopted homeland. From today onwards I was no longer Miss Jones of Flat 6, Morton House, Wandsworth; I was *Mademoiselle* Jones of Les Tuileries, a little cottage that I'd found on the Internet in the hamlet of St Amans de Pierrepoint. How cool was that?

Well, not very, according to my friends. There had been a real tumbleweed moment when I'd dropped that particular bombshell. I could still picture their looks of complete disbelief that a confirmed city girl like me would even entertain the idea of moving to the country. They really didn't get my need to change my life and slow down a bit, or understand that I felt I couldn't do this just by moving to the Home Counties, as my sister had suggested.

'Yes, but why France?' Daisy had asked me on that fateful evening when I'd told her.

I couldn't really explain why France. It was just something I wanted to do while I was still young enough to give it a try. Still, at least they had come round to the idea in the end.

The plane taxied to a halt outside a small metal hut, which, I was reliably informed by Ms Know-all in the next seat, was the airport terminal building. I'd been expecting the airport to be something along the lines of Exeter, or maybe even Bristol; but frankly, I'd seen bigger village halls than this. Blimey, I thought, how on earth did O'BrianAir ever find this place, never mind decide to operate flights to it? It was little more than a runway in the middle of open fields.

Tripping gingerly down the aircraft steps in my heels – well, a girl had to keep up appearances, even in the French countryside – I paused for a moment to breathe in the pure, clean air of rural France. The pollution of central London was a thing of the past for me now. I took a deep breath.

'Jesus Christ!' I spluttered. 'What on earth is that awful stench?'

A few hundred metres away I spotted a large herd of doe-eyed, cream-coloured cows all lined up along a fence like a welcoming committee. A mist of flies hovered around them. Cows mean only one thing to me. Cowpats. And these cows were filthy. Nothing like the ones in the butter adverts at home.

Up to that point, my only real taste of country life was when a client had invited me to his country house for a weekend shooting party. It hadn't been my sort of thing in the slightest and I certainly didn't see myself as a tweed and wellies girl; but sometimes you just have to take one for the team. His 4,000-acre estate had been put to good arable use, so to me the countryside was a fragrant place, heavy with the rich smell of ripening corn. I was the first to admit that my idea of rural life came from *Country Living* magazine rather than *Farmers Weekly*, but I still hadn't expected it to be this smelly.

At least the sun was shining. A brief twinge of pity for my friends, stuck in their dull offices in cold, rainy London, pricked my consciousness. OK, so the weather had been beautiful when I left, but it made me feel better to imagine it that way.

I tottered across the tarmac towards a sign saying *'Entrée'*, that hung drunkenly over a doorway leading into the terminal. Inside, I found myself sweltering in the intense heat of a single room which served as either Arrivals or Departures depending on the time of day, but had certainly never been blessed with anything as twenty-first century as air conditioning. Within seconds, little rivulets of sweat started to course down my back and the fetid smell of several hundred perspiring bodies assaulted my senses.

Everyone was crowded round a rather Heath Robinson baggage reclaim belt, which was little more than a long table with rollers. Through the plastic flaps in the wall, I could just make out a sturdy, thickset man, complete with bushy moustache, frantically slinging all the cases onto the table. The eager hands of the passengers propelled them along the rollers to their owners, while the unclaimed ones were left to drop unceremoniously onto the floor. Until I was sure I was going to stay in France, I had decided to downsize my life into one very overstuffed suitcase. The rest of my belongings were in my parents' loft.

Barging my way desperately through the milling passengers, I just managed to catch sight of my beloved vintage Louis Vuitton suitcase (genuine, of course) as it arced off the baggage reclaim belt and onto the cement below. To my horror, it sprang open as it hit the floor, spilling out my clothes and worse still, my best La Perla lacy knickers which were immediately trampled underfoot. Silently I cursed my sister for losing the key.

Uttering cries of 'Excuse me' and *'Excusez-moi'*, one of the few phrases I remembered from my GCSE French (which I'd failed dismally), I pushed through the crowds and threw myself down on the ground to wrestle my clothes from beneath the feet of my fellow passengers.

'Do you mind?' I shouted crossly, trying to extricate a pink thong from around the ankle of a military-looking man.

'What in God's name are you doing woman?' he boomed in a clipped, upper-class voice.

'Isn't it obvious? I'm trying to get my knickers off...'

'I *beg* your pardon?' he choked; his large, veiny nose glowing purple and his eyes bulging.

'No, off you, not off me! Look!' I pointed at his feet.

The man looked down to see a tiny scrap of material wrapped around his size ten Church's brogue.

'Call those knickers? More like bally dental floss if you ask me.'

I smiled weakly as he lifted his foot to release my thong, while I scrabbled around on the floor, shoving assorted items of well-trodden clothing back into the case.

With all items restored to their rightful place, I straightened up, smoothed down my ruffled hair and joined the queue for what was laughingly called Passport Control – just the one very grumpy looking border guard sitting behind a little wooden desk. Thinking I'd better give home a quick ring to say I had arrived safely, I rummaged in my handbag for my mobile. Pressing the 'on' button, I waited for it to burst into life. Nothing. The little phone icon had a nasty black bar going through it.

'No network, *mademoiselle*,' said a lady standing near me, her English heavily accented, 'you cannot get a signal 'ere. You 'ave to use the phone box.'

'Does it take bank cards?' I asked.

The lady looked at me quizzically. 'Cards? Non, *espèces* only, 'ow you say, cash.'

'Cash? Gosh, I haven't seen a phone box like that for years. How quaint. OK, thanks anyway, um, *merci*,' I said, wishing it had occurred to me to bring some euro coins as well as notes.

As the queue gradually got shorter, I indulged in a little bit of people watching. There seemed to be far more English voices than French. In fact, it reminded me of a donkey sanctuary what with all the braying that was going on. When I finally got to the head of the queue, I wished the border guard a cheery *'bonjour'* and handed over my passport. He looked at it closely then looked at me. All right, so my passport did make me look like a member of a terrorist cell, but wasn't it a universal truth that passport photos made you look either slightly deranged or like the latest mass murderer?

He narrowed his eyes, studying me from beneath a pair of spectacularly shaggy eyebrows, then slapped my passport closed and shoved it back at me with a gruff *'merci'*. I had hoped for something a little more auspicious to mark the beginning of my new life in France. Surely it warranted bells and whistles or something? Taking my passport and suitcase, I headed outside to the taxi rank – except there didn't seem to be one. I threaded my way through groups of hugging relatives and friends to have a better look. Nope, there definitely wasn't one. Maybe you just had to wait and one would turn up.

Lugging my increasingly cumbersome suitcase to the front of the terminal building, I cursed my decision to make a pair of spike-heeled Louboutins the footwear of choice for the trip. There wasn't even a proper footpath, just what looked like builders' rubble everywhere. Not ideal in heels. Must be all those builders from Birmingham emptying out their boots before they start their new lives as retired brain surgeons, I thought, making my way carefully along the path.

From out of nowhere, a huge people carrier with blacked-out windows purred up to the kerb, the rear door sliding open automatically before it had even stopped. A young woman wearing oversized sunglasses which covered half her face pushed past me and, almost knocking me off my feet, jumped into the back.

'Well don't mind me!' I shouted crossly.

The woman didn't even look up as the door slammed shut and the car took off at speed. I glared up the road after it.

'It was her, I'm telling you Mum,' I overheard a teenage girl say as she passed me.

'It can't have been. What would *she* be doing here?' her mother replied.

Who? I thought, wondering if I dare ask them. In my line of work, I mixed with famous faces all the time and although I had only glimpsed the woman briefly, she certainly didn't strike me as anyone I should have known. Oh well, now I'd probably never know.

Dumping my suitcase on the ground, I sat on it and waited for a taxi to arrive... and waited and waited. Half an hour later I was still sitting there, increasingly hot and bothered and wondering whether I would ever make it to Les Tuileries this side of Christmas. By this time, the airport was deserted, my fellow passengers had long since left. Who would have thought it? An airport deserted in the middle of the day. Where were all the flights? In desperation, I went back into the terminal building in search of someone, anyone, who might be able to help me find a taxi.

'Hello, hello. Anybody there?' My voice echoed around the empty building. 'Hello? Please, is anybody there?'

I heard the muffled sound of footsteps and eventually a door opened, revealing a middle-aged woman with a shock of frighteningly orange hair.

'*Oui?*'

'Do you speak English... er, *parlez-vous anglais?*' I asked hopefully.

'A little bit. Can I 'elp you?' replied the woman.

'I need a taxi, *un taxi*. To St Amans de Pierrepoint.'

'A taxi, *hein?* You call Gérard. I give you his number. He 'as a taxi. He will come.'

She scribbled a number down on an old boarding card and handed it to me.

'Um, there's one other *petit problème, madame*, I don't have any coins on me, only notes. Could you change a fifty-euro note?'

The woman raised her eyebrows so far that they disappeared into the orange thatch.

'I am not *une banque, mademoiselle*.' Muttering to herself, she rooted around in her pocket and withdrew a handful of cash mixed up among a load of old sweet wrappers.

'*Tenez*,' she said, handing me a euro before disappearing back into the bowels of the terminal building.

'*Merci, merci, madame*,' I called out to the woman's departing back. She responded with the slightest of Gallic shrugs.

Thankfully the telephone was working, a welcome change from the ones near my flat in London. Not that I ever used them of course, who did these days? After a few rings, a deep male voice answered the phone.

'*Allo, oui*.'

'Er, *parlez-vous anglais, monsieur?*'

'*Non, désolé, français*.'

Bugger, bugger, bugger! I took a deep breath to compose myself.

'*Je voudrais un taxi* to St Amans de Pierrepoint from the *aéroport*,' I said in my best French, hoping I had got my tenses right. Never mind integration, it was conjugation that really mattered.

The man replied in a machine-gun staccato of completely unintelligible French. I didn't catch a single word. Damn, I thought, wishing I'd put more effort in to learning the language. A friend was studying French at night school and had given me some tapes. I could say a few useful sentences, but I had completely overlooked the fact that the French would then reply to me in, well, in French. I hadn't a clue what he was saying. I decided to keep it simple.

'*Taxi, oui ou non, monsieur?*'

'*Oui, mademoiselle*,' the voice said slowly, over-enunciating as if speaking to a slightly stupid child. '*Cinq minutes*.'

Cinq, cinq? That's five. Five minutes. Brilliant!

Outside, I slipped my aching feet out of my shoes, perched on the Louis Vuitton and for the first time since arriving in France, sat back and took stock of the surroundings. The sun shone down from a cloudless, blue sky with just the faint wisps of a vapour trail breaking up the vast cerulean expanse. I slipped off my jacket and took advantage of the wait to catch a few rays. No more spray tans for me now, I thought, remembering the embarrassment of standing in my kitchen, stripped down to a pair of paper knickers and a fetching plastic cap while Kelly, the local beauty therapist, did her work with a spray gun.

Tilting my face skywards, I felt the sun turning my cheeks pink. It was heaven... if only that God-awful smell would go away. Still, wasn't this so much better? Life in London had become such a slog recently and I'd been overtaken by a sudden urge to get back to the land and grow my own vegetables. It was quite out of character considering that I originally came from Beckenham, and struggled to keep alive the little pots of basil and coriander on the kitchen windowsill in my London flat. I'd even thought about joining the Women's Institute. Instead, I had bought a copy of *Smallholder,* 'the leading monthly magazine for the amateur small farmer' the cover told me; as well as a rather lush shabby-chic Cath Kidston gardening set – currently unused.

It had seemed serendipitous to come across an old school friend, Polly, on Facebook. She had moved to France to 'live the dream' a few years previously and now ran a bed and breakfast in the Loire Valley. It had piqued my curiosity. I'd always found the idea of moving out of London unthinkable, but the more I talked to Polly, the more intrigued I became.

There was a real sense of community in the French countryside she had told me, unlike London where I barely even knew my neighbours. Mind you, with Tattooed Mary and her Rottweiler in the flat next door, I wasn't sure that being friends with your neighbours was all it was cracked up to be. It didn't matter how many times Mary told me he was a pussycat, every time I met the huge, slavering beast, I expected to lose an arm at the very least.

Polly had told me how everyone looked out for everyone else in the country and hardly a day went by without some shiny, happy local leaving a box of muddy potatoes or a few freshly laid eggs on the doorstep. I could just imagine if someone left something on my doorstep in Wandsworth. It would be gone in a nanosecond.

Yes, this was altogether much better. I checked my watch. The taxi should be here any moment now.

Chapter Two

Half an hour later, I was still sitting there staring hopefully up the long, straight road that led from the airport. Gérard, the errant taxi driver, clearly had a different understanding of *'cinq minutes'* than I did.

So far, the first impression I had formed of France was, well, that it was all very... empty. The stinking cows, chewing the cud and contemplating me with their large, brown eyes, were my only companions as far as the eye could see. They were starting to give me the creeps.

In the distance, a cloud of dust finally heralded what I hoped was the arrival of Gérard. An ancient Peugeot 106 slid to a halt. Hmm, not much chance of air conditioning in that then, I thought.

Gérard, a small, squat man in old jeans and a T-shirt that showed evidence of the remains of his breakfast and possibly last night's supper too, jumped nimbly out of the car, bid me *'bonjour'* with a toothless grin and swept up my suitcase. He pulled on an old piece of baling twine that was fed through a hole where the lock should have been, and the boot popped open. I wondered what he'd last had in the boot. Fowl of some sort judging by the amount of feathers and what looked suspiciously like bird droppings, and now he was about to put my favourite suitcase in there.

'Non!' I shouted a little too loudly, making him jump back like a scalded cat. He shoved my bag at me.

'I'll keep it with me thanks,' I smiled at him, feeling a little mean that I had spoken so sharply.

Gérard shrugged and motioned for me to get in the back. From close up it appeared that it had been some time since his last close encounter with soap and water, and possibly a toothbrush, not that there was that much left to brush. I wondered whether I'd still be able to get my teeth whitened here.

I handed him the address of Les Tuileries and Gérard took off at an alarming pace, all the while babbling on at me in unintelligible French whilst the ancient Peugeot bounced and rattled over the pitted road surface. Yet again, I wished I'd paid more attention to French lessons at school. Mind you, the very idea that I would one day move to France would have been laughable back then. Even the welcome, but sadly short-lived, addition of a very cute language assistant from Paris wasn't enough of an antidote to the linguistic Temazepam that was Madame Martin's dreary lessons.

Winding down the window a bit to get some cooler air circulating around the stuffy car, I leaned back and shut my eyes. I'd done it. I was in France. This was the start of my own 'French Dream'. As the wind tousled my hair and Gallic love songs spilled out from the crackly radio, Gérard hummed along softly. All was well with the world. My eyelids grew heavy and within minutes, I had drifted off into a light sleep dreaming of feeding my chickens, weeding my vegetable plot and bottling my delicious homemade jam while the smell of freshly baking bread wafted from my Aga – did they have Agas in France? It was a scene straight out of one of those French lifestyle magazines that

I'd been devouring hungrily for the past few months, and here I was, in the middle of it.

I was jolted awake as we went round a sharp bend and suddenly, in front of us and taking up practically the whole of the road, was an enormous agricultural machine. I shouted at Gérard who, startled, wrenched the wheel to the right and slid by the huge mechanical beast with millimetres to spare. I breathed again, we had made it. Suddenly I let out a scream as the old jalopy slid gracefully into a huge ditch, like a seal slipping off an ice floe, and came to rest on its side, wheels still spinning, churning up clouds of dust that floated in through the open windows.

Inside the car, I lay on my side, held in place by my seatbelt. My suitcase, which had been on the seat next to me, was on top of me, along with assorted detritus that had been in the seat pockets. As the dust settled, a quick check of my limbs revealed that nothing was broken and I struggled to undo my seatbelt. Gérard was already scrambling over the passenger seat to climb out through the door, a purplish bruise that was starting to form on his cheek the only visible evidence of how close we had come to disaster. He pulled open my door and pushed the suitcase out of the way, before hauling me rather inelegantly up and out onto the road with surprising strength for such a small man. The only casualty was my blouse, which caught on the window winder and tore open. Gérard averted his eyes chastely as I quickly pulled it together. Apart from that, we seemed to have escaped unscathed. The monster machine, a combine harvester, had stopped a bit further up the road and the driver was already racing back to the scene of the accident.

'*Ça va?*' he asked us, a worried look on his face.

Gérard nodded in the affirmative and with a dip of his head towards me said, '*Anglaise.*'

'Are you all right, *mademoiselle?*'

I nodded. Tears pricked the back of my eyes as I struggled not to cry. This was definitely not in the little tableau I'd created in my dream.

'*Oui*, yes, I'm OK.'

The driver made me sit down on the verge and produced a bottle of lukewarm water from one of the many pockets of his combat trousers. Gérard swilled his mouth out and spat noisily into the ditch before handing me the bottle. Eeuugh, I thought, but my mouth was full of dust and my throat was as dry as an African riverbed; so wiping the top vigorously on my skirt (and noticing that the combine driver took the opportunity for a quick peek at my legs), I drank deeply.

'*Crachez, mademoiselle,*' said the driver, feigning spitting.

Well this was a fine start to my dream; sat at the side of a road, filthy, my blouse torn, my hair hanging in dusty rats' tails and being told to spit in the dirt. The only spitting I had planned was at wine tastings at the local vineyards. On the positive side though, I had to admit, our rescuer was really quite cute. Out of the corner of my eye, I studied him more closely; he was tall and strong with thick, wavy chestnut hair and light hazel eyes that gave him an almost ethereal appearance. He had a bit of the look of Channing Tatum about him, just slightly more rustic. From the rolled-up sleeves of his shirt I could see tanned forearms, knotted with muscles, and through his combat trousers, I could make out a pair of seriously impressive thighs. He had full lips, perfect for... Oh, for heaven's sake, I told myself, you've only been in France for a few hours and you're already acting like a love-struck teenager. I gave him my best winning smile. Not easy when your face is covered in dust and your blouse is torn, revealing rather more *décolletage* than was probably decent in these parts. He looked at me strangely. Maybe this was considered a bit too forward out here in the sticks.

Pulling a mobile phone from his pocket, he punched in a number, speaking more quick-fire French that I couldn't understand. When he finished, he turned to me and choosing his words carefully, explained slowly in English that his brother would be along in a few minutes with his tractor to pull the car out of the ditch. As we waited, my phone suddenly sprang to life, emitting a symphony of beeps. Well, at least I now had a signal. I looked at the list of texts, mainly from my friends, wishing me luck in my new life. To them, my new life was just going to be one long round of sunshine and chilled *rosé*.

Not so far, I thought.

There was one from Madame Mollet, the letting agent:

> I am afraid I have a meeting and cannot come to Les Tuileries today. The key is in the post box. I call tomorrow. *Cordialement*.

The knight in shining armour came and sat down beside me.

'Julien d'Aubeville,' he said offering me his hand. Suddenly feeling very self-conscious, I took his hand and introduced myself, holding onto it for just a moment longer than necessary.

He pulled it away. 'Ah, you have a good French name, *hein?*'

I'd never really thought about it but, rolling off his tongue, it certainly sounded French and maybe even a little bit sexy.

'So where are you going?'

'To St Amans de Pierrepoint. Do you know it? I've rented a cottage there.'

'St Amans? Yes, I know it well. Our farm is only about half a kilometre from there. If you like, when we've got the car out of the *fosse*, the ditch, I will take you there.'

'Would you? That would be really kind. I don't think Gérard's car will be going far.'

A loud chugging engine and a whiff of diesel signalled the arrival of the tractor to pull the car out of the ditch. A young man jumped out and strode purposefully towards us. I did a double take, turned to Julien and then back to the newcomer.

I took in the same wavy, chestnut hair, hazel eyes and slight look of Channing Tatum. Hmm, things were really starting to look up.

Julien noticed me looking from him to his brother and back again.

'Yes, we are identical twins. Well, nearly identical. I am of course much better looking. This is my brother, Louis.'

'*Enchanté,*' Louis said putting out a work-roughened hand and giving me the once-over in a way that made me ever so slightly uncomfortable again.

I watched, fascinated, as the two brothers hitched up a cable to the back of the old Peugeot and then Julien leapt nimbly into the cab.

'*Vas-y,*' shouted Louis, giving his brother the thumbs up. Slowly and carefully, they started to winch the poor old car out of the ditch. It creaked and groaned arthritically as it inched out and I could hardly bear to watch. I was sure that the newly redesigned Peugeot wouldn't make it in one piece, but despite all indications to the contrary, within minutes it was upright and back on the road.

Julien stopped the tractor, climbed down from the cab and Gérard walked round the car to inspect the damage amid much huffing and scratching of his head.

'*C'est foutu,*' he announced sadly.

I looked to Julien for a translation.

'He said it's fucked.'

I resisted the urge to smile at his use of an Anglo-Saxon expletive, but looking at the damage to the car, I had to agree he had a point.

'You speak, er, good English,' I commented.

'No, I swear good. My English is actually quite shit. Me and Louis worked in Ashford in Kent for a while but it's the *trou du cul* of England so I came back.'

Trou du cul? I guessed it wasn't a compliment.

'Right. Yes, it's not a great place really,' I replied, making a mental note to Google Translate *trou du cul* as soon as I could fire up my laptop.

'OK, are you ready?'

'Yes,' I replied. 'Oh, wait a minute. My suitcase.'

Julien retrieved it from the back of the car and then put it in the cab of the tractor. He offered me his hand to help me to my feet and motioned for me to get in. I rated my chances of successfully climbing onto the tractor in heels as somewhere between nil and not a chance and in any case, my precious Louboutins were now ruined beyond any hope of repair.

'Oh well, new life, new footwear, I suppose.' It was clear that killer heels would be completely impractical in rural France. I bent down and removed them, planted a kiss on each toe and with all my strength, hurled them into the undergrowth. They might make a nice home for a mouse or something. Brushing my hands together, I hitched up my skirt and with a helping hand from Julien and a push from behind from Louis (though I did wonder if he really *needed* to touch my bum), I scrambled into the tractor, a knot of childish excitement in my stomach. I'd never been in a tractor before.

'It is not very comfortable,' said Julien, 'and you must hold on tight.' I looked for something to hang on to. '*Non*, you must hold on to me,' he smiled.

Oh well, if you say so I thought, wrapping my arms around his muscular chest and feeling the warmth of his back pressed into my breasts. I was sure I could feel his heart beating a little faster than was normal and I smiled to myself. There had definitely been a *frisson* of something between us.

We bumped along in the tractor, every rut in the road making me more aware of the hard muscles of Julien's body pressed up against me, separated only by my filmy blouse and his work shirt. I wondered how long it would take to get to Les Tuileries, secretly hoping that it would be a while. As we continued along the road for several miles, I had a panoramic view of the countryside from my vantage point in the cab. It stretched on endlessly but was worryingly devoid of any people. Where on earth were they all? I was just starting to wonder if I had picked the only part of France where cows outnumbered humans three to one when the tractor turned sharply up a hill.

'This is the road to your new home,' smiled Julien, a broad grin spreading across his face. 'That is our farm.' He pointed to a crop of buildings spread across the lower slopes.

'We are almost... *voisins*, how you say, neighbours. St Amans is just at the top of the hill.' His accent turned my knees to jelly.

The road wound its way up the hill, crossing over a little river that, Julien told me, gave the valley its name. Finally, we rounded a sharp bend into the hamlet. A cluster of pale stone houses of various shapes and sizes lined the main road, if you could call it that. A little lane led off to the left and what appeared to be a very grand house, almost a mini-chateau, sat shielded behind a dense row of poplars.

'*Salut*, Martine!' Julien called to a middle-aged woman tending chickens in her garden. She waved gaily to him and continued with her work. I couldn't help noticing that she appeared to be wearing a nylon housecoat topped off with a nice pair of pink, fluffy bedroom slippers. My friend Charlotte had a family holiday home in northern France and had told me about the dreaded nylon housecoat. God, French chic certainly did seem to have bypassed this little corner of France.

'*Salut*, Laure,' he called to a younger woman who had appeared at the door of the house. She didn't respond, preferring to look out at the world through a curtain of stringy hair.

I looked around, a rising sense of panic gripping me. Where was the local shop, an *épicerie* or *boulangerie* or something? Where was the village café where I had imagined myself spending lazy afternoons sipping a chilled glass of *rosé*? In fact, where was everything? All I could see for miles around were fields and cows and more fields. It was all very beautiful but I had no idea that it would be so remote. Maybe I should have put a bit more thought into choosing where to live rather than just relying on places I'd heard of and the number of hours of sunshine. Apart from Martine and Laure, I still hadn't seen a soul and I somehow didn't think that they would ever be up for a night of clubbing.

'Um, where's the nearest shop... *magasin*?' I asked.

'Rocamour is the nearest village but it only has a post office and an *épicerie*. You go that way,' he said pointing behind him to a road that wound up the other side of the valley.

'Bussières is about five kilometres away. It is bigger and has a supermarket and a bank, a few restaurants, a pizzeria, that sort of thing.'

'What about a nightclub... you know, dancing?'

Julien laughed. 'Oh, you have to go about twenty kilometres to Villeneuve de Beaumont for that, well, unless you enjoy a *thé dansant*. They are very popular round here.'

'Dancing tea? Oh, tea dances. Not quite my thing. So what do people do for entertainment round here then?' I asked, slightly nervous about his reply.

'Well, we have the *loto* every month, I think you call it bingo...'

Oh God, it was getting better by the minute!

'... we have the *quatorze juillet fête* for Bastille Day...'

So that's thirteen days sorted. What about the rest of the year?

'... we have the *marché gourmand*, the gourmet food market in July and August...'

More promising, I thought, but it certainly didn't sound like this place was the entertainment capital of rural France.

'*Voilà!*' announced Julien as we turned into a long driveway. At the end of it was a gorgeous, pale-stone cottage, almost the colour of buttermilk. As we got closer, I saw a blowsy honeysuckle weaving its way up the stones and around the front door in a still life which was straight out of a *Country Living (France Special)* magazine.

On the old stone wall opposite, a pale ivory climbing rose threatened to overcome me with blooms in a few weeks. There were hundreds of tiny rosebuds twisted up like sweets in wrappers. Faded blue shutters were fastened back to reveal windows hanging with hand-sewn linen café curtains and on every windowsill a riot of red, scarlet and white geraniums tumbled over the edges of faded terracotta pots. I was transfixed. More than that, the first stirrings of love for this little cottage fluttered in my heart like a butterfly. I silently thanked those French property websites which had been my guilty pleasure for the past few months and which had led me to Les Tuileries. I could hardly believe that I was renting this place for half the price of a one bed flat in London. *And* it had a swimming pool. In fact, I could sell my flat in Wandsworth, buy a farmhouse and a few acres in France and still have change to tide me over until I found a job.

'You can let go now,' smiled Julien.

'What? Oh, sorry.' For a few moments I had lost myself in the beauty of my new home and hadn't realised I was still hanging on to him.

'*Allez hop,*' he said, jumping nimbly to the ground in one swift movement.

I passed down my suitcase before hitching up my skirt to tackle the steep tractor steps. Thank goodness I'd ditched the Louboutins. I started to climb down, keen to show Julien that the city girl could handle a tractor like a pro, but unaware as I did so that my skirt had snagged on a sharp piece of metal. Jumping to the ground, there was a loud rip; it had torn from hem to waistband, a half-pace away from the lovely Julien, leaving me with my knickers on show for all the world to see. In horror, my face scarlet with embarrassment, I grabbed the remnants of my torn skirt and pulled the back together trying unsuccessfully to cover my modesty.

'*Oh là là,*' Julien laughed. 'You English girls are very, how you say, advanced?'

'I think you mean forward,' I muttered, turning to find that we were not alone. An elderly French couple were huddled together, a look of total bewilderment on their faces.

'*Ah, Monsieur Brunel, Madame Brunel, je vous présente votre nouvelle voisine, Mademoiselle Jones.*' Then to me, he whispered, 'Meet your *voisins,* your neighbours.'

'This hardly seems the right moment,' I hissed back.

Momentarily wrong-footed, I fixed my warmest smile on my face and advanced towards the couple, hand outstretched in greeting, The old woman looked me up and down disapprovingly and I could feel the beginnings of a deep blush creeping up my neck. Behind me Julien snorted. Here I was, on my first day in my new home, standing in front of my new neighbours with my underwear hanging out and no shoes on. Monsieur Brunel seemed less bothered by my appearance and stepped forward to shake my hand, a salacious glint in his eyes as they flicked down to my cleavage. Madame Brunel quickly whipped off her housecoat –

boy, was the nylon thread count high in these parts – and shoved it roughly at me with a look of mild disgust. Then turning on her heel, she grabbed her husband's sleeve, pushing him in front of her up the driveway, all the while berating him in rapid-fire French. I thought I detected just the hint of a smile on her hen-pecked husband's weather-beaten face. Madame proceeded to deliver a fierce slap across the back of his head and shouted something unintelligible. I could take a rough guess at what it was. Probably the most fun he's had in years, I thought, as without realising what I was doing, I slipped the housecoat on to cover myself up.

Turning to Julien, I picked up my suitcase and headed for the front door. The key should be in the post box according to Madame Mollet's text. But where was the post box? I looked around the front door but there was no sign.

Julien watched me curiously. 'What are you searching?' he asked eventually.

'Looking for,' I corrected. 'The letterbox.'

'The *boîte à lettres* is at the end of the drive.'

'Could you? I'm not really dressed for it.'

Smiling, Julien set off up the driveway, following in the footsteps of the departing Monsieur and Madame Brunel, and returned a few minutes later clutching a large brown envelope. I took it from him and as I ripped it open, a large bunch of keys fell out into my hand. There must have been at least ten of them and some were exactly like the sort of keys you'd see hanging from the belt of a jailer in a costume drama. I decided to look at all the paperwork in the envelope later.

Trying each one in turn, I finally found the one that unlocked the door. Pushing the handle down, it swung open, releasing a blast of warm and slightly musty air. I stepped inside. I found myself standing in a small hallway with exposed stone walls; the shutters were closed and the change in light momentarily disorientated me. Ahead of me was another door which I pushed open and walked into what looked like the lounge. As my eyes adjusted to the light, I could make out the interior of a large country kitchen through a door at the end. I peeped in and saw an old-fashioned range stove set in the recess of a chimney, not quite an Aga but good enough, and what appeared to be a huge stone sink and a small fridge. Apart from that, the cottage looked suspiciously bereft of furnishings.

Another door at the other end of the lounge led me into an empty room. The cottage was, it seemed, completely bare. Not a stick of furniture anywhere.

'*Bon*,' said Julien, 'I must go to help with Gérard's car.'

I thanked him profusely. 'Maybe I'll see you soon?' I said.

'Yes, maybe, now that we are neighbours.'

He winked at me, then turned and with a cheery wave stepped out into the honey-coloured sunlight leaving me wondering whether that was a promise of things to come or just my overactive imagination.

Left on my own for the first time in my own little cottage, I had a 'Julie Andrews' moment and swung round, arms outstretched, like Maria in *The Sound of Music*. 'I'm here,' I cried then, catching sight of myself in the glass of the door, 'and I'm already in a bloody housecoat!'

Chapter Three

Breathing out a contented sigh, I sat down on the step to read the contents of the envelope that I was still clutching in my hand. There was a letter from Madame Mollet handwritten in that particular flowing, French style that I remembered from a school exchange trip to Paris. It put my own childish scrawl to shame.

Mademoiselle,

I am so sorry that I cannot be there to meet you. There has been a problem with the furniture for the house. It should have been delivered yesterday but the van broke down. Monsieur Marin, the landlord, has assured me that it will be delivered by the end of the day today.

Also enclosed are full instructions for the cooker, the hot water...

I carefully folded the letter away. There would be plenty of time to read all that later. For the moment, I wanted to slip into something a little less revealing and a little cleaner, have a good look around my cottage and maybe take a quick dip in the pool. I picked up my suitcase and wandered from room to room, finally setting it down in the room which I decided would be my bedroom. It was large and airy with exposed stone walls and a door that opened onto a little patio at the side of the house, the perfect place to relax with a nice glass of chilled *rosé* in the evening.

Flicking the catches of the suitcase, I opened it and contemplated for a minute the devastation that had been caused at the airport. I then upturned it in the middle of the floor and rummaged around the clothes, shoes and well-trodden underwear before finally picking out a short denim skirt and a linen blouse. I stretched luxuriantly. It was so lovely to be here, finally, in my little home in France. Fishing my sunglasses out of my handbag, I slipped my feet into a pair of sparkly flip-flops, wiggling my toes deliciously. Fancy being in flip-flops in April, I thought.

From the lounge of the cottage, French windows led out onto a terrace in the garden. An ancient vine grew up a pergola overhead and a couple of old wrought-iron chairs were placed around a vintage bistro table just calling out to be shabby chic'd with a spotty oilcloth and some coloured-glass hurricane lamps.

Do they call them French windows in France, I wondered? I knew the French called a condom a *capote anglais* or English cap rather than a French letter – one of the few things I remembered from the school exchange. Outside, the spring sun broke through the trees in shafts of light the colour of melted butter. I could see that the garden had potential, not that I knew much about gardening. Goodness knows, my previous attempts at growing anything had been a disaster. It was hard enough trying to remember to take my make-up off every day, never mind water the plants.

The lawn sloped gradually down to the edge of the hill, where it dropped away sharply and amid the undergrowth, I could just make out a ruined building, probably an old shepherd's hut or something. The view was magnificent and I felt my spirits lift. Rolling hills, a patchwork of a hundred different colours from burnished gold to a deep green, spread out in every direction.

One side of the garden was edged by a dry stone wall that was just a fraction too tall for me to look over. Wondering what was on the other side, I slipped off my flip-flops and found some footholds on the rough stones; grabbing hold of the top of the wall, I pulled myself up just far enough to peep over.

On the other side was a beautiful three-storey square house, the mini-chateau I had seen from the road, with stone steps leading up to a balustraded veranda that wrapped around the first floor. A stunning pool, complete with waterfall, was surrounded by some seriously chichi sun loungers, while exotic plants flopped over the lips of huge terracotta amphorae. Someone clearly had some serious money here. It seemed so incongruous in this little French farming hamlet.

Even more incongruous, a convertible Mercedes and a Porsche Cayenne people carrier were parked in front of the house and I was sure that the people carrier was the one I had seen at the airport. I was too engrossed in the splendour of the neighbouring property to notice an angry-looking woman bearing down on me.

'Oi! What do you bleedin' well think you're doing?' yelled the irate woman in the flat estuary vowels of Essex. 'Piss off out of here, bloody nosy Frogs.'

'Um, actually I'm English,' I shouted back.

'Whatever! Just piss off outta here, silly bitch. Stop spying on me.'

This wasn't going well at all.

'Gosh, sorry,' I called. 'It's just I've only moved in today and I was wondering who my new neighbours were.'

Despite the woman's enormous sunglasses and large floppy sunhat, her face was vaguely familiar but I couldn't quite place it.

'Yeah, well you've seen all you're gonna. Now bleedin' get out of here.'

'Sorry, sorry,' I called, embarrassed, and jumped down from the wall more than a little taken aback by my first meeting with my new neighbour. Hopefully the next meeting would be a little more positive. But who was she? I was absolutely sure I'd seen her somewhere before.

At the end of the garden was the swimming pool. I smiled. I actually have a pool, I thought. A closer look, revealed water that was a rather unattractive shade of *crème de menthe* green, decidedly slimy-looking and certainly not fit for human use. A big, fat bullfrog croaked loudly then hopped into the water with a plop. My stomach gurgled loudly and I remembered that I hadn't eaten since the overpriced, undercooked toastie on the plane.

A brisk walk to the village, Rocamour, was what was needed so I could buy myself a few provisions until I could sort out a car. I had told the estate agent that the rental property had to be within walking distance of a village with shops and about one and a half kilometres didn't seem that far. Grabbing a scarf to protect my pale English shoulders from the sun, which was surprisingly warm for April, and some more suitable, if less fashionable footwear – I'd made that mistake once already – I headed off in the direction of the road that Julien had shown me earlier.

It was a new experience to be so carefree. No job to tie me down, no boss to nag at me to meet deadlines, no dreadful journey on the Tube while paunchy middle-aged men took advantage of the movement of the overcrowded train to cop a quick feel of my bum.

St Amans de Pierrepoint was far smaller than I'd imagined and wasn't exactly the country idyll I had expected. To be honest it was a bit tatty and unkempt. Ten houses or so freckled the hillside, barns tumbling down in various stages of decay. Keeping watch over the hamlet was an old *manoir* that had definitely seen better days. It was a handsome house built of the same mellow pale stone as the other houses, but on a grander scale. There was a certain beautiful symmetry to it and its setting, amid an abundance of shrubs and fruit trees, was quite magical. It was a shame to see that the shutters were closed and it appeared that no one was living there. Apart from the stone it was quite unlike most of the other houses which looked like they had probably started out as one room, then gradually been extended over the centuries. I had heard that they used to build the houses with a space underneath to keep the livestock overnight; apparently, the heat of the animals' bodies would warm the room above. Call me pampered but I prefer central heating.

Everything had a certain chaotic quality, sort of wild and undisciplined. Further down the lane a flock of hens pecked and scratched happily, their rich brown feathers reflecting the sun. I watched them for a few minutes. I'd never really liked chickens except roasted or in a nice korma, finding them a bit too like dinosaurs with feathers when you got close up. It was the eyes that got me. They followed you everywhere and seemed to look right into your soul.

Strolling on down the road, I passed an old barn, half-ruined, with roof timbers exposed like an animal skeleton in the African bush. An old cart with only one wheel was resting in its dark interior, as if waiting for someone to come and hitch up a horse and take it out. Next to it, piles of wood were neatly stacked, old roof timbers by the look of it, and bizarrely, an old toilet painted with blue flowers. People would pay hundreds for that in Portobello Road, I thought to myself.

I'd been so intent on inspecting the old barn that I'd hardly noticed the gap in the trees, which offered the most spectacular vista. I gasped. It was so beautiful. To one side, it was heavily wooded with scrub oak, thin trunks, like spiky fingers, poking up through the earth. To the other, newly planted wheat fields stretched as far as I could see and at the bottom, a little river flashed Morse code to me in the sunlight.

On the opposite side of the valley was Rocamour, so named because of a huge rock that used to overhang an old picnic area where marriages were reputed to have taken place.

I had read the story about the origins of the name on an expat website. Unfortunately, during one such marriage, the rock inexplicably parted company from the hillside which had cradled it for centuries and fell onto the wedding party, killing everyone. Their bodies remain to this day entombed beneath the rock, captured in time. Still, at least the bride would never have to worry about her husband forgetting their wedding anniversary.

The village was what was known as a *bastide*, a fortified enclave built high on a hill so the local lord could keep an eye open for invaders, usually English ones, during the Hundred Years War. Judging by the number of British people reported to live in the area, it had clearly been a wasted effort.

A lone tractor puffed its way up the hill burping out little clouds of smoke from its exhaust and a bit further over, I could make out a small figure hunched over rows of vines on terraces carved out of the hillside. I marched down the hill with a purposeful stride, reasoning that the sooner I got to the bottom, the sooner I could start up the other side to the village. I was dying to see what it was like and had tried to google it before I left, but apart from some historical stuff like the rock, I had no idea what to expect.

I stopped briefly to pet a fat white pony that whickered softly as I passed. Limpid brown eyes peeped out from behind a long forelock and he reminded me of the ponies in the Norman Thelwell books that my gran kept in her toilet. I rubbed his soft pink nose and pulled up a handful of grass which he ate as if he hadn't been fed in months.

'You little piglet,' I said, smiling. As I walked on down the hill, the pony followed me meekly, matching me stride for stride. As we reached the end of his paddock and he could follow me no more, he whinnied pathetically for me to come back and pet him again.

'Later,' I called out to him, 'later.'

Further down the lane I came to a beautifully maintained vegetable plot. Alan Titchmarsh would have been green with envy at the neat rows of plants. Along the far boundary, several rows of vines stood to attention basking in the sun that would shortly nurture their grapes. There were no houses nearby and I wondered who the plot belonged to. Whoever it was clearly spent a lot of time on it.

At the bottom of the hill, I stopped on the little bridge and watched the river running beneath. Silver slivers darted about in the water and further downstream I caught sight of the brilliant rainbow plumage of a kingfisher waiting patiently for his moment to dive under the water for his lunch. I turned and leaned against the bridge, allowing the sun to fall on my face, warming me gently. Bliss! This time last week I would have been doing battle with the London crowds, like a salmon trying to swim upstream, getting my ankles kicked, deafened by the traffic, head pounding from the continuous honking of car horns. And now? I listened. Nothing, no thing. Not. A. Thing. Even the faint whirr of the tractor's engine had faded. For a London girl like me, it was quite disconcerting.

The road to Rocamour wound up on the opposite side of the valley so, checking both ways, I stepped out into the road. I had, of course, forgotten that in France they drive on the right so my look right, look left and look right again should have been reversed. As I stepped into the road, out of nowhere, a speeding car hove into view, the driver honking wildly when he saw me. Caught by surprise, I leapt backwards straight into the ditch behind me, a ditch which I painfully discovered was full of stinging nettles.

'Ow, bugger, shit!' I shouted, trying to extricate myself without doing any further damage. Scrambling up the bank onto the side of the road, I sat down to rub my itchy legs. Country lore told me that wherever there are stinging nettles, there are dock leaves, but looking around there was nothing but recently mown grass. I sat for a minute, watching as blotchy patches appeared on my bare skin and cursed my luck at falling down two French ditches in one day.

Bloody driver didn't even stop, I thought, as I pushed myself off the ground and nipped sharpishly across the road, making sure to look the right way this time, before continuing up the hill towards Rocamour. It was certainly much steeper than I'd thought and within minutes I was breathing heavily, feeling the sweat on my back. Stopping, I bent over, hands on knees, to try and catch my breath. So much for a gentle walk into the village each morning to buy freshly baked croissants! And so much for the expensive gym membership that I'd been forking out for the past two years. I continued on, thinking that I'd never felt more unfit in my life and by the time the final bend was in sight, my thighs were burning and my chest was on fire.

I stopped again, pretending to admire the view, as a gaggle of noisy ramblers, most of them older than me by a good twenty years, strode past with no signs of flagging. Surely I should be fitter than this? With a final push, and determined not to be beaten by a bunch of Saga louts, I rounded the bend into the village.

Chapter Four

A blue and white sign announced that I had finally reached Rocamour. On my left was the church that I had just been able to make out from my garden. It was bigger than I thought it would be, far too big for what seemed like such a small village. The clock appeared not to have moved for many years and was suspended in time at three thirty-five. Next to the church was a small *épicerie*. I'd check that out later but right now, I had more serious work to attend to.

Across the square I saw the village café, its outdoor terrace shaded by scarlet awnings in sharp contrast to the bright green foliage of a huge lime tree. Tables were spread out in the shade, many of them already occupied and it obviously did a good lunchtime trade. Oh yes, this was much more like it. People!

Choosing a table in the sun so I could catch a few more rays, I flopped down in a seat, completely exhausted. An elegant, perfectly coiffured waitress appeared at my side and looked me up and down with a slight whiff of distaste. I imagined how I must look; stung legs, beetroot-red face and hair looking like it hadn't had close contact with a grooming implement for some time. I flattened down my dress and tried to smooth my hair in a feeble attempt to make myself more presentable.

'*Mademoiselle*,' asked the waitress imperiously, '*que désirez-vous?*'

Désirez? Desire? She must be asking what I wanted to drink.

'*Un* beer?' I said hopefully. Alexandre Dumas, when he came to England to learn the language, had said that English is just French badly pronounced so I worked on the premise that 'beer', pronounced with a vaguely French accent, would do the trick. The waitress sniffed and turned on her heel, disappearing into the gloom of the interior of the café. I breathed a sigh of relief when she returned a few minutes later with a glass of ice-cool beer, condensation running down its sides.

'*Trois euros, mademoiselle*,' she said placing a till receipt in front of me.

Nearly three quid for a glass of beer? That's a bit steep, I thought, it's not even a pint. No wonder they don't binge drink in France! I rooted round in my purse and handed her the fifty-euro note.

'Sorry,' I apologised, 'it's all I have.'

The waitress's glare was only marginally warmer than a nuclear winter as she flounced off into the bar, before returning a few minutes later with a small saucer piled high with euro coins.

'Sorry, it's all *I* have,' she said with a sarcastic smile.

I took the change without comment. Not much point upsetting her any more than I already seemed to have done. Sitting back, I contemplated my surroundings and fellow patrons of the Café du Midi. If I closed my eyes, I could almost be back home, there were so many English voices. Must be a popular spot with holidaymakers I thought, sipping on my ice-cold beer. Picking up the menu to see what was on offer, the prices seemed eye-wateringly high for a small village café. It was important to pace myself on the money front until I found a job, so eating here on a regular basis was definitely out for the moment.

Opposite, the little village shop seemed to be in darkness. Funny, I thought, you'd think they'd be open to take advantage of all the lunchtime trade. A sign on the corner pointed to *La Poste*, the post office and another to a *quincaillerie*. I had no idea what that was and made a mental note to add it to my growing list of words to check out in my dictionary.

Stretching out my stinging legs, I pulled my skirt up slightly in the hope that the sun might do something to disperse the ugly-looking white lumps that had spread across them from ankle to knee. I closed my eyes and tilted my face up towards the sun. A cold beer and sunshine in April. Heaven.

'*Mince alors!*' exclaimed a male voice behind me. (I made a mental note to look that one up too). 'What has happened to you this time? Another accident? You are certainly accident lying down!'

Julien! I scrabbled to pull my skirt down. Lying down... lying down? I was nonplussed.

'Oh, accident prone. Accident prone, that's what you mean.' Google Translate had a lot to answer for.

'Some lunatic Frenchman nearly ran me over and I had to jump out of his way. I ended up in a ditch... for the second time today. It's becoming something of a habit. No real harm done,' I continued, noticing his concerned look, 'just fell into a load of stinging nettles. Hurts like shit... *merde*,' I added.

Julien smiled. I hadn't noticed the dimple in his left cheek before. It gave him an air of vulnerability that I found very attractive. To be honest, I found just about everything about him attractive.

'Can we join you? Louis will be here in a minute.'

'Yes, of course,' I moved my bag so he could sit down next to me.

'Are you eating?' he asked.

'No, not today. Another time maybe.'

'And you are settling in all right?'

'So far, so good. Well, apart from all the ditches I keep falling in to, I suppose.'

From behind my sunglasses I studied his face. He really was gorgeous. There was something about him that made me want to just reach out and touch him.

'So...' we both said at once. I laughed, feeling suddenly very self-conscious.

'Ah, *l'anglaise* again,' said Louis as he pulled up another chair without waiting to be asked and sat down. The moment was lost.

'Something to drink?' asked Julien, nodding his head towards my half-empty glass.

'Oh, thank you but no. If I have one more drink at lunchtime, I'll be sleeping all afternoon. No, one is my limit, especially if I'm not eating.'

'That is *pas normale* for an *anglaise*, an English girl. I heard you all drink like a *poisson*... a fish,' said Louis. I wasn't entirely sure whether he was joking.

'You know, you really shouldn't believe everything you read in the papers,' I replied.

Louis just shrugged his shoulders.

'So,' he said as his brother disappeared into the bar to order them both a drink and something to eat, 'you have been to this part of France before?'

'Well, not exactly. I've been to Paris but not here. I've not had much chance to spend time anywhere really, what with work and all that. I used to work in PR. Celebrities and stuff.' He looked decidedly unimpressed.

'But still, you made the decision to move here. *C'est bizarre*,' he said breathing out in a long, low whistle and shaking his head.

I bristled ever so slightly. Put like that, it did sound pretty naive.

'Well, how much different can it be here than in England? I'll find myself a job. I'm not worried what I do. It doesn't have to be anything high powered, I'm happy to work in a bar or something as long as I can make enough to live on. My friend Tania moved down to Dorset, which is very rural and found herself a job straight away.'

'*Sacré bleu*, I have a real *lunatique anglaise* here. Whatever *you* read in the newspapers is probably not true, or possibly it is true in Paris, but certainly not down here in *la France profonde*. *Chômage...*' Louis searched around for the word '... inemployment...'

'Unemployment,' I corrected, a snarky note slipping into my voice.

'*Un*employment,' he repeated, emphasising the first syllable, 'is over ten per cent in the country, maybe up to twenty-five per cent in the *ados*... the young people. And they are French. They have no problems with the language. How you think that you will find a job? You don't even speak French. Even to work in a bar you almost have to go to the *Fac*... the university now. Look at Noélia,' he nodded his head towards the waitress who was leaning on the door frame looking like someone had stolen her favourite teddy. 'She has a *licence* in law from Bordeaux and she still can't get a job.'

God, I thought, no wonder she looks so pissed off!

'Well there seem to be loads of English people here, maybe I can find a job with one of them,' I replied defensively, hoping for Julien to reappear. They may have been identical but their personalities were very different and Louis was making me feel slightly uncomfortable.

'Pah,' Louis almost spat, 'they mostly work on the black, you know, cash only. You need to find a proper job so you can get healthcare and pay your taxes, get yourself a French pension.'

I hadn't even given that side of things a second thought. I had just assumed I'd find a job, apply for it, get it (of course) and then the rest would fall into place.

The throaty roar of a car engine put paid to any further discussion on the subject as a Mercedes convertible, which I knew belonged to my bonkers neighbour, raced into the village and turned sharply into the square behind the church. The woman I'd had a run-in with earlier was at the wheel, hair flying out behind her and the same oversized sunglasses shielding her eyes. The clunk of a car door closing was swiftly followed by her appearance – young, spray-tanned a rather alarming shade of orange and wearing a tiny sundress that erred only just on the side of decency and left little room for imagination – or lunch. Long legs led down to a pair of Jimmy Choos that I knew didn't leave much change out of £1,000. She seemed so out of place in this little French village.

I suddenly had an epiphany. 'Bloody hell!' I exclaimed loudly. All heads swivelled in my direction.

Louis looked at me as if I had lost my mind, though in fairness that was pretty much how he'd been looking at me since the whole 'moving to France' conversation.

'I know who that is,' I hissed in his ear. 'That's Tracey Tarrant.'

She'd been a runner-up in one of the interminable talent shows that had filled my Friday nights, losing out to some boy band from Dagenham. Her record label had dropped her after her second album bombed and rumours had recently appeared in the tabloid press of a very ill-advised affair with a married footballer. So *this* is where she'd disappeared to. Just wait until the girls back home heard about this one! I whipped my mobile out of my pocket. Damn! No signal again. I watched as Tracey made her way round the terrace until she found a table on her own at the back, half hidden from passers-by. No one seemed to take much notice of her.

Despite the shade from the lime trees, she kept her sunglasses fixed firmly on her face and seemed at pains to hide herself.

Shortly afterwards the reason became clear. The Porsche Cayenne, the one with blacked-out windows from the airport, purred into a parking space in front of the village shop.

The doors opened and a heavily-muscled leg, clad in shorts, appeared from the door, closely followed by the six-foot two-inch frame of… flaming hell… it was him!

'Warren Hartson!'

It seemed that there had been more to the rumour than just idle gossip, and with his media darling of a wife apparently playing away from home with some actor in Los Angeles, he was clearly putting his free time to good use.

I leaned across the table towards Louis.

'Do you know who that is?' I hissed. 'It's only Tracey Tarrant. She nearly won a talent show a few years ago and there's been a rumour that she's been having a fling with this married footballer – and that's only *him*, Warren Hartson, he plays football for Chelsea.' I waited for a response. Louis looked at me, baffled.

'Him I have heard of. He is good but he is not Zizou,' he whispered back. 'But her, I have no idea who she is. Is she unwell? She is a very strange colour.'

Ignoring the urge to ask who on earth Zizou was, I pressed on.

'You must have heard of her. She had a single out that went to Number One. It was called "Light Up My Love".'

Louis frowned and shook his head. 'The French radio stations are not allowed to play much foreign music. Anyway, we have our own celebrities here, so we are not much interested in yours. Johnny Hallyday has a *château* very close to here.'

It was my turn to look baffled. 'Johnny who?'

Louis looked almost offended. He turned to Julien who had finally arrived back with the drinks.

'Elle ne sait pas qui est Johnny Hallyday!'

Julien feigned turning away and walking off in disgust then turned back to me smiling,

'You don't know Johnny Hallyday? You have much to learn about France. You have the Internet at your house?'

I nodded. 'Well, as soon as I get connected I will have.'

'Then you must look him up. He is a legend in France, a real legend.'

I wondered if something had been sadly missing from my education. If he really was that famous, surely I would have heard of him?

The two brothers and I chatted companionably for a while longer until lunch arrived. I had to admit it looked divine and I was suddenly very hungry. A large salmon steak nestled in a seasonal salad dressed with a sublime-smelling balsamic dressing, all on a large, oval white plate. It looked like something out of *Jamie Oliver Does France* rather than the kitchen of a little café in a rural village.

'Gosh, that looks amazing!' I exclaimed.

'Oh yes, we have a great chef here,' said Julien.

'*Eh, Jacques, viens, il y a un de tes compatriots,*' Julien called out to a thirty-something guy who had appeared by the door to the café, his chef's whites marking him out as the one who had prepared all the fabulous food.

He sauntered over to check out the new English girl and I took a moment to take him in. Tall, long-legged, short hair styled in a brush cut and a rangy, loose-limbed walk. Cute, I thought. There was certainly no shortage of lush men in this village!

His whites had the name 'J Tournier' embroidered on the chest. A real French chef, I thought.

'Ey oop lass,' he said in the broadest of Yorkshire accents. My heart sank.

'He is also English but he has married a French woman,' said Louis, as if that forgave him his transgression for being a foreigner.

Hmm, I thought, I'm sitting in deepest France surrounded by British people in a French café with an English chef. This wasn't exactly what I'd signed up for.

'Jack Tournier,' he said, stretching out his hand to shake mine. 'Another newbie eh?'

'Very,' I replied, 'I only arrived this morning.'

'Blimey, and you've already met these reprobates. Bad luck eh!' He laughed, clapping the Twin Hunks on the back.

'They had to drag me out of a ditch... well, not me exactly, more the car I was in.' I smiled.

'Crazy Gérard was picking her up from the airport,' said Julien.

'Oh well, that explains a lot,' he laughed. 'I'm surprised he was even sober at this time of the day. He's usually unconscious by mid-morning.'

'What?' I said. 'You mean he's a rampaging alcoholic with a taxi licence?'

'Yes, that's about it. Welcome to France, where we shrug our Gallic shoulders at "Elf and Safety".'

'So do you own this place then?' I asked.

'No, more's the pity. Claire and Stéphane own it but they are away visiting their grandchildren near Nice.' He got up from the arm of the seat he had been perching on.

'Well, back to the coalface. Looks like it's going to be a busy lunchtime session. Nice to meet you. Drop in any time.'

'Yeah, I will,' I answered smiling up at him. 'Thanks. Nice to meet you too.'

Jack turned and retreated to the kitchen.

'Well boys,' I announced, standing up to leave, 'I'd better be getting off. I need to do a bit of shopping then get back for the arrival of the furniture.'

'No one will come during lunchtime, this is France,' said Julien. 'Your delivery men will be in a café somewhere having a big lunch and a carafe of wine. And the shop doesn't open until three o'clock either.'

'Three o'clock!' What am I supposed to do until then? What happens if people can only shop in their lunch break?'

'Then it's tough luck, innit,' came a voice from the shadows. 'They only seem to work a few hours a day. Does my bloody head in. Lazy bastards.'

Every head on the terrace turned in the direction of Tracey Tarrant but she just ignored them all and went back to texting on her smartphone while Warren Hartson glared at her. I sat down again, a little embarrassed at being the cause of her outburst.

'This is France,' said Julien. 'Lunch breaks are for lunch, not for shopping. Here food is to be savoured. Most places outside the towns close for two hours for lunch.'

'So my usual half an hour for a sandwich and a latte at my desk wouldn't go down well here then.'

'I think the French would probably go on strike,' he smiled.

I smiled back. 'Yeah, I've heard it's your national sport.'

'Let me buy you some lunch. It's the least I can do after what happened earlier.'

'Well, in that case… thank you, lunch would be lovely.' I smiled back at Julien and our eyes held each other's. For a moment, it was as if there was no one else there. It felt like one of those seminal moments in an old black and white film, when the hero and heroine realise they are falling in love. My heartbeat quickened.

The loud scrape of a chair being pushed back broke the moment.

'I'll get some more drinks.' Louis practically stomped off towards the bar, leaving me wondering what on earth his problem was. Julien watched him go but I couldn't read the expression on his face.

Chapter Five

The church bell striking three times was my cue to leave. I thanked Julien for lunch and waved goodbye, having first exchanged phone numbers, and wandered across the road to the little *épicerie*. The owner, a middle-aged lady with aubergine-coloured hair, was just putting out a sandwich board announcing she was open for business.

They certainly like their extreme hair colours here I thought, making a mental note to wait until I next went back to London to get my hair done.

I was really looking forward to stocking up on the lovely fresh fruit and vegetables that I had heard about. The French only ate food that was in season apparently. No carbon footprint the size of a yeti to bring mangetout from Kenya for them. If it wasn't in season, they didn't eat it. I'd also heard that this was the area for *foie gras*, which had become a bit of a sore point back home. It wasn't really my thing either but I would put money on the French not giving a damn about whether force-feeding geese was politically correct or in line with current animal welfare concerns. They'd just eat it.

Wishing the proprietor *'bonjour'*, I went inside to see what delights it held. The interior was gloomy and having been shut up for several hours in the warmth of the midday sun, very stuffy. I could just make out racks of wilted lettuces and wrinkled carrots. I picked up a cucumber but its flaccid body drooped in my hand so I quickly put it back. I'd seen fresher fruit and vegetables in the rubbish bin of my local corner shop back in London. The shelves contained a paltry selection of biscuits, instant coffee and tinned vegetables. If the dust on the tins was anything to go by, they had been there for some time. I didn't dare look for 'sell-by' dates.

A cold cabinet at the front of the shop was home to a few slabs of dry cheese, their surfaces like a lunar landscape, full of crevices and cracks, and some sorry-looking packs of reconstituted ham, not even the proper stuff. It reminded me of a shop I used to go to with my grandmother in Norfolk run by a mad old woman with no teeth. It wasn't what I was expecting. Wasn't France the home of gastronomy?

I found a reasonably firm lettuce, some tomatoes that didn't threaten to explode in my hand, coffee, Liptons Yellow Label tea (well, it was tea of sorts), a bottle of cheap *rosé*, a couple of baguettes – I could keep one till the morning – and the world's most expensive pint of milk. One euro sixty for a pint! I could buy four for that money at home. I took my basket to the till and handed it over to the lady with the aubergine hair who proceeded to chat to me in French.

'No *parle français*,' I said feeling my face redden. 'Sorry.'

'Never mind, you will learn it soon enough,' the woman replied in nearly flawless English. 'You're new here aren't you? I haven't seen you around before. Are you on holiday?'

'No, I've moved here for a while, I'm renting Les Tuileries.'

'Really? Old Monsieur Marin's place?'

'Yes, that's the one. You speak amazing English. Where did you learn?' I was genuinely impressed.

'Oh, just from having some English friends and wanting to learn it. You should find yourself some French lessons. The Alliance Franco-Brittanique in Bussières does free ones. You can just drop in on a Saturday morning. That is market day too. They have an informal coffee morning. It starts about ten o'clock.'

'Really? I'll have to give them a try. If I'm going to be here for a while, I need to get to grips with the language.'

'That lot over there…' she nodded her head towards the café, 'most of them have been here years and can still barely speak a word. That's one of the reasons I decided to learn English. It's no good if I can't talk to my customers.'

'But shouldn't they be learning French? I mean, we're in your country.'

The women just gave me a knowing smile. 'You can get to know some other English people at the club too.'

'More English people? I'd quite like to get to know the French.'

'Well, yes, but it is also important to have friends that you can talk to and laugh with. I still do not understand the English sense of humour or the Welsh accent for that matter! The French here are very inward-looking. Most of the people in the village have lived here for generations. They are all married to each other or at the very least their second cousin's goat.'

I looked shocked.

'You mean, you haven't noticed that they all have six fingers round here?' She winked at me.

I smiled back awkwardly, hoping that the French family who had just come in didn't understand her.

'I'm from Paris,' she continued, 'so I'm definitely not from *le coin,* you know, the area. They dislike us Parisians more than the foreigners. I'm just trying to find a buyer for the shop and then

I'm moving back up to the north. They are a little less inward-looking there.'

'I'm sorry to hear that. Every village needs a shop. Well, I'd better get on. Thanks so much for the heads-up on the French classes. I really appreciate it.'

'You're welcome. See you again. By the way, I was only joking...'

I turned and smiled, giving her a 'yeah, you got me' look.

'... about the goats.'

I set off down the hill, stopping at a terrace in front of what I assumed was the village hall. 'Salle des Fêtes', it said in big letters above the door. It sounded so much nicer than 'village hall' or 'community centre'. A place where happy things took place. Leaning on the railings, I had an almost 180-degree view across the valley. It simply took my breath away. Rolling fields gave way to the rise and fall of hills which broke like waves across the countryside. I picked out several small churches, more like chapels, dotting the landscape. Small clusters of houses spread out around them and bullet-like poplar trees pierced the clear blue sky. A little road, almost empty of traffic, wended its way between twin rows of plane trees towards Bussières in the distance.

It reminded me a bit of Wiltshire. Here and there were small copses of oak, chestnut and beech trees, resplendent in their new spring coats, and above my head, birds of prey wheeled and swooped on their unsuspecting victims. The thin blue vein of the river threaded through the valley, bridged by little stone crossings, glittering in the sunshine. I could hardly believe that this was my home. How lucky was I?

Reluctantly tearing myself away, I picked up my bags and walked at a leisurely pace down the hill. I'd forgotten how hot it was and before long, I had embarrassing dark patches of perspiration spreading under my arms. Crossing the road carefully this time, I checked to the left and right. I'd spent more than enough time in French ditches since my arrival this morning.

As I trudged up the hill towards St Amans de Pierrepoint, I became aware of a sound that I hadn't noticed on my way down. Running water. I couldn't quite pinpoint where it was coming from but it was certainly nearby. Peering through the undergrowth, I could just make out a pond hidden behind the trees. A bit further up the road, where the trees thinned out, I found a gap and went through to have a look. It was like something out of a fairytale. A stream ran down the hill over a series of little waterfalls. Shafts of sunlight broke through the trees and glinted off the surface and the water was so clear, I could see the pebbles at the bottom of the stream. It looked so enticing and my throat was burning. I'd never drunk water that didn't come from either a tap or a bottle. Dare I? Surely it couldn't be any worse than the water in London. That was just recycled sewage, wasn't it? Cupping my hands, I dipped them into the coolness, drew the water to my mouth and sipped it. It tasted good, slightly metallic, definitely not Evian, but cold and refreshing. I drank a little more then sat down and dipped my toes in the water at the place where it ran off down the hill. It was far colder than I'd imagined and it cooled my tired feet. I wiggled my toes, delighting in the feeling.

In the distance I could hear a car making its way at speed up the hill. As it drew level, I saw Tracey Tarrant at the wheel. It slid to a halt by the little pond and her not-so-dulcet tones called out to me.

'What the 'ell are you doing there?'

'Well, I'm just resting my feet. It's a hard walk up that hill,' I replied, wondering how someone with a singing voice like melted chocolate could have a speaking voice like someone splitting granite.

'Wanna lift?'

I thought for a moment. I didn't relish the thought of the long walk up to St Amans de Pierrepoint, but then equally I didn't relish the thought of even a few minutes in the company of the mouthy Tracey.

'Umm...'

'Well don't bleedin' put yourself out.' Tracey started to put the car in gear.

'No, sorry, I didn't mean to be rude. I'd love a lift.' I collected up my shopping, loaded it onto the back seat then got in next to Tracey.

Tracey gunned the engine and we shot off up the hill, scaring a rabbit that had unwisely chosen that moment to run across the road. Fortunately, the journey was too short to strike up any meaningful conversation and I was thankful when we pulled into the driveway of my neighbour's ritzy pad.

'Fancy a drink?' asked Tracey. I thought I detected an almost pleading note in her voice.

'Thanks, but I can't. I've got delivery men coming this afternoon with furniture for the cottage. Another time maybe?'

'Whatever.' Tracey turned and headed towards the house.

'Bye then,' I called at her retreating back. Tracey waved a heavily-ringed hand dismissively without even so much as a backward glance.

God, what a hideous woman, I thought. Just goes to show that you can give someone money but you can't give them class. She's absolutely the last person I wanted to spend any time with.

Lifting my bags out of the back of Tracey's convertible, I headed towards the sanctuary of Les Tuileries. It was a relief to step back into the cool of the little cottage and I took off my shoes so I could feel the cold terracotta tiles underfoot.

In the kitchen I unloaded my shopping, putting the milk, wine and salad stuff into the little fridge, then made myself a cup of coffee and cut some cheese and a piece of baguette and went out into the garden. There was a small outbuilding by the pool and looking inside, I found a couple of old but usable sun loungers. Dragging one out, I positioned myself by the Chartreuse-coloured swimming pool. It was so lovely just to sit. Sit and do nothing. I felt my shoulders relax and the tension flow out of me. This was bliss. Absolute bliss. I polished off my baguette and cheese, which actually tasted far better than it looked, and waited for the arrival of the furniture.

Chapter Six

'Knock, knock. Hello... anyone home?' called a man's voice, breaking into my daydreams. Stretching out my aching neck and back, I dragged myself reluctantly up from the sun lounger, presuming it was the man to deliver the furniture.

I opened the door to find a middle-aged couple standing on the doorstep. They were well dressed and had that polished, beatific look that could only mean one thing. Jehovah's Witnesses.

'Hello,' said the woman. 'Do you worry about the state of the world?'

I was slightly taken aback that she was English.

'Er... I've not really given it that much thought to be honest. I do worry about global warming though.'

'And Jesus?'

'What? Does he worry about global warming too?' I smiled but they just looked at me blankly. 'Look, I'm sorry, I've just moved in today and I'm a bit worn out from the journey. I don't mean to be flippant. I know it's just part of your religion to go out and try and convert people but my mum is a Wesleyan and my dad a lapsed Catholic so my religious upbringing was nothing if not confused. Just give me the magazine and I'll make a donation to your church. Hang on a sec.'

I went to find my purse and came back to the door. They were still standing there, smiling beatifically so I handed over a few euros and took the magazine the man offered.

'Thanks,' I said, giving the cover a brief look.

'If you ever need us we have a stand at the market in Bussières,' he said

'Great. I'll bear that in mind. Have a nice day.' I closed the door firmly and went to the bedroom window to make sure they were leaving. I had envisaged going to the market for fresh produce rather than religious instruction. This place was certainly full of surprises.

I went back outside to my sun lounger but no sooner had I sat down when there was another loud knock. Please don't tell me they've come back to try and save my soul, I said to myself as I went to the door.

When I opened it, a man of similar age to me was standing on the doorstep.

'Hi. I'm Nick. Got some furniture for you,' he said as he planted a kiss on each of my cheeks.

I recoiled slightly, unused to someone I didn't know invading my personal space like that. In London I'd have probably floored him.

'Oh, don't worry,' he said noticing my unease, 'you'll get used to it. Everyone does the *bisous* round here. That's French for kisses. It's rude not to.'

'Oh, right,' I answered. The thought of having to kiss Madame Brunel made me faintly uneasy.

'You were expecting me, weren't you?'

'Yes, yes, sorry, it's just that, well, I was expecting someone French.'

'Yeah well, this is Little England. Rumour has it there are still a few of the locals left here and there.' He smiled, eyes sparkling, clearly mocking me. 'Nah, I do all of Sylvie's, Madame Mollet's, removals. She says she doesn't trust the Frenchies not to nick everything.'

I was a little taken aback. 'Sorry?'

'Dodgy lot, the frogs, you make sure you're careful round them. Anyway, where do you want this stuff?'

'Umm... Let me see what you've got and then I can decide where you can put it.'

Nick opened up the back of a rusty old transit van that was stuffed to the gills with furniture; most of it looked like it had been knocked off from a charity shop, and not a particularly upmarket one at that.

'Hmm, not exactly The Conran Shop is it?' I started rummaging through the back of the van. It looked as if there were a couple of beds, a sofa, an armchair, a table and chairs, some wardrobes and sundry bits and bobs.

'OK, let's get it inside. Have you got someone to help you unload it?'

Nick looked sheepish. 'I was kind of hoping you could give me a hand.'

I sighed to myself. Oh well, what the hell. I'd been in a tractor, two ditches and a death-trap taxi so far today. What difference would it make to have another new experience – furniture removals?

'OK, let's start with the bedroom furniture,' I said, motioning at Nick to grab the other end of the bed. 'On the count of three, one, two, three, lift...'

One hour, several broken nails and a skinned knuckle later, the little stone cottage was looking a bit more like home. A rather lumpy-looking double bed took pride of place in the master bedroom along with what was a really quite a nice old bedroom suite of a dark oak wardrobe, tallboy and bedside cabinets with a linen fold design. I'd found an old wooden lamp that would have been more suited to my grandmother's house but it would do for the moment and at least it offered me some sort of light for reading at night. I placed it on the bedside table and stood back. Not bad. A bit rustic perhaps but never mind. I had every intention of filling my home with gorgeous shabby chic (rather than just shabby) French antiques but there was plenty of time for that.

In the lounge, or *salon* as Nick kept calling it, I'd got a sofa, which was just about retro if you were being generous, an armchair, a coffee table that looked as if it had been hewn from an ancient oak tree and quite likely had, a couple of reproduction end tables and an old analogue television that weighed more than the rest of the furniture combined. It had taken ten minutes to carry it into the house, with me having to stop and start constantly to save myself from dropping it. Now it sat perched on a rather flimsy-looking table that threatened to collapse under its bulk at any moment.

The second bedroom was sparsely furnished with just a bed and a canvas wardrobe but the big mystery was still the toilet and bathroom which I had yet to locate.

'Hey Nick, do you know this house at all?' I called to him as he connected the gas bottle to the cooker in the kitchen.

'Yes, why?'

'Well I can't find the bathroom.'

'Ah, the bathroom...' he answered mysteriously. 'Madame Mollet didn't tell you about the bathroom then?'

'Tell me *what* about the bathroom?' I was worried now.

Nick led the way through the kitchen and to a door which I had assumed led to a pantry, and with great ceremony, flung it wide open.

'TA DA!' He stood back to reveal a kind of wet room affair with a bit of a 'Colditz meets Ray Mears' theme going on. There was a shower with a concrete floor set with hundreds of pebbles and a half wall of glass bricks but, worst of all, the toilet was little more than a hole in the ground with a white porcelain surround and two plates for the feet.

I gasped and fell silent. This couldn't be it, surely? I felt myself starting to panic. 'I can't... I can't use that thing... Jesus Christ...'

'Oh, it's not that bad really. Lots of the old French prefer them. Turkish toilets they're called,' said Nick helpfully. 'Very popular with the Arab ladies as well. Apparently it's easier with their long dresses. I did the bathroom. Do you like it?'

'Well as I'm neither an old French woman nor an Arab...' I was gobsmacked. 'Didn't you think to put a bloody pedestal toilet in?'

Nick looked hurt. 'I thought it had a certain rustic charm.'

'Rustic charm?' I flopped down on one of the kitchen chairs while Nick stood around awkwardly shuffling from one foot to the other and taking a sudden interest in his shoes.

'Would you use it though? I mean, would you?' I asked.

'Well, um, I suppose...'

At least he had the decency to look a bit shamefaced.

'OK, no, I wouldn't use it but what about the shower?' he said, trying desperately to move the conversation away from the hole of doom. 'Great isn't it? My boys collected all those pebbles themselves from our garden.'

'Lovely, I'm sure,' I answered with just a tiny hint of sarcasm in my voice.

'Oh, and by the way, a little tip for you, free, gratis and for nothing.'

He was starting to get on my nerves with all his south London bonhomie.

'Get yourself a Sky box and card and then you can pick up English telly. You really wouldn't want to watch the crap on the French channels, trust me.'

I was struck by just how little I already trusted Nick but I thanked him for the advice anyway.

'There's a satellite dish here already. I put it up myself,' he told me proudly.

Bloody marvellous, I thought. It probably only picks up Bollywood.

'Well, I'd better crack on. Places to go, people to see and all that.'

I didn't respond.

'Listen, I'm a bit of a DJ on the side. Used to do some of the big clubs, you know, Ministry of Sound and all that, before we moved out here.'

I suspected that the nearest he'd ever been to the Ministry of Sound was one of their albums in HMV. I thought back to what the woman on the plane had told me about everyone having these fantasy lives. Maybe she was telling the truth.

'I'm doing a gig up at La Fontaine in Bussières on Saturday. It's in the square opposite the church. My wife, Libby, will be there, she'd love to meet you. There aren't that many young people around here so it would be great for her to have someone her own age to talk to. Eight-ish?'

'Yeah, we'll see. Not really sure what my plans are just yet.'

I was too upset about my Turkish privy to think about what I would be doing at the weekend.

'Right then, I'll be off.' Nick made a hasty exit and the last I heard of him was his transit van coughing its way down the hill back to his house with his proper toilet.

I sighed. I'd been doing a lot of that on my first day in France. I headed to the bedroom to sort out my clothes, which were still lying in a heap on the floor and wondered just how much use I'd have for that Phase Eight suit and the Joseph linen trousers. From what I'd seen so far, with the obvious exception of Tracey, it seemed like casual-casual was the preferred dress code. Oh well, a good excuse for a new wardrobe, not that I ever really needed one. One by one, I hung up my clothes, smoothing them over a little, then set about sorting my underwear, removing the ones which had footprints on from their unscheduled outing at the airport, and putting them aside for the wash. That little job done, I lay down on the bed. My early morning was catching up on me. I'll just close my eyes for a moment, I said to myself. It was the last thing I remembered before drifting off into a deep, dreamless sleep.

Jolted awake in what seemed like only moments later, I was surprised find it was nearly dark. I reached for my watch from the bedside table. It was gone nine o'clock. I'd been asleep for over four hours. Stretching languorously like a cat, I briefly considered just staying in bed but knew that I'd then be awake at four in the morning twiddling my thumbs and wondering what to do with myself. In any case, I hadn't even made up the bed.

I wandered into the lounge and decided a spot of telly was what was needed. The old set buzzed and hummed before springing to life and for a moment I thought I was in some kind of parallel universe. The screen filled with a talent show suspiciously like the one that Tracey Tarrant had been on, just in French.

The sets were the same but the three judges were certainly different. There was a slightly 'mutton dressed as lamb' older woman, a youngish man with a 1980s-style haircut and someone who looked like he'd taken the wrong turning on his way to the *Question Time* studio. A young girl was on stage, ready to sing. She was dressed in a minidress, over-the-knee socks, platform shoes and the biggest pair of geek glasses I'd ever seen in my life.

The backing music started and the girl opened her mouth to sing. A thin, reedy voice came out as she wailed her way through 'Chasing Pavements' by Adele or 'shazing payments' as it came out. God, I thought, it's good to see that the auditions are every bit as bad here as they are at home!

I grimaced. It really was dreadful but I felt strangely compelled to watch it. Car-crash reality television in French. Maybe life wouldn't be so different after all.

After a few minutes, I couldn't stand it anymore and flicked over to another channel which was showing a gritty police drama, all sludgy colours and pouring rain. Trying hard to follow what was being said, I stared at the television until my eyes started to hurt. This was no good. What I needed was a good dose of *Corrie* or *EastEnders*. I'd look into the Sky thing the next day. Turning off the television I wandered into the kitchen where the bottle of *rosé* I had bought earlier was chilling in the fridge. Oh well, the house may not have a proper toilet but at least I can open a bottle of wine. The French windows were still open and despite the late hour, it was warm outside. Clutching my wine glass, I stepped into the garden.

It was incredibly dark, far darker than at home. I chided myself. I had to stop thinking of England as home. This was home now. I'd never really thought about how little of the night sky you could actually see in London. I sat down on the ground and tried to count the stars. Above me, I quickly identified Ursa Major and Ursa Minor, The Plough, Orion – I was a bit of an anorak where constellations were concerned thanks to an ex-boyfriend with aspirations of becoming an astro-physicist. In the heady thrall of new love I had set about devouring my dad's copy of Carl Sagan's *Cosmos* with the same single-mindedness I'd later put to good use in my university degree. The ex had been unimpressed with my failure to grasp the Heisenberg Uncertainty Principle and had gone off to Switzerland to work on the Large Hadron Collider at CERN.

Lying down on the cool grass, I gazed at the night sky above, and with no light pollution to spoil things, it was a mass of stars. The Milky Way was as clear as the pictures I'd seen in *Cosmos*. Hundreds of bigger stars were suspended in a pale wash of smaller ones that swirled across the sky. It was amazing. I took out my phone to text the girls back home.

'Lying on my back looking at a million stars. What are you doing?'

Pressing the send button, I could just imagine where they were now. Fighting their way home on the Underground after an evening standing in an overcrowded bar shouting at each other over the noise, slinging back vodka jellies. Now actually...

No, this was my life now. I had said goodbye to the breakneck pace of London life and *bonjour* to the peace and beauty of rural France. I sighed deeply, feeling a wave of unadulterated contentment wash over me. And then the first mosquito bit.

Chapter Seven

'Twelve, thirteen, fourteen. Bugger, fifteen mozzie bites!'

I examined my arms and legs in the mirror to see if I had any more. I could cope with the ones on my body; it was the red, pulsating ones spotting my face that were the problem.

Today was market day in Bussières and I was desperate to go and check out the French lessons at the club, but I looked like I'd gone down with a nasty case of the pox. This really wasn't how I wanted to meet people, especially after the debacle with Monsieur and Madame Brunel. I was quite sure they would be dining out on that story for years. Damn it, I thought, I'll just have to brazen it out. I opened the wardrobe door, pulled out a large, floppy sunhat, and tried it on. In the right light, it cast enough of a shadow across my face to make me look secretive and mysterious rather than the last square meal of the local mosquito population.

And there was also the fact that Julien had offered to give me a lift. He had been on my mind a lot since our meeting in the café, in fact, since he nearly ran me over in the combine harvester if I was being honest, and every time a message arrived on my phone, I grabbed it excitedly in case it was him. Eventually, a few days later he did send me a message apologising for not contacting me sooner and asking if I wanted to go to the market on Saturday. I skipped around the room for a good half hour after that.

Turning back to the mirror, I dabbed some concealer on the worst offenders. It didn't really help much. There was no getting away from the fact that I looked like a teenager (which was good) with a nasty dose of acne (which wasn't). Last time I had seen Julien I had just had my second French Ditch Adventure and I was really hoping to make a slightly better impression this time. It wasn't looking good.

Going into the kitchen, I took the remains of the previous day's baguette, some butter and jam from the fridge and arranged it all on a plate before heading out to the little table in the garden and the early morning sunshine. I paused to listen for a minute. Nothing. Just the happy trilling of the birds as they swooped among the trees. I still couldn't get over the peace and quiet here.

I tried to break the baguette – but it was like reinforced concrete. Overnight my lovely, fresh bread had turned into an offensive weapon. I banged it on the table and ducked as a piece splintered off and shot past my head. Oh well, maybe just coffee then.

At the sound of tyres crunching on the gravel drive, I grabbed my bag and hat and rushed outside to meet Julien who was just climbing out of an old Renault 5. Dressed in a pair of straight-legged jeans, which showed off his rather excellent thighs, and a tight white T-shirt, he looked good enough to eat. Wicked thoughts flashed through my mind that made me blush.

'Hey neighbour, how are you?' I said coolly.

'Good,' he said leaning down to plant a kiss on each cheek. '*Mon Dieu*, what happened to your face?'

'You're not supposed to comment,' I smiled. 'The least you could have done is warned me that you have mosquitoes the size of jumbo jets here. All I did was lie out in the garden...'

'After dark?'

'Yes, after dark,' I continued.

'Well you must use lots of *citronelle*… you know, insect stuff, to keep them away. You know we breed them especially to like English blood. Well, we have to get our revenge for Mers-el-Kébir somehow,' he smiled.

'*Your* revenge?' I smiled, even though I wasn't entirely sure who or what Mers-el-Kébir was. 'Who gave us *Come Dine with Me* and *Fort Boyard*? That's revenge enough in my books.'

'Ah yes, a bit of our great French culture, that you English are so fond of,' he said. 'Anyway, look, I have something for you.'

I looked around, curious, then turned back to him, shrugging my shoulders.

'The car,' he said, laughing.

My mouth fell open and I stared at him, speechless.

'Look, it is just an old one that has been sitting around doing nothing on the farm for years. It is no beauty but it works. It is yours until you find something better.'

'Oh my God!' I cried, aware that my voice had climbed about two octaves. 'I don't believe it! Thank you so much!'

Sensing an opportunity, I flung my arms round him and squeezed him tight, enjoying the feel of his taut body through his shirt. I pulled away and looked up at him, seeing my face reflected in his velvet brown eyes. For a split second, I thought time had stood still. The only thing missing was the violins.

'OK, let's go,' he said, pulling away and opening the car door, the slightest hint of colour showing in his face. I instantly felt stupid. Here I was, only a few days into my new life in France and already throwing myself at the first friendly face. Pull yourself together, I chided myself. You don't need a man. You are a strong, independent woman. Who was I kidding?

Julien stood back and let me climb in to the driver's seat.

'OK, have you ever driven a left-hand drive car before?' I shook my head. It seemed very weird having the gearstick on the other side. Oh well, I thought, I'll soon get used to it.

Julien ran through everything: the indicators, the gears, the air conditioning.

'Whatever you do, don't leave the aircon running with the engine off or you will flatten the battery,' he told me. 'Are you ready?'

I put the car into reverse, eased out the clutch and manoeuvred it gingerly backwards round the side of the cottage, then headed up the drive. At the top, I had to think for a minute about which side of the road I had to be on, but as I'd seen all of three cars on the lane since my arrival, the chances were it wouldn't really matter.

I passed Laure in her front garden and waved and smiled but was rewarded with nothing but a wary stare that followed me until I rounded the corner to head down the hill out of the hamlet.

As we passed the vegetable garden that I had noticed on my first day, I saw an elderly man stooped over a hoe, tending to his crops. I tooted the horn and waved. He stared back at me. What *is* it with these people? I thought. They all seem so unfriendly. I wave, they stare. I wondered whether to broach the subject with Julien, but not wanting to seem critical of his fellow countrymen, I let it go.

'*Salut*, Hubert,' Julien called out of the open car window. The old man waved and the shadow of a smile passed across his face.

Oh fine, I thought, bristling ever so slightly, ignore me, why don't you? 'So, who's that then?'

'Him? That is Hubert Marcel, he lives in the house down the lane just before yours, you know, the one with all the rubbish in the garden?'

'Can't really say I've noticed but then it's a bit tucked away I suppose. Maybe I'll pop round and say hello.'

'Watch him, he's an old dog.'

'Oh come on! Him? He's got to be at least eighty.'

'He's fifty-three.'

'Ah.'

As we drove past, I caught sight of a woman coming out of the shed behind Monsieur Marcel. She was wearing a tiny gold bikini and heels, the perfect outfit for gardening. She swaggered over to Monsieur Marcel, her rather ample *décolletage* bobbing as she walked, and planted a kiss on his cheek. He squeezed her bottom playfully.

I nearly drove the car into a tree. Clearly there *was* life in the old dog. 'So, er, who's the woman?'

'Oh, that's Christine. She used to be married to his brother.' Julian told me matter-of-factly.

I arched my eyebrows. Maybe Claudine in the shop was right about all the intermarriage. 'His brother? Did he die or something?'

'Oh no, Hubert's wife ran off with Christine's husband last year. They live down in Marseilles now.'

'Escaping the scandal eh?' I smiled knowingly at Julien. He looked at me nonplussed.

'No, he was transferred with his company,' he replied, clearly thinking this sort of wife swapping was the most natural thing in the world.

'Oh… right.' Life in the country was clearly never boring.

At the bottom of the hill, I turned right towards Bussières. With the window down, the wind in my hair and a gorgeous man in the seat next to me, I thought I'd never been happier.

The tensions of London were slowly washing away. I could feel my shoulders dropping gradually and the constant knot in the back of my neck was hardly noticeable any more. Fields of young wheat waved languorously in the sun. The sky was the fresh blue of cornflowers and puffy, white clouds scudded across it at a leisurely pace. That seemed to sum up this little part of France to me. Leisurely. Everyone seemed to have more time. No one was rushing around with a Starbucks in one hand and a sandwich in the other; in fact, no one was rushing at all. I smiled to myself and thought, you clever girl, you've done the right thing.

My mind went back to the moment I had broken the news of my move to my friends. It was on my birthday and I had planned to meet up with my best mates at The Archangel, my favourite restaurant. With a few bottles of the bubbly stuff pre-ordered and a table booked for eight o'clock, I was ready to party.

I had worked in celebrity PR since leaving university and although my friends thought it unspeakably glamorous, especially as I worked with so many famous faces, the truth was I'd had enough of my boss, a misogynistic public school idiot who had changed his name from Clive to Zane to try and be cool. The job paid well but I rarely seemed to have the time to spend it, what with the twelve-hour days I regularly worked. I had been starting to wonder if there was more to life than collapsing in front of the television each evening.

It all started when I'd had a full day ahead of me accompanying one of our clients, Kitty Moseley, to a photo shoot for a Sunday supplement. Kitty was probably the most temperamental and demanding of the not-quite-supermodels and while her agent might describe her as 'elfin', 'a stunning pre-Raphaelite beauty' and 'a consummate professional', I'd describe her as a pig from hell.

Things had got off to a bad start when I forgot to order Kitty's super-skinny double latte with extra foam and a shot of vanilla. Well I hadn't actually forgotten, it was more that I hadn't been told that Kitty was incapable of functioning without one. Kitty had thrown a complete hissy fit and insisted that her Reiki master, a pumped-up body-building type with the unlikely name of Derek, be summoned so she could get her chakras re-aligned before she could *possibly* start work. Kitty retired to the dressing trailer to have them put back wherever they were supposed to be, leaving Bruno, the photographer, and the rest of the crew to spend the next two hours glaring at me. Mind you, judging from the moaning that was coming from the dressing room, I was fairly sure that it was more than just Kitty's chakras that were being re-aligned.

When we eventually got to work, Shitty Kitty, as I now called her under my breath, insisted that make-up be on standby after every single shot as she had discovered... shock, horror... the most enormous spot on her chin, so enormous that no one in the room except her could see it. Meanwhile, her personal assistant, an Eastern European called Evelina, who towered over everyone in a pair of 6-inch heels, stood off camera telling her she was 'so beautiful, darlink' every few minutes until I thought I might just barf right there on the floor.

Shitty Kitty got more demanding as the day wore on but the last straw was a request for a particular, and very hard to find, bar of organic chocolate. Sometimes I felt more like a glorified babysitter than a PR professional. I was tempted to remind her of the link between chocolate and bad skin but decided that it might be wiser to let that one go. Bearing in mind the theme of the shoot was 'urban decay' and we were filming in a derelict warehouse in an unfashionable part of the East End, the chances of finding anything more than a bar of Dairy Milk were fairly hopeless. I tried to explain politely to Kitty, but the look she bestowed on me could have frozen the blood of an Eskimo so as the clock ticked relentlessly down towards eight, I set off in the pouring rain to find a taxi and a bar of chocolate.

What felt like hours later and £40 lighter, I arrived back at the shoot with possibly the only bar of this particular organic chocolate in the whole of the East End. I walked through the warehouse door, chocolate held triumphantly aloft.

'Here you go! Who's a clever girl then?' I said to an empty room.

Where the hell were they all? A noise behind me made me swing round and I came face to face with a man-mountain with a flattened boxer's nose and a snarling Alsatian at his heel. I saw my whole life flash in front of me as I pressed myself against the wall.

'Sorry, love, don't mind Brutus here, he's a big softie really.'

I looked at the dog, took in the bared teeth and strings of drool hanging from each side of his mouth and thought I might beg to differ.

'I'm the night watchman. No one here I'm afraid. They left about an hour ago. I'm just locking up now.'

'What? But... but...' I was beside myself with rage. 'She insisted she had to have this bloody chocolate. I've traipsed halfway round frigging London trying to find the exact one she wanted. It's my birthday and I'm supposed to be sitting in a restaurant in the West End with my boyfriend and a bunch of friends, not standing in some godforsaken warehouse running errands for that... that...'

'Sorry love,' the night watchman said. 'You want me to get you a cab or something?'

'Oh, yes, sorry, yes please.' I felt near to tears at the unfairness of it all.

Twenty minutes later, as I sat in the back of a cab watching the rain drumming on the windows and the long queue of traffic up ahead, I knew I'd be lucky to make The Archangel before ten o'clock the next morning, never mind that night. I tapped out a quick text to Alex, my boyfriend.

'Gonna B L8. There ASAP. Hugs xx'

Almost instantly, my phone dinged and Alex's reply appeared on the screen.

'Hurry up, we're all waiting for you. What time? X'

'Well thank you so much for your sympathetic reply,' I muttered to myself in a snarky voice, sticking my tongue out at my mobile. NEVER! I tapped in before deleting it.

'10ish. Start without me.'

He didn't even bother to reply to that one.

With time on my hands and the traffic showing no signs of moving I started to reflect on my life. I was exhausted and just recently the bad days had started to outnumber the good ones. On the one hand, I did love my job, at least there was never a dull moment, but on the other hand, I knew I wanted something more. A gentler pace of life maybe? God, was this the first sign of a mid-life crisis? I was expecting that to start around forty-five, not twenty-eight.

My phone sounded the arrival of a new message. Alex, I thought, but it wasn't him. In fact, I didn't recognise the name at all and stared at it for a second, trying to work out who it might be. Funny how you do that, isn't it? It's like getting a letter and recognising the handwriting on the envelope, then spending ages trying to work out who it's from. I clicked it open.

'*Bonsoir,* thank you for your interest in Les Tuileries. I can confirm that it is available to rent if you are still interested...'

I frowned at the screen, thinking it must be meant for someone else. Suddenly it dawned on me. A few weeks ago, after another particularly rough day, I'd been trawling the French property sites that my old friend Polly had suggested to me, and found a lovely cottage for rent. On the spur of the moment, I had sent an email asking if it was available. This must be it. I smiled to myself. It wasn't really a serious enquiry. I'd email back and make up some excuse. I clicked on 'reply' and began to type, then stopped. *Maybe*, I thought.

Eventually, over two hours late, the taxi pulled up outside The Archangel. I paid the driver the equivalent of the GDP of a small African nation and headed inside. My friends were sitting at a table, tucked away in the corner. I stopped to watch them. Alex was in full flow telling one of his dreadful jokes, Charlotte, my best friend since forever, was already a bit the worse for wear, no doubt something to do with all the empty bottles littering the table. Daisy, my sister and her boyfriend Finn, were creased up with laughter at Alex's joke. Justine and Suzy, my old university friends, were deep in conversation. From the debris on the table, I could see that they had started without me. I felt ever so slightly annoyed that they really hadn't waited. It was my birthday after all. On impulse, I took my phone out of my pocket, scrolled to my emails and clicked on 'send'. Hundreds of miles away, in the south-west of France, another phone announced the arrival of a new message.

Alex looked over and saw me. 'Hey, birthday girl,' he called. I smiled at him and walked over to join them.

'Hi sis,' said Daisy, 'bad day?'

'Pretty much. By the way, I'm moving to France.'

Chapter Eight

The little town of Bussières, normally deserted save for a few elderly women sitting on the benches in the square, was buzzing with people. The square had been completely taken over by stalls, some with brightly coloured awnings, others with umbrellas in stands, shading the merchants from the sun.

Julien directed me into a small car park behind the village square. In the shade of a row of plane trees old men in black *bérets* were playing *boules*, the sound of their light-hearted shouting and joshing mingled with the gentle thwack of the metal balls that they were throwing with alarming accuracy. On the benches which lined the pitch, rows of elderly women sat, shoulder to shoulder, some gossiping, some knitting, others just watching the world go by. It was the perfect French scene. Someone waved. It was Louis.

'*Salut,*' he called. He spoke briefly to his opponents and came towards us.

'Well, you two don't make it easy, do you?' I said after we had exchanged kisses.

'I'm sorry?'

'Look at you both in white T-shirts and jeans. How's a girl supposed to tell you apart?'

'I've already told you,' replied Julien, 'I'm the good looking one!' Louis threw him a withering look.

'Oh, yes, so you like to think. Can I just take him a moment?' He put his arm round his brother and led him away, talking quickly, their heads close together. Even if I understood French, I would never have been able to work out what they were saying. They stood a little way off and it was clear that what Louis had to say, Julien didn't want to hear. There was a lot of gesticulation and for a brief moment, I saw him look over at me, suddenly making me feel very ill at ease. I was fairly sure Louis was talking about me.

A few minutes later, Louis headed back to his *boules* game, giving me a brief wave as he went.

'Everything OK?' I asked as we headed for the market.

'Yes, fine. It was just something about the farm.'

I had an uncomfortable feeling that he wasn't telling the truth.

'*Bon,*' said Julien, 'first we have to buy you a *panier*, a basket. No proper French woman would be seen at the market without one.'

Sure enough, everyone around me seemed to have a hessian basket, from which peeked out fruit or vegetables and the odd baguette here and there.

At the corner of the market, I could see a swarthy-looking man was standing amid a colourful spread of bags. 'Over there,' I said, pointing to the stall. We wandered over to have a look.

'*Bonjour, la belle mademoiselle,*' he said, bowing gracefully to me. After that, I was lost. He launched into his well-rehearsed sales patter while I stood looking on hopelessly.

'What did he say?' I asked Julien.

'Well after he told you that you were the most beautiful woman in the market today...'

I laughed. 'Charmer!'

'... he said that he has the best selection of bags in south west France and that you should have this one with the blue to match your eyes.'

Market-trader speak was clearly pretty similar the world over. I picked up the basket that the man was pointing out. It was a basket. I'd never had one before. They weren't really de rigeur in Knightsbridge. It wasn't Mulberry but it would probably do.

'How much is it?'

The man, anticipating the question, launched into another long spiel. I turned to Julien.

'He said that he sold the same basket to the Comtesse de Lavaur only last week and that normally it would cost fifty euros, he has to feed his family, eight children you know, but he said it is yours for twenty euros.'

'Deal.' I rooted in my bag for my purse and handed over a twenty-euro note in exchange for my new shopping basket. The man thanked me elaborately, wishing me a pleasant day in very broken English, before moving on to the next customer.

'OK,' said Julien, 'now you are practically French.'

I smiled up at him. 'You're so being so kind to me, Julien. Thank you. I really appreciate having someone take me under their wing.'

'Under their wing?' He looked confused.

'I mean, to take care of me, show me the ropes, that sort of thing.'

'Bof,' he said shrugging in that particularly French way, 'it is nothing. Anyway, you are a nice girl. Who wouldn't want to help you?'

I could think of one or two back in London who wouldn't exactly be queuing up. I doubted that the lovely Kitty Moseley would pee on me if I was on fire, but what did that matter? I was in France with the best-looking man in the northern hemisphere.

I felt a funny, fluttery feeling in my stomach again. It wasn't like me to be so demure. Normally I'd have had a few drinks, thrown my arms around him and then regretted it all in the morning. He was different though. I liked him. I mean, really liked him.

'Listen,' he said, 'I have to go and do some things. It's all boring stuff, for the farm. Do you want to stay here and I will meet you again in one hour?'

'Oh, yes, OK,' I replied, trying to mask my disappointment. 'Maybe we can get a coffee or something when you get back? Shall we meet in the café on the corner?'

He did the *bisous* thing on both my cheeks and walked off through the market. I watched him go. He really was rather splendid. I sighed then set off to explore, deciding to do the full tour before buying anything.

It was a far cry from my local market which was the place to buy pet food, cheap batteries and knock-off CDs. There were stands selling fruit and vegetables, wrinkled old farmers selling eggs and a few onions, *boulangers* with bread of every shape and size imaginable, fresh flowers, a fishmonger with a giant pan of paella bubbling away, scenting the air with delicious smells, there were even plastic crates of fluffy rabbits. I stopped to pet one through the bars. I hadn't really expected pets to be on sale.

'You want?' said the woman who seemed to be in charge of the stall.

'Oh, no, it's all right. Thanks anyway.'

Before I had a chance to object any further, the lady had grabbed the rabbit out of the crate by the scruff of its neck and shoved it in my arms. The little rabbit nuzzled into me and I stroked it gently, tickling it behind its ears.

'Is good rabbit, *mademoiselle*,' said the woman. She squidged the rabbit's tummy. 'Very good, he grow big, many meals. Look.'

I obediently felt the rabbit. 'Yes, he's certainly well-fed.'

The woman nodded enthusiastically.

'You know they're for eating, don't you?' said a voice I recognised behind me. 'She means that it'll give you many meals.'

I spun round to find Nick, the furniture man, standing behind me with two scruffy kids in tow.

'What?'

'Look, didn't you see those ones there?'

I looked over. A row of skinned rabbits, eyes staring blankly, were laid out in a chiller cabinet.

'Omigod!' I hugged the little rabbit to my chest, shielding its eyes from the sight of its cousins, stripped and peeled and ready for the pot.

'Yeah, it's the staple diet around here. Chicken is too expensive but rabbit is dead cheap. Most of the oldies keep a few rabbits for the pot.'

'My dad lets us shoot them with his gun,' said the taller one.

'Then we skin them with our Swiss army knives,' said the smaller one. He drew a knife out of his pocket and waved it in my face.

'Bloody hell, put it away. You'll get arrested,' I said hastily.

'Oh, don't worry,' said Nick, 'it's all a bit different here. If you go over the other side there's a stall that sells everything from hunting knives to switchblades. All perfectly legal. Most kids round here carry a knife.'

I made a mental note not to tangle with any of the local teenagers on a dark night.

'These are my kids by the way. This is Beau,' he motioned to the older one, 'and this is Rip.'

'Not big on long names then?' I laughed, wondering who on earth would call a child Beau, especially one like this who, with his buck teeth and mouth-breathing, was anything but.

'Yeah, well with me as their dad I knew there was a fair chance they wouldn't be that bright so I wanted something that would be easy to spell.'

I frowned and looked at him. Was he joking or not?

'Well, better crack on. Don't forget Saturday night in La Fontaine if you're stuck for something to do. It's just over there.' He pointed to a rather run-down bar with cheap plastic chairs and tables outside. Certainly not the sort of place I imagined myself spending too much time.

'*Mademoiselle?*' said the stallholder, holding her arms out for the rabbit, which was now fast asleep in my arms.

'*Non,*' I shouted, rather louder than intended. '*Combien?*'

The woman held up ten fingers.

'*Oui,* yes, I'll take it.'

The woman held out a box and motioned for me to put the rabbit inside. With the box securely taped and my purse ten euros lighter, I headed back towards the car with my new friend. I had made some impulse purchases in the past but never a rabbit.

'You'll be fine in here with the windows open,' I told it. 'I won't be too long and you won't be rabbit pie.' I peeped through the holes in the box and the rabbit looked back at me with wary eyes.

Back in the market square, I continued my wanderings, gradually filling my basket with some freshly baked bread, a bag of huge local tomatoes, a frilly lettuce, still damp with morning dew – or that's what I told myself at least.

'*Mademoiselle*, you want some cheese? The best cheese in France.'

A young man in a *béret* and a smock was holding out a chunk of soft cheese on the blade of a knife. Thanking him, I carefully took it and popped it in my mouth. It was strong, but not 'old socks' strong. I remembered something Alex had said to me before I left. 'Never trust a country that has four hundred cheeses, all of them *Brie*.' I realised how little I had thought about Alex since I got here.

'You like?' asked the man earnestly. 'It is made by my family for generations. My great-*grandpère* created the recipe and passed it down the family. It is made from sheep's milk on our farm in the foothills of the Pyrénées.'

I listened as he described the little mountain farm, the flock of rare French sheep and his ancient *Papi*, bent over a vat of cheese, stirring it, pressing it into moulds, smearing it with pig fat (actually I could have done without that little snippet of information) and bandaging it, then taking it to mature in a cave in the hills. I was lost in his description and all the while he talked, he fed me small pieces of cheese. The whole thing was quite mesmerising.

I could hardly wait for him to finish so I could tell him that I would definitely love to buy a piece of his family's heritage... sorry, cheese. He cut me a small wedge, wrapped it lovingly in greaseproof paper, then slipped it into a brown paper bag.

I stared at him, open-mouthed. The best part of twenty-five quid for a bit of cheese? He looked back at me, impassively, knowing he had led me past the point of no return. Handing the package to me, I was too embarrassed to say no so I took it and gave him a bundle of euro notes in return.

He handed over my change and thanked me for my custom.

I stomped off, angry with myself for being taken advantage of. Maybe Alex was right about the French. Maybe they couldn't be trusted. I stopped myself. I'd been ripped off. It happened everywhere. I pushed the unwelcome thought away and set off to find the Alliance Franco-Brittanique, which was, after all, the main reason I had come into town. It was the drop-in coffee morning today and I wanted to find out about French lessons.

The club was on a road off the market square in a dismal little building that looked like it may have started life as a cowshed and hadn't really progressed much since. I pushed my sunglasses up on top of my head, opened the door and walked into a hallway which was lined with notice boards advertising local traders, items for sale, pets, local clubs and societies. I browsed the notices. Keep Fit. Not quite Zumba but it might do. Scottish country dancing. Nope. Bridge Club, Mah Jong, Cribbage. There seemed to be a bit of a pattern emerging. A sign by the notice board indicated the 'English Library' with a big arrow pointing to a door on the right. That might be worth a look.

Pushing open the door, I walked into a room that was barely bigger than a broom cupboard, with every space on the wall crammed with shelves of books. An older lady with half-moon glasses sat behind a desk rummaging through an index box full of library cards. She looked up, smiling vaguely, as I walked in, before returning to her rummaging.

I wandered down the rows of books: Barbara Taylor-Bradford, Catherine Cookson, Jilly Cooper, Danielle Steel. Not really my thing to be honest.

'Are you looking for anything in particular?' The lady at the desk peered over the top of her glasses at me.

'Umm, do you have any Catherine Alliott?' I asked.

'I'm not sure I'm familiar with her I'm afraid.'

'Wendy Holden?'

'Err...'

'Jodi Picoult?'

'We've just had this very nice book returned,' the woman suggested hopefully, holding up a book that would definitely have appealed to my mother, but sadly not to me.

'Thanks but I think I've already read that one,' I lied. The poor woman was only trying to be helpful after all. 'By the way, where is the coffee morning?'

'Just down the hallway dear, last door on your right. I think Priscilla and Jeremy are hosting it today.'

Priscilla and Jeremy... Prissy and Jerry, I thought as I headed off to meet my doom – or at least that's what it felt like. With names like that it didn't bode well. I paused for a moment, my hand on the door handle. Deep breath, I told myself.

Pushing open the door I walked in, a fixed smile plastered across my face. Conversation stopped and twenty heads swivelled in my direction. Twenty old heads. I was probably the youngest by about forty years.

'Hello, dear,' came a voice from across the room, 'can I help you?' A shrew-like woman in her sixties came towards me, pulling a cardigan around her bony chest despite the warmth of the room. Her long, grey hair was pulled back into a tight bun and everything about her screamed 'anally retentive'. It had to be Prissy, I thought.

'Um, yes, no... um... sorry, I'm in the wrong place. I was looking for the... the...' My voice petered out. 'Toilets?' Oh for heaven's sake, I thought, why did I have to say that?

'Next door along dear. You're new here aren't you?'

'Yes, quite new. I've been here a few weeks now. I'm living up at Les Tuileries.'

'Oh yes, the one with the creative sanitary facilities,' said the woman, smirking. 'No wonder you want to use ours.'

'Ah, I see the reputation of my lavatorial arrangements precedes me. Anyway...,' I crossed my legs and feigned desperation. 'Got to go, literally. See you again.'

I hurried from the room, pulling the door closed behind me. In the hallway, I collapsed against the wall. God's bloody waiting room. That's all I needed. French lessons would have to wait. I could surely find them somewhere other than there. Looking at my watch I realised that the hour was nearly up. Time to go and meet Julien. Slipping my sunglasses down over my eyes, I stepped back out into the street and headed for the café.

Up ahead I caught sight of one of the Twin Hunks through the crowd. Julien or Louis? Julien, I thought, definitely. I stepped out to try and catch him up but then stopped abruptly, as if I'd walked into an invisible wall, so abruptly, in fact, that the lady walking behind cannoned into me.

'*Excusez-moi, madame.*'

The woman glared at me and carried on walking. I had lost sight of the twin in the crowd.

The terrace of the café was busy but there was one table in the corner, shaded by the awning. I sat down and pushed my bag under the table, still perturbed by what I had seen, or at least, thought I'd seen. The waiter came to take my order but I told him that I would like to wait for my friend.

Julien arrived a few minutes later and sat down opposite me, stretching out his long legs and running his fingers through his hair.

'You have ordered?' he asked.

'No, I thought I'd wait for you.'

Julien signalled for the waiter to come over. 'What would you like?'

'Do they do lattes?' I asked.

He laughed. 'I will get you a *grand crème*. It's the nearest thing we have.'

He called a waiter over and put in his order. The waiter had the slightly crazed look of someone who was not quite managing. He repeated the orders back in slow, broken French.

'Oh, are you English then?' I asked. 'Because if you are, you can just talk to me in English.'

He replied to me in French.

'No, you see I'm English so it's OK. I can see you are struggling.'

The waiter scowled at me. 'I've got to learn French. It's taken me two years to find this job but they'll only keep me on if I can speak the language.'

Two years to find a job as a waiter in a café? I wondered if I had overestimated my own chances of finding work.

The coffees on order, Julien asked me what I'd bought in the market.

'Well, you know, just the usual. A baguette, some fruit and vegetables, oh, and a rabbit.'

'A what? A rabbit?'

'Yes, well, you see it was going to be sold for food and I couldn't stand it. It was curled up in my arms and all warm and fluffy...' a smile started to form on Julien's lips, '... and I just, well, bought it. It's in the car. I'm going to keep it, you know, for a pet.'

Julien roared with laughter. '*Mon dieu*, you have a lot to learn about life in the country. Here we keep things only for eating, well, apart from dogs and cats of course. Rabbits are not pets, they are food.'

I looked down into my lap, feeling ever so slightly silly.

He leant across the table and pushed a strand of hair back from my face. 'You are so funny, *ma belle*.'

Instinctively, I put my hand up to cover his, feeling the roughness of his palms against my face, so different from the city-soft hands of Alex.

'*Voilà*,' said the waiter exuberantly as he put our coffees down on the table. The spell was broken. Opening up the paper on the cube of sugar, I dropped one into my cup and stirred it slowly.

'I could have sworn I saw you earlier,' I hesitated. 'Um...' I hesitated again, wondering whether to go on or not. 'With a woman. You were kissing her.' I looked up at him.

'Me, *non*, it's not possible,' he replied almost too quickly. 'It must have been Louis.' For a split second, I thought I saw a shadow cross his face.

'Well, it's not as if it's anything to do with me anyway. I mean, we've only just met.'

Oh for heaven's sake, I told myself, just shut up!

I stirred my coffee intently, feeling stupid and embarrassed at the turn of events. Julien looked away.

'Oh look, I'm sorry. That all came out wrong. Let's just forget it shall we? Look what I bought in the market.' I fished in my basket, coming out with the bag containing the world's most expensive piece of cheese. 'Do you want to try it? It's made to an old family recipe in their farm in the foothills of the Pyrénées.'

'Let me guess. By Guillaume, the one over there in the *béret*,' said Julien, pointing across to the cheese stall where another unsuspecting couple were listening intently to the story of the family *fromage*. 'We're nearer to the Pyrénées than that cheese has ever been. He buys it from a supermarket in Bergerac and he lives in the HLM, the public housing, in Bussières.'

'What?! He charged me twenty-five bloody euros for it!'

'He does it all the time to the tourists.'

'But I'm not a tourist, I live here,' I protested.

'I know but you have to understand that around here if you can't trace your family back to the Hundred Years War you will always be a foreigner or a tourist. Still, at least you are not from Paris. They are even less accepted than foreigners.'

'So I heard. But why?'

'Oh, you know, they are so different to us rural people, arrogant, rude, condescending...'

Yes, that sounded about right I mused, thinking back to my experience on a school exchange. When I was thirteen, I had spent a thoroughly miserable week in France with Elise, a precocious Parisian girl. Elise clearly felt that the little English girl was far too provincial and set about making sure I knew how inferior I was to a cool *parisienne*. She had taught me all sorts of words which were totally unsuitable but which I had then used to shocking effect in Madame Martin's French lessons on my return. We finished our coffees in companionable silence. Despite my earlier *faux pas* it felt so comfortable being with him. There was no need to talk to fill the silence.

'Come on, we should go. There's a bored bunny waiting for us in the car.'

'Bored? It is a rabbit. It doesn't get bored.'

I threw him a withering glance then smiled and gathered up my bags.

'Just a moment, I need to do something. I'll be back in a minute.'

He got up and walked over to where Guillaume, the cheese man, was counting the money he had swindled from the unsuspecting tourists. I watched him go. I could watch that rear view all day I thought. Meanwhile, an unsuspecting Julien was having a very animated conversation with Guillaume who was looking very sheepish. Julien saw me and waved me over.

'*Voilà,*' he said handing me twenty-five euros. 'A refund for your overpriced cheese.' Guillaume shrugged his shoulders and smiled, giving me one of those 'well you gotta try' looks.

I rummaged in my basket and handed back the cheese but he held up his hands. 'No, *mademoiselle*, you can keep it.'

Back at the car park, the *boules* players were gradually packing away and a tablecloth had been spread over one of the benches. A few bottles of red wine were opened and one of the old ladies was slicing *saucisson*, another a *Brie*, while a third tore apart a baguette. It was so simple but looked divine. So much better than the homogenised sandwiches that I was used to. As I opened up the boot to put my basket in, a black streak shot out, making me jump back and cry out in surprise. A pile of chewed cardboard was all that remained of the box that had held the rabbit and with its first whiff of freedom it had taken off, jumping down from the boot and zigzagging its way across the car park. People leapt out of the way of the speeding bunny as it shot between their feet.

Sadly, freedom was short-lived, as was the rabbit. From nowhere, a little russet spaniel appeared, yapping as it gave chase, and in fright, the little bunny shot across the road, straight into the path of a car.

I screamed and covered my eyes as a squeal of breaks heralded the end of its life. I peered through my fingers, hoping against hope that the rabbit had made it across the road. My mouth dropped open in horror as the driver of the car hopped out, picked up the dead rabbit, flung it in his boot and drove off, tomorrow's dinner no doubt sorted.

I stood there, stunned.

'Welcome to the countryside.' Julien put his arm around me and gave me a hug.

Chapter Nine
Six Weeks Later

The weeks flew by, with one sultry day slipping into the next. So far, all the niggly little things had gone swimmingly. I had the internet set up, the phone was connected and Nick had sorted out Sky TV so I could even watch Corrie if the mood took me... which it didn't. He'd even arranged to have the pool cleaned and the once green and slimy water was now clear blue.

I watched my pallid skin turn a light mocha and my hair bleach blonde in the sun. It used to cost the best part of £150 at Franco's but here was nature doing it for free. The bad old days in London were becoming little more than a distant memory.

Mind you, so was a pay cheque. My savings, such as they were, seemed to be disappearing rather faster than I'd anticipated. Things were just so much more expensive than I'd imagined. I needed to start looking for a job.

I was still trying to shake the feeling that I was on holiday and for the moment at least, I was happy with my own company and with the solitude of my little cottage. Being so totally alone in such peace and quiet was unusual. I'd wondered if I might hate it but in fact I didn't, not so far, at least. I hadn't seen Tracey Tarrant since the day I arrived, though I knew that she was still there, holed up with her footballer, inexplicably beyond the reach of the paparazzi it seemed, and I still hadn't organised any French lessons. Oh well, one day.

I turned over on the sun lounger and unhooked my bikini top so I could get a nice even tan. I sighed contentedly and dozed in the late May sunshine, half-listening to the frantic chirruping of the cicadas. God they were noisy! The glass of chilled *rosé* I'd had with my lunch made me feel sleepy and before long I had dropped off, dreaming, as I did rather too often these days, of Julien. I was sure he liked me but he kept holding back. We had met up several times for drinks, even for lunch once or twice, although if I was being honest with myself, it was more that we both ended up in the café at Rocamour at the same time. He flirted with me and I with him but then something always seemed to stop him making that final move. Fortunately, the Julien of my dreams was a little more forward.

We lay tangled up by the side of the pool in the woods. Julien brushed my hair from my face. I looked up into his eyes which were heavy with lust, my mouth parting slightly. He leaned towards me. Finally he was going to kiss me. He drew nearer and nearer. Our lips met. He tasted of...

... grass? My eyes sprang open.

'Bloody hell! What the...'

A large horse, ridden by an even larger woman, was nuzzling my face... in my garden... by my pool! I hate horses. Little ponies are fine, but this huge beast... I lay rooted to the sun lounger, fingers gripping the towel underneath me as I tried to calm myself.

'GET. IT. AWAY,' I said to the woman, slowly and carefully enunciating my words.

'Oh, don't be such a girlie, he just wants to say hello, don't you Kaiser?' boomed the woman, dismounting so heavily that the ground shook. 'Just need to use the lavvy. Don't worry, know the house well. I can find my own way.'

I sat up and she thrust the reins at me. I stared, open-mouthed. The cheek of the bloody woman!

'Just a minute...' I shouted as my visitor, oversized rear end clad in tight jodhpurs which gave the unfortunate impression that she had a couple of puppies romping inside them, strode off towards the house, unzipping her jodhpurs as she went.

I held the reins distastefully between my thumb and forefinger and stared at the horse. It stared back. It was a huge black and white thing with hairy feet and hooves the size of dinner plates. It soon got bored with the Mexican stand-off and its head went down to crop the grass on my lawn. I wasn't entirely sure what to do so I opted for just sitting still and hoping that it would ignore me.

Several minutes passed before the woman returned, tucking her shirt into her jodhpurs as she walked.

'Don't mind me using the facilities do you? Got caught short, what.'

I opened my mouth to protest that actually, I wasn't keen on strangers rocking up and using my toilet, but before I had a chance to say anything, the woman bellowed at me.

'Ride, do you?'

God, couldn't this woman do anything quietly?

She stuck out her hand before I had chance to answer. 'Clarissa Blythe-Cholmondeley-Walker,' she said, 'but most people call me Chummy. Won't bother with that bloody kissing lark. Damned unhygienic if you ask me.'

I breathed a small sigh of relief and shook her hand, wincing slightly as Clarissa's calloused hand crushed mine in a vice-like grip.

'Heard some new blood had moved in. Glad to see the back of the last incumbents to be honest. Came to see if you were a horsey gel. Would be good to have someone to ride out with, although Kaiser's safe hacking out on his own. Goes in front or behind quite happily.'

I tried to conceal a smirk. 'Uh, no, not really. I'm kind of frightened of them,' I admitted.

'Stuff and bloody nonsense. I'll let you ride Kaiser here, he's a real school master. Can be a bit forward going on open ground and goes like a bloody rocket if you give him his head but he's got a lovely light mouth and great elevation.'

I frowned. What sort of strange language was this woman talking? 'I quite like cats though,' I added hopefully.

'Cat lover, eh? Want to get yourself down to that cat charity place in Bussières. Bunch of bloody do-gooders if you ask me. Always on about neutering the feral cats. Just shoot the buggers, I say. You want to get yourself a nice Labrador or something.'

'Um, actually I'm a little bit allergic to dogs.'

Clarissa looked at me witheringly. Clearly in her eyes I was beyond any hope.

'Well, anyway, having a little *soirée* tonight and thought you might fancy coming along to meet a few of the chaps. Sevenish? I'll send the old man to pick you up. That way you can have a few bevvies. Rodders can go for a few hours without a drink, bless him.'

I opened my mouth to say thanks, I really fancied an early night but Chummy was already heaving herself back up into the saddle, poor Kaiser having to brace himself to take her weight.

'See you later. Seven.'

I watched her ride off, ample behind jiggling in time with the horse's footsteps. Footsteps or hoof steps? I would rather hack my leg off with a rusty nail file than spend a few hours with Clarissa and her friends.

Four hours later, having failed completely to come up with a single reasonable-sounding excuse for not going, I was sitting in the passenger seat of Chummy's Range Rover listening to her husband Roddy, ex-Grenadier Guards, wittering on in a voice that was so plummy that his upper lip didn't even move.

'F'nah, f'nah, f'nah...'

I smiled and nodded. I could have been agreeing to have his lovechild for all I knew. Mercifully the car journey was short and within a few minutes, we were turning into a long sweeping drive lined on either side by cypress trees.

'F'nah, f'nah, f'nah...'

Yes of course I'll dress up in a French maid's outfit and whip you with a wet haddock, I thought, starting to enjoy my little game.

The car turned between two impressive stone pillars.

'WOW!' I exclaimed as a miniature Disney chateau appeared in front of us. Perfectly symmetrical, its tall, narrow towers pointed up towards the scarlet-hued early evening sky. The sun, dipping low, bathed the red brick in a warm, rosy glow and sparkled off a lake set back behind the chateau, surrounded by parkland and woods. The gravel driveway formed a perfect semi-circle edged with lavender and pale pink roses. Steps, flanked on either side by topiaried box trees, led up to a plain, white front door directly below a wrought-iron Juliet balcony. It was, quite simply, divine.

Roddy came around the car to open the door for me then led me up the steps into a magnificent panelled hallway with rich, chestnut parquet floors.

'Here she is!'

Clarissa swept into the hallway, like a galleon in full sail, dressed in a flowing tent dress.

'Hello, Clarissa, so kind of you...'

'Chummy, name's Chummy. Only people who call me Clarissa are Mater and Pa.'

'Err, Chummy.'

'Come on through and meet everyone.'

She led me through a cavernous music room with a grand piano in the corner and out through French windows dressed in sheer muslin onto a raised terrace overlooking the lake.

'This is the most amazing house, Cla... err, Chummy. How long have you lived here?'

'Had it for years now. Rodders bought it from the dosh he got from a business deal.'

Must have been some deal, I thought, but before I had a chance to wonder, Chummy whispered to me, 'Iran', before tapping one side of her nose and giving me a knowledgeable look. I had absolutely no idea what she was talking about.

Chummy clapped her chubby hands. 'Chaps, she's here. Come and say hello. Rodders, bring some bubbly.'

A glass of champagne was thrust into my hand as Chummy led me round the small gathering making her introductions.

'Squeezy and Quentin, live over the hill, Le Cornau. Binky and Teddy here are in the village.'

'So where do you live?' asked Quentin

'I'm renting Les Tuileries in St Amans.'

'Aaaahhh,' they all sing-songed in unison, giving each other knowing looks. I looked at them quizzically, hoping someone would enlighten me.

'Why do I feel like I'm the only one who isn't in the know? It's not the toilet is it? Honestly, I've got used to it. It's a bit rustic but I've got thighs of steel now,' I said slapping them firmly.

They looked bemused. Clearly it wasn't the sanitary facilities that had them all winking at each other.

'Don't you know about the last tenants?'

The voice, with the faintest hint of a Welsh accent, belonged to a stringy woman who had obviously spent far too much time in the sun. Coal-black, mean-looking eyes peered out from a leathery, wrinkled face framed by a harshly-chopped dyed black bob. She looked a bit like a tortoise in a wig.

'I'm Muffy by the way. Pleased to meet you.' She stuck a thin, calloused hand out.

'So, what's the story then?'

'Religious cult.'

'No! Really? At Les Tuileries? Do tell.'

'I always knew there was something wrong with them. They didn't mix with anyone. Not like Gerry and Barbara who lived there before. They were just like us, lovely people.'

Maybe they just had an allergy to people with ridiculous names, I thought, groaning inwardly. I thought I'd left this sort of attitude behind.

'... spawned loads of brats, never let anyone in the house and they were... you know...'

I looked quizzically at her. 'What?'

'You know.'

I raised my eyebrows in question. 'No, sorry, you'll have to give me a clue.'

'Foreigners.' She said foreigners in the same way as you'd say 'syphilis' or 'paedophile'.

'But we're foreigners too aren't we?' I was genuinely puzzled.

'No, not foreigners like us.'

'Like what then?'

'Well, you know, they were... black.'

I looked at her, horrified. Surely this sort of bigoted attitude didn't still exist in the twenty-first century, even out here?

'So that makes them a religious cult? Maybe they were drug dealers too or running a white slavery ring? Come on, that's a bit racist isn't it?'

I tried hard to be polite but this stupid, ignorant woman had really got my back up.

'Oh, don't mind her. She wouldn't recognise a racist comment if it ran up and stuck a burning cross on her lawn would you, Muffy, dear?'

A young girl in her early twenties, with the self-assuredness that comes with money and privilege, walked across the terrace swinging her hips like a supermodel, lustrous chestnut hair flowing down her back like a shampoo advert.

'I'm Cecilia. Cecilia Blyth-Cholmondeley-Walker but you can call me CeeCee. Nice to meet you.' She put out a hand with long, manicured fingernails and shook mine firmly. 'Yes, she's my mother,' she said, nodding towards Chummy. 'Who'd have thought, eh?'

There was certainly little to link the tall, lithe CeeCee with the rotund, lumpy Chummy.

'I can't stand bloody horses either. Come over and sit down,' she said, motioning to a low rattan sofa a little way away from the others. 'Let's leave the oldies to themselves. All they ever talk about is how France is like England in the 1950s anyway.'

'What? You mean racism, wife-beating and rickets?' I smiled.

Cecilia sniggered. 'Oh, I can see you and I are going to get along famously.'

'And wait till I tell you who's living next door to me,' I whispered into her ear.

Chapter Ten

I sat out on the terrace with my regular breakfast of croissants, which I picked up each morning from Claudine's shop, and a big mug of *café au lait*. I was going to have to cut down on the croissants though I thought, feeling the slight pinch around my waist where my shorts were digging in. Better still, I should be walking to the shop, not taking the car. Ah well, I'd start my croissant-free diet next week. I licked my buttery fingers and took another sip of coffee as I heard yet another car making its way up the hill. It was unusually busy in the otherwise sleepy little hamlet. The road ended in open fields just past Les Tuileries so normally the busiest it got was the farmer pootling along in his old white Citroën van to check on his crops. Strange.

Curious to know what was happening, I downed my coffee, grabbed my sunglasses and set off to investigate. I didn't have to go far. It seemed that my neighbour, Tracey Tarrant, was the reason for all the action. The tall, wrought-iron gates to her house were surrounded by what looked suspiciously like paparazzi. Seedy-looking men with long-lens cameras strung round their necks hung about chatting and smoking, every now and then glancing through the bars of the gates towards the house.

Hanging back a bit, looking more than a little bemused at the press invasion, were Monsieur and Madame Brunel, Martine and Laure in their housecoats and Monsieur Marcel. Just to make it really French, Martine's chickens had come along too. I smiled at my neighbours and was rewarded with a row of blank looks. Clearly the fact that I was also a foreigner meant I was guilty by association and, in any case, Madame Brunel had definitely not forgiven me for our first meeting. When I'd returned her housecoat, clean and folded, she had just snatched it from my hand and slammed the door in my face before I'd even had a chance to say thank you. She probably took it straight out the back and ritually burned it to cleanse herself of the evil of the foreign whore. Monsieur Brunel, on the other hand, definitely had a twinkle in his eye whenever I saw him, although his wife had clearly banned him from any further contact with me. I was almost certain that I could detect the slightest hint of a smile, even now.

'Excuse me,' I said to the least scary-looking of the photographers, a smallish man with a shaved head and several cameras trampolining on his rather ample belly, 'what's going on?'

'It's Tracey Tarrant, innit,' he replied. 'We've been looking for her for weeks, ever since she run off with our boy, Warren. His missus is not happy at all.'

'Well that's a bit rich coming from her. She's not exactly living a nun's life in LA is she?' I said, feeling a moment of pity for Tracey. Yes, she was a bit brash and vulgar, but there was also an air of vulnerability about her that I found intriguing. She held the world at arm's length, scowling and swearing at anyone who got too close. She'd been the subject of more than a little media bitching and 'Tracey shows her flabby thighs' type stories. The *Daily Mail* had even published that photo of her getting out of a car in a tight dress and no knickers. They must have had to lie on the floor to get that one.

'So how did you find her?' I asked. 'I mean, she's been here for weeks and she's not exactly been hiding herself.'

'Beats me. Maybe there's still honour among thieves, so to speak, you know the expat *omertà*. Don't tell on us and we won't tell on you. Anyway, we got a tip off from someone who had "inside information".'

My stomach lurched, thinking about the conversation I'd had with CeeCee at her mother's party the previous week. She couldn't have, could she?

'So, um, who was it?' I asked, nervously.

The man tapped the side of his nose, then went back to his vigil.

'So, is she even there? I don't see her Merc,' I said.

On cue, the silver convertible purred round the corner with Warren at the wheel and Tracey in the passenger seat, a scarf wrapped around her head making her look a little like Audrey Hepburn, just more orange. Seeing the press pack, Warren jammed on the brakes and the car skidded to a halt. I saw Tracey's stunned expression, mouth open in a perfect O. With the sort of quick thinking that had made him the star striker for his team, Warren rammed the car into reverse and shot backwards, only to meet Julien coming round the corner in his tractor. They were caught, like love rats in a barrel.

The paps engulfed them in seconds, cameras flashing in their faces as they tried to fend off the hordes. The photographers shouted evermore provocative questions looking for the one shot that they could sell to the tabloids, while Tracey tried to fight her way out of the car and make for the safety of her house. Warren sat there motionless, his face in his hands. I looked on in horror. Whatever I thought of Tracey, this just wasn't fair. A sense of righteous indignation made me push my way through the rabid photographers. This was a moment for the sisterhood to stand up against the common enemy. Sharpening my elbows, I barged towards her. As we met, Tracey's face twisted into a mask of rage.

'You bloody bitch. You did this didn't you?' she screamed, loud enough for the paps to stop their clicking and fall silent.

'But... no...'

'I knew it the moment I saw you, knew you'd be trouble, nosy cow. I said to Warren we was in the shit. How much d'you get from them? Must have been worth a few hundred quid, eh?'

I looked at her in shocked silence as Tracey launched at me, punching me squarely in the nose. I fell backwards on the ground, my sunglasses spilling off my face. Tracey threw herself on top of me, slapping and punching as I tried to protect myself.

The paps, realising they had been gifted *the* picture, possibly of the year, snapped away, leaving me at her mercy.

Suddenly I felt Tracey's weight being lifted off me and opened my eyes to see Julien with his arms around her, restraining her. She was no match for his strength and he picked her up, feet flailing as she tried to kick him, and carried her back to Warren, who was by now standing by the car looking on, about as much use as a chocolate teapot.

'Get her out of here,' Julien snarled, pushing Tracey roughly towards Warren.

I sat on the floor, blood dripping from my nose, tears making tracks down my dusty face. Julien picked me up gently, retrieving my sunglasses from the nettles at the side of the road, and led me towards Les Tuileries and sanctuary, the staccato clicking of shutters the only sound. Well, that and Madame Brunel's loud 'tsking' as we passed by her. I felt the eyes of my neighbours bore into me. What must they think?

The cool, darkness of the cottage was like a womb, keeping me safe from the troubles of the outside world. I sat on a chair in the kitchen holding a bag of ice to my eye while Julien tenderly bathed the blood from my face with balls of cotton wool dipped in salt water.

'Ooowww,' I winced. 'Sorry, I feel such a baby.'

'Keep still and it won't hurt so much,' he said, reaching for more cotton wool. 'Well, I think your modelling days are over for a while,' he smiled, trying to cheer me up as he gently dabbed at my nose.

'How bad is it?'

'Not good but at least nothing seems to be broken. Let me finish up here and you can go and look in the bathroom mirror.'

My face throbbed and I was fairly sure that I would have the mother of all shiners by the next day.

'*Bon*, that's the best I can do,' he said, tipping the bloody water down the sink.

I went into the bathroom and turned on the light over the mirror to get a better look. My eye was starting to close and the beginning of a purple bruise was taking shape underneath it. My nose was swollen, but fortunately still in one piece and my lip was split. I looked like I'd just gone through a couple of rounds with a heavyweight boxer. God, where did Tracey learn to punch like that? I could feel the first twinges of anger building up in the pit of my stomach as hot tears pricked the backs of my eyes. I'd only been trying to help and I'd never have told on her. That just wasn't me at all. I bet it was that bloody CeeCee. There was a loud rap on the front door.

'Julien, could you go and see who it is please?' I called from the bathroom.

A few minutes later he tapped lightly on the door. 'It is the *gendarmes*.'

I went cold, feeling suddenly faint. Brilliant! Now I was going to be arrested for public affray. I'd had a morbid fear of the police ever since the local bobby had come to my primary school when I was growing up. Standing at well over six-foot six-inches, PC Berry had put the fear of God into my seven-year-old self, and from then on, I followed the letter of the law to the last full stop. I'd never even had a parking ticket.

'Shit, what do they want?' I asked him quietly, my voice shaking with nerves.

'They want to know if you wish to *porter plainte*, you know, press charges against Mademoiselle Tarrant.'

I leaned on the sink, relieved that they hadn't come to cart me away.

'Tell them no, would you?'

'I think you'd better come and talk to them yourself.'

'Do I have to?'

'Yes, come on. It is only the officers from Bussières, nothing to worry about.'

'*Oh là là, mademoiselle,*' said one of the officers, drawing in his breath sharply as he saw my bruised and puffy face.

'*C'est bon,* really, it's not nearly as bad as it looks.'

'They don't speak English, shall I translate?'

'Yes please, but just tell them that it's OK. I don't want to press charges.'

A long conversation ensued with much gesticulating and shrugging and the occasional question thrown my way. I tried to keep up with what was said but in the end gave up. Turning from Julien to the *gendarmes* and back again was making my head hurt. If this is what it took when I didn't want to press charges, I could only imagine how much more complicated it would be if I did. Despite everything, I didn't really blame Tracey. That sort of intrusion into your life was enough to tip anyone over the edge. I wondered whether I might just be going a bit soft in my old age.

Eventually the *gendarmes* seemed happy that they had everything they needed and I had a mild case of repetitive strain injury from signing my name so many times. The French certainly loved their form filling. Bidding me a good day (well, it could hardly get any worse), they left.

'I must go too. My tractor is still sitting on the hill and I must move it.'

'Thanks so much,' I said, 'really. Thank you.'

He didn't say anything, just enveloped me in his arms. It was the last straw for me. The tears came and I sobbed into his shirt while he stroked my hair, gently kissing the top of my head.

'I was only trying to help her,' I sobbed. 'I didn't tell them she was here. I'd never do that to anyone... I might think it, but I'd never do it. I can't stay here now. Madame Brunel hates me. I can't imagine what the others think either. I feel completely and utterly humiliated.'

'Listen, what is it you say in England? Today's news is tomorrow's chip paper? Something like that. By next week it will all be forgotten and everyone will have someone else to talk about.'

I smiled up at him. 'Thanks, but I'm not so sure. Listen, you go. I'll see you soon.'

He cupped my face in his hands and kissed me gently on the lips. I tried to kiss him back but the pain of my split lip made me wince. I stood back to let him out of the cottage. Bloody typical, I thought as I watched him leave, the nearest we get to full-on kissing and I've got a fat lip. I went back to the kitchen, pulled out a chair and sat down, head resting in my hands as I felt my lip and eye throb in unison.

A few minutes later, there was a gentle tap on the door. Fearing it was the paparazzi again, I dropped to the floor and commando crawled to the window where I could just about get a clear view of who was on the doorstep.

Pulling myself up slowly, I peeped out of the window, straight into the face of Laure, who was peering through it, her hand shading her eyes. It was hard to tell who surprised who first. Both of us screamed and jumped.

I opened the door, intending to apologise for frightening her, but before I'd even had a chance to say *bonjour*, she thrust a tube of cream into my hand and made a rubbing motion on her face, indicating that I should use the cream on my bruises.

'Arnica,' she said, smiling shyly.

I was genuinely touched at the unexpected display of kindness and without thinking, threw my arms around her neck and hugged her tightly. I felt the young woman stiffen in my embrace and knew that, once again, I had transgressed another of the unspoken rules of the French countryside.

'Sorry, *désolée*,' I said, releasing her straightaway. Laure scurried away like a scalded cat, the chickens running along behind her.

'Cocked up again,' I said out loud.

Opening the fridge, I helped myself to a glass of ice-cold *rosé* and went outside to sit by the pool and consider my future. France certainly wasn't what I had imagined. I realised how wrong I had been to think it would be just like home but in a different language. Maybe I'd been stupid to think that it was that easy just to take off and start a new life somewhere else. I hadn't planned it, the spontaneity of my decision making me feel a bit like a modern day adventurer, but even I had to admit that the secret to any sort of 'adventuring' was planning. After all, Sir Ralph Fiennes didn't conquer the North Pole on a whim and a prayer.

I desperately wanted my friends around me now, even Alex. He drove me mad sometimes but we always had fun and he gave the best hugs. He was a bit like an old woolly jumper. Comfortable, but a bit scratchy in places. I suddenly realised that I missed London, my friends and my mum and dad, and that I had neglected them since I had left. I had been so wrapped up in my new life that I had barely spared a thought for theirs. The Brits I had met were all a lot older and I felt I had little in common with any of them. I had thought there would be more people of my own age here but most people, even the French I'd met, were nearer to my parents' age than mine. I had also expected there to be more clubs to join and activities to take part in, but so far, apart from the classes at the Club in Bussières, I hadn't found anything. CeeCee had seemed like a breath of fresh air, but in reality, back in London we would move in completely different circles and I wasn't sure I could buy into this idea of being friends with people just by virtue of a shared nationality. I'd had high hopes for my friendship with Nick's wife but my trip to his disco at La Fontaine had been depressing to say the least. 'Ernie, the Fastest Milkman in the West' was almost impossible to dance to and his wife, Libby, a frazzled, nervy woman in clothes that could have done with a good wash if I was being honest, was never going to be my new best friend. Nick seemed to make sure every hour of her life was filled with doing 'important jobs' for him and I knew I would have little in common with a woman who had to ask her husband's permission to go out.

The peace of the countryside *was* lovely but in the last few days I'd realised I was starting to miss the buzz of the city, the cafés and restaurants – it was fair to say that the famed French gourmet food was little in evidence in this part of France, from what I had seen. It was all duck, duck and *canard* and what the French couldn't put in a can wasn't even worth thinking about. I thought back to the series made by a certain celebrity chef about the cuisine of south west France and came to the conclusion that he must have been taking mind-altering drugs, which, bearing in mind his spaced-out appearances in the tabloids recently, wasn't beyond the realms of possibility.

My view of France came from books, magazines and *A Place in the Sun*; the reality, I was starting to realise, was a bit different. Even the job front was proving a challenge. I had bought all the local papers and scoured the job sections but there was nothing, unless I wanted to work in the local chicken factory – even if they would give me a job with my limited French. No, not even limited, more like non-existent; besides, it wasn't quite what I had in mind.

I'd never felt quite so alone in my life. Alone was starting to feel like lonely. Lying back on the sun lounger as tears streamed down my face, I stared long and hard at the clear blue sky. It was another lovely sunny day and the promise of more to come. But was it enough? After all, there was more to life than good weather.

Chapter Eleven

'Jesus Christ!' I was glued to the television screen, eyes wide in horror. The breakfast television presenters were doing their round-up of the front pages of the national press and there I was, in all my glory, on the front of the seediest tabloids with Tracey Tarrant sitting on my chest laying into me like a woman possessed. I sank down on the sofa as the two presenters read the story of my fracas with Tracey. It had, it seemed, made all the British papers. One had run a particularly unflattering 'knicker shot' of me sprawled on the ground. Thank goodness I had worn some decent underwear. I quietly fumed.

'So who is this mystery woman and why was she brawling with Tracey Tarrant in public? Could this be another strand in the complicated web that is the love life of Warren Hartson?' asked the presenter.

I snorted my coffee. Me and Warren Hartson? As if! I wouldn't touch his sort with a barge pole. Overpaid tosser!

Pressing the button on the remote control, I turned off the television in disgust. My head was still throbbing, my eye was almost completely closed, and this wasn't making me feel any better.

I sat out on the terrace in the sun, unsure what to do next. The last of the milk had gone and yesterday's baguette was today's offensive weapon so I knew I had to go up to the village for supplies, but could I bear it? Maybe no one had seen the television report and I knew that newspapers didn't arrive in the village shop until the following day… Oh, for goodness sake, who was I kidding? I knew they all watched British television; the constant dialogue about the latest plot lines from *EastEnders* and Corrie at the café was testament to that; and they were constantly moaning about the British news. They would be up there, crowded round a newspaper, sniggering at my misfortune.

Nothing for it but to 'man up' as Alex would have said if he was here. No point hiding at home. If people knew, then so be it. There was always that expat *omertà* that the photographer had mentioned. Maybe they'd close ranks around me.

Time for 'the hat' again, I thought. Last time it was to hide my mosquito bites, this time it was my black eye. Life so far had been nothing if not eventful. I went into the bedroom and rummaged around for it on the top of my wardrobe. Shaking it out, I placed it artfully on my head, trying different angles to ensure the maximum amount of shadow to hide my bruises.

'Right, time to face the music,' I said to my reflection in the dressing table mirror.

Picking up my car keys, I held my head high and set off for the village. Halfway down the hill my mobile suddenly sprang to life. It was like the 1812 Overture played in its entirety. I pulled in to check who was texting me and saw a steady stream of texts coming in. It seemed as if everyone had seen the story. A full five minutes later my phone was still binging with incoming texts and Facebook messages. I had a look at the first few.

Daisy: 'Bloody Hell, girl, what have you been up to?
Call me xxxxx'

Charlotte: 'It was you, wasn't it? Always knew you'd be
famous! Lol J'
Alex: 'OMG! What's been going on. Call, text, anything
but soon x'
Alex: 'Give me a buzz soon as x'
Alex: 'CALL ME'
Alex: 'Call me PLEASE!'

Parking up in the square, I headed into the shop, ostensibly to
buy my baguette and milk, but really to check that they didn't
have any of the day's papers. I surreptitiously flicked through the
English language papers on the revolving stand. Everything was
dated from the day before. Sighing with relief, I went to the till
to pay. Claudine gave me a sympathetic look and diplomatically
didn't mention my black eye.

The terrace of the café was fairly busy with the usual suspects
and I could hear the gentle hum of their conversation wafting
across the square. They'd probably been there since breakfast
waiting for the sun to come over the yardarm, which seemed to
happen about ten o'clock in the morning round here, so with any
luck they had missed the news. I decided to go and get myself a
coffee.

As I reached the terrace, there was a group of people huddled
round a table deep in animated conversation. It could only be
one thing. Before I had time to turn round and walk away, the
conversation stopped and they all turned to look at me. That's
twice I've stopped the conversation since I got here, I thought.
Someone giggled.

There was nothing for it. With head held high, I pulled out a
chair and sat down, adjusting my hat downwards to hide my war
wounds. The same supercilious law-graduate server, Noélia, who
had been there on my very first visit, came to take my order.

'*Vous désirez un café? Un thé? Un coup de poing?*' She threw me another of her spectacularly sarcastic smiles.

I was flustered. 'Um, er, I'm sorry, I didn't understand the last bit?'

'She asked if you wanted a punch,' said a voice from a table behind me. 'I think it's her idea of humour.'

Evil thoughts ran through my mind as I ordered myself a coffee, 'with milk and no violence', matching sarcastic smile for sarcastic smile.

'I don't suppose you've heard the last of it,' said the woman again.

I turned to her.

'God, is there anyone who doesn't know about it?'

'Probably not. It's the most exciting thing that's happened since the *maire* of Laborie bought a Harley-Davidson and roared off into the sunset with the woman from the cleaners in Bussières. I'm Sam, by the way.'

'Hi. I'm guessing that you already know who I am.'

'Well, I won't pretend I don't. Do you mind if I join you?'

'No, be my guest,' I said wearily.

'Listen,' said Sam. 'I work for *The Expat Times*, "The Premier Newspaper for the Expat Community".' She said the slogan in a deadpan voice.

'They've asked me to come here to find out the "story" behind the story. To be honest, my credentials as an investigative journalist are a bit flimsy. I've no idea how to hack your phone and I don't know any private detectives. I'm more used to writing about recipes for chutney and reviewing amateur dramatics, so if you'd rather not talk to me I'll just pretend I couldn't find you.'

'What? A journo with a conscience? That's got to be a first,' I said teasingly.

'Yeah, well, *The Expat Times* isn't exactly *The Times* is it, whatever the editor might like to think.'

'So how did you find me?'

'We got an anonymous tip-off at the office.'

'So much for the expat *omertà*,' I sighed, 'clearly I don't qualify. Look, to be fair, I think I've kind of had my fill of newspapers for the moment if you don't mind. I spent enough time dealing with the press when I lived in London so I was hoping to leave all that behind.'

'Really, what did you do in London? Off the record, of course.'

'Is there such a thing with journalists?' I gave her a wry smile. 'OK, well, I worked for a PR agency. Celebrities and films. Press liaison, media relations, that sort of thing.'

'Really? We've got a few celebrities round here too.'

'I know, Johnny Hallyday.'

'And that guy who was in a 1970s sitcom, what's his name?'

'Sorry, probably a bit before my time.'

'Yeah, well, if he didn't live here I probably wouldn't know his name either. And now you are a lady of leisure?'

'Lady of *enforced* leisure. I'm looking for a job but not really taken with chicken plucking, which seems to be about all that's on offer.'

'I know. It's not easy is it?' Sam thought for a moment. 'You know, I've had an idea. How are your writing skills?'

'Good, very good in fact. Why do you ask?'

'We need a new feature writer on the paper. I know it's not exactly your area but there's not much call for celebrity PR in these parts. How about we cut a deal? You tell me what happened at Tracey's house and I'll have a word with the editor. What do you think?'

'I think you need to speak to your editor first before I say a word.'

'Give me five minutes, OK?'

Sam grabbed her phone from her bag and walked over to the other side of the square.

I watched as she talked and gesticulated, feeling ridiculously nervous. I'd done board interviews at one of the top PR agencies in the country and here I was with my stomach in knots over some little local newspaper I'd never heard of. But this could be a turning point in my new life. I couldn't deny that the money situation was making me nervous and this could be my way out.

After what seemed an age, Sam turned and headed back to the café. I tried to read her expression. Sitting back down at the table, she smiled.

'He's got a feature for you to write and if it works out, he'll take you on. Here's his number so give him a buzz and he'll brief you.' She took a shorthand notebook out of her bag and scribbled down a number and handed it to me.

'I think this calls for a celebration. How about lunch? My treat in return for the inside story on the "Tarrant Tussle". Might even stretch to a glass of the fizzy stuff.'

'Lovely,' I said, feeling quietly thrilled. 'Here's hoping that I didn't get this black eye for nothing.'

I took my sunglasses off to show Sam the damage.

'Ouch! Looks nasty. I heard that there are a few photographers who've been on the wrong end of Tracey's right hook in the past.'

'Well, I wish I'd known that before,' I laughed. 'Right, what's on the menu then?'

Sam called the waitress for some menus and ordered a couple of glasses of champagne just for good measure. The waitress reserved one of her most imperious smiles for this request. Champagne by the glass was clearly sacrilege in her world.

'Gosh, what's her problem?' Sam asked, clearly irritated.

'An "I've got a degree in law from Bordeaux University and I'm working as a waitress" sort of problem.'

'Ah well, I can understand that. I've lived in France since I was small, I've never even been to school in the UK, but they still think of me as being *anglaise*, which is shorthand for bottom of the pile when it comes to handing out jobs. It's not easy being a foreigner in France, even one who's lived here for years. Before I got this, I struggled for years even to find work as a cleaner. You might say "we're all Europeans" in England, but here it's "we're all French and you are Europeans". And you don't even need to be a foreigner. People from other parts of France are just as much outsiders. I met a woman in Bussières a while back who told me she understood how difficult it was being a foreigner because she was from the Charente, which is only a few hours away from here!'

'God,' I laughed, 'it's a different world, isn't it? I wonder how many of the people in the village have ever been to London or even Paris for that matter.'

'I doubt whether half of them have even been to Toulouse. Right, what are you ordering?'

'Hmm, I fancy a salad I think. I've got a bit of a croissant baby going on here.' I patted my stomach. 'If I don't cut down a bit, I'll be spending the summer dressed in tents. What's that one? *Salade de gésier*?'

'Ah yes, deliciously French if you like a spot of duck gizzard.'

'Duck what?'

'Gizzard. It's like a secondary stomach that a duck has which is full of grit...'

'Stop right there. Euuww, it sounds disgusting,' I said as I wrinkled my nose.

'Well, I'm going for the chicken Caesar. Will you order for me whilst I go and powder my nose?'

'Sure thing. Now, what shall I have?'

Noélia came and stood by the table, order book and pen poised.

'Can I have a minute?'

'No, we are busy. It is late. I need your order now or the kitchen will be closed.'

'But it's only one o'clock,' I said through gritted teeth.

She shrugged her shoulders.

'OK. Chicken Caesar for my friend and… oh, I don't know. What do you suggest?' I smiled, thinking this might be a way to get the stroppy waitress on my side.

'If you would like a nice local dish, I would suggest *salade d'andouillette*. It's a type of local sausage.'

'Yes, that sounds nice. I'll have one of those.'

As she headed back into the kitchen, I became aware of the sound of singing. It sounded like 'La Marseillaise', the French national anthem. Round the corner came a middle-aged man wobbling dangerously along on a bicycle, clearly drunk.

As he neared the café, singing off-key, the wobbling reached a critical point and the bike disappeared from under him, depositing him in a heap in the road. He lay there motionless.

'Oh my God!' I cried, my hand going to my mouth, as a car sped into the village narrowly missing the inebriated body.

Without thinking, I rushed into the road. 'Someone call an ambulance,' I shouted.

An uncharitable snigger spread around the terrace of the café. 'I wouldn't bother with him, love. That's just Armand, the village drunk,' called a tattooed man in a Spurs football strip.

God bless the Brits abroad, I thought.

'*Monsieur, monsieur*, you have to move.' I shook his shoulders but he just grunted and rolled over, settling comfortably in the road. The alcohol fumes coming off him could have knocked out an elephant at twenty paces.

I tried to sit him up so I could get my arms around him and drag him towards the pavement, but he was a dead weight and every time I managed to get him sitting up, he would flop over to one side before I could get a good grip on him. It was like juggling with an octopus.

'Oh for God's sake,' I muttered under my breath as another burst of 'La Marseillaise' made me jump, 'give me a break will you?'

'Never a dull moment with you around, is there?' I looked up to see Sam standing over me, a broad smile on her face.

'Sam, thank God. Give me a hand here will you?'

Taking one arm each, we strained and pulled until Armand's snoring bulk was safely deposited out of harm's way. I picked up his bike and wheeled it to the pavement, propping it up against the wall.

'Bloody hell, he weighs a ton for such a small man. Better stick him on his side, just in case.' I rubbed the small of my back. 'Come on, let's get our lunch.'

We sat back at our table and I made sure I glared at the assembled diners who had done nothing to help.

'There's a law in France about failing to help someone in need, you know,' I said loudly. I remembered reading about it a while back. Something to do with Princess Diana's death and the paps taking photos rather than getting help.

Noélia suddenly appeared next to us holding two plates loaded with food.

'*Salade César* for you *madame*,' she said putting one down in front of Sam, 'and for you, *mademoiselle, salade d'andouillette*,' putting the other plate in front of me with a flourish and a slight smirk. I thought I detected the slightest intake of breath from the diners nearby.

'Er, thanks,' I said, looking at the pale, whitish sausage nestled among the salad leaves and tomatoes.

'*Andouillette*? You're adventurous,' said Sam pulling a slightly disgusted face.

'Why? Noélia suggested it,' I replied.

She was lingering by the door of the café, watching us, the faint smirk lingering on her lips.

'I must admit though, it's a bit smelly,' I remarked.

I picked up my knife and fork and cut into it before popping a bit in my mouth and chewing enthusiastically. I smiled at Sam. The smile started to fade almost as quickly as it had appeared and was replaced by a look that was a cross between horror and desperation.

'Bloody hell,' I said, my mouth still full of *andouillette*, 'what is this stuff? It tastes like… like… shit. Literally.'

'Pig's colon sausage?'

I gagged. Flapping my hands in front of my mouth, I motioned to Sam to pass me a serviette and spat the foul-tasting sausage out into my hand.

'Pig's colon? What the…'

'It's the colon that gives *andouillette* its particularly "fecal" taste. I call it the sausage of the eternal stench.'

'That bitch! It smells like a public toilet during a cholera epidemic.' I pushed my plate to one side.

'What have you done to upset her?' Sam asked. 'I mean, *andouillette*? It's only one step down from a full-on fatwa.'

'I wish I knew. She's been like this with me since day one. How's your chicken Caesar?'

'Lovely actually. Do you want to share?'

'No but thanks anyway. My mouth still tastes like a sewage farm.' I took a large swig of my champagne. 'There, that should deaden the taste buds a little bit.'

'Look,' Sam dug around in her bag, pulled out a plastic carrier and passed it under the table to me. 'Scrape it all into this then she'll presume you've eaten it. Don't let her think she's got one over on you.'

Surreptitiously, I tipped the remains of my salad into the bag and slipped it into my handbag, hoping to goodness that it didn't leak, then I put my plate back on the table and placed my knife and fork neatly side by side.

A few minutes later Noélia stopped at our table.

'How was your meal?' she asked, looking directly at me.

'Delicious, thanks.' I pushed my empty plate towards her. She picked it up with just the merest arch of a perfectly plucked eyebrow and stalked off.

'Ha! One to you,' smiled Sam. 'More champagne, I think.' She called Noélia over again. 'We'll have the rest of the bottle, please.'

We sat, drank and chatted well into the afternoon. It was so nice to find someone who I seemed to have so much in common with and to be able to tell my side of the Tarrant saga. A few more like her and I'd be sorted. The champagne and sunshine combined to make me feel slightly light-headed, with that nice fuzzy feeling you get right before you've had too much.

'Hello.' I froze at the sound of a familiar voice, that nice warm feeling evaporating in an instant. Turning in my seat, I shaded my eyes against the sun.

'Alex? What the hell are you doing here?'

'Well, if you'd answered your phone or sent me a text I probably wouldn't be but I saw the news and the bloody mess you'd got yourself into, so I cancelled all my meetings and flew straight over.'

'But why Alex? I'm fine. I can look after myself.'

'Well, I might beg to differ on that one.'

I glared at him, feeling a rising tide of annoyance at his attitude. Sam coughed politely.

'Oh, sorry, Alex, this is Sam. Sam, this is Alex, my, my…'

What was he? Surely he didn't still think he was my boyfriend did he? But the way he was looking at me, with that proprietary way than men have, made me wonder.

Sensing my discomfort, Sam jumped in. 'Hi Alex, nice to meet you. Can I get you a glass of something?'

'Thanks, but no. I've been mainlining coffee since early morning so I think I'd better steer clear of any stimulants for a while.'

Alex pulled out a chair, sat down and stretched out his legs. He had been a rower since he was kid and still had the physique of an athlete despite the fact that his arms got more exercise lifting drinks than they did with a blade these days. We all stared uncomfortably at each other. A hush had descended over the terrace as everyone sensed an oncoming drama.

'Look, you guys obviously have stuff to talk about and I'd better get back to the office,' said Sam. 'Here's my card. Give me a call and we'll get that feature sorted out.'

She handed me a business card, then wished Alex goodbye and kissed me on both cheeks. 'Don't worry about the bill. I settled it earlier,' she called over her shoulder. 'Speak soon.'

I picked up my champagne and sipped it, secretly wanting to down it in one to give me a bit of Dutch courage.

'Alex, you can't just march in here like this. Sam and I actually had some business to discuss. How on earth did you get here anyway?'

'Plane, then I got a taxi from the airport. Cost me a bloody fortune. I only came up to the village to try and find out where the house was, so it was a bit of luck to find you here.'

'Yes, wasn't it?' I answered snippily.

'So how's things? Apart from the neighbour situation of course.'

'Good.'

'Got a job yet?'

'No, not yet. I've got a few possibilities but nothing firm. I'm doing a piece for a local newspaper which might lead to something. That's what Sam and I needed to talk about before you came barging in.'

'Look, I've come to take you home. It's obvious you aren't coping here.'

'I'm sorry?'

'Oh come on, you've got no job, no friends to speak of...'

'Excuse me, Alex, but did you not just arrive to find me in the middle of a business lunch? And who says I've got no friends? I may not have a London-style social life but that's not what I'm here for.'

'And what are you here for? God knows why you want to live in the arse-end of the universe.'

'*Trou du cul,*' I said flatly.

'What?'

'That's what you call it in French. *Trou du cul*. It literally means bum hole.'

'Yeah, well, thanks for the French lesson. Come on, it was all a nice idea but enough's enough. It's been one disaster after another ever since you got here, from what Daisy's been telling me. Face up to it, darling, you're just not cut out for The Good Life. I saw Zane the other day and he said he'd always have you back at the agency.'

'Oh, and how is Clive?' I said, emphasising his real name, 'and less of the "darling" too.'

I picked up the paper napkin and started shredding it into tiny pieces.

'Alex, I'm fine, honestly I am. I really like it here and…'

'Look, let's go back to the house and get you packed up. I've booked you a ticket on a flight back to London tomorrow morning.'

'You've. Done. What?' I said quietly through gritted teeth.

On the neighbouring table, an elderly, prune-skinned woman and her equally wrinkled husband were watching our conversation as if it was a Wimbledon final, heads swivelling first to me, then to Alex and back again.

'Look,' I said in a whisper, 'we can't do this here. Let's go back to the house and we can talk about it properly.'

I picked up my bag and with a tight smile at the next table, I stalked off towards my car. Alex ran to catch up, taking my arm. I shook him off crossly. As we passed the still sleeping body of Armand, the old drunk farted loudly and mumbled *'bravo'* under his breath.

'Bloody lowlife,' Alex growled.

'Oh, leave him alone, he's not doing anyone any harm. If he wants to rot his liver that's his call.'

'Please don't tell me we're going in that rust bucket,' he laughed, pointing at my cherished Renault 5.

I threw him a withering look and opened the door to let him in.

'I'm sorry if it's not up to your usual standard but I moved here for a different life. Here we don't judge people by the car they drive. In any case, it was lent to me by one of my neighbours. Can you imagine that happening in London? It would end up on eBay before you could say "Buy It Now".'

As we drove out of the village, the landscape spread out in front of us. I caught my breath, as I did every time I saw it. This is what people meant when they said something was uplifting. I felt my spirits soar.

'Look Alex, look at that view. Isn't it amazing? It's just so beautiful. I mean, where could you get that in the UK?'

'Dorset, Wiltshire, Devon.'

We drove the rest of the way in an uneasy silence.

Chapter Twelve

'Well, this is it,' I said, as we turned into the long drive down to Les Tuileries. We pulled up at the side of the cottage and got out.

'Yes, it's quite pretty I suppose. A bit quiet though.'

'Strangely enough, Alex, that's what I like about it.'

I pushed open the door and motioned for him to come in.

'Don't you lock your doors then?'

'What for? Who'd even find the house all the way up here?'

'Yes well, you'll invalidate your insurance.'

I sighed. He has no beauty in his soul, I thought. His father had been a Lloyds of London 'name' and Alex had followed him into insurance broking, although he insured ships rather than houses.

'Can I get you anything? You must need a caffeine fix by now.'

'Yeah, that would be good. But do you have any proper milk? Not that disgusting UHT stuff.'

'Things have moved on a bit. We even have indoor plumbing now.'

I wondered what he would make of my own indoor plumbing, which was, it was fair to say, somewhat behind the times. The fact that it was indoors was probably the best thing you could say about it.

'I'll make the coffee,' I said going into the kitchen, leaving Alex to get settled in the lounge. It gave me a few moments to reflect on how much things had changed between us in a few short months. The comfortable relationship we had once shared had become decidedly stiff.

'Do you want it with some frothy milk?' I called.

'Whatever's easiest.'

As I stirred the two mugs of coffee, Alex came into the kitchen. He stood behind me and slipped his arms around my waist, kissing me gently on the neck. I felt myself stiffen slightly. I felt Alex stiffen too, but his was a different sort.

'Oh baby, I've missed you...'

For the briefest of moments, I thought, to hell with it, but then Julien's face flashed across in my mind. No, it wasn't going to happen. It wasn't right.

'Look Alex,' I said, untangling myself from him, 'I can't do this. Things have changed. I've changed. I know your intentions are good but...'

He stopped and looked at me. Cupping my face in his hands, he lightly kissed the end of my nose.

'You're right. I'm sorry. I'm being a complete idiot here, aren't I? It's just that, I don't know, I thought we had something and then you just decided to up and leave.'

'Alex, I asked you to come with me but you didn't want to. Anyway, you'd hate it here. It's too quiet for you. Come on. Let's go and have our coffee.'

I picked up the mugs and took them into the lounge. Alex followed and flopped down on the sofa, pushing his hair back and stretching out his long legs.

'I'm shagged out,' he said, yawning. 'Big day yesterday. Board meetings and all that.'

'Not as big as mine,' I said, smiling.

'Well, you have a point there.' He picked up his coffee and sipped it thoughtfully.

We both started to speak together.

'I'm sorry…'

'I'm sorry…'

'OK, you first,' I told him.

He sighed and rested his head on the back of the sofa. 'I'm sorry I was such an arse in London, so dismissive of your plans, I didn't give you any support. I guess I was a bit jealous that you had the courage to follow your dream. You are probably one of the strongest, most self-sufficient people I know. If anyone could make a life here, you could. But the thing is, I really miss you.'

I looked at him, finding this outpouring very out of character. He wasn't the sort to normally wear his heart on his sleeve. I put my head on his shoulder and he slipped his arm around me and kissed the top of my head. We sat there in silence, deep in our own personal thoughts.

'Look, I'm absolutely knackered. Would you mind if I went to lie down for a bit?'

'Alex Cameron, you're not trying to lure me into bed are you?' I teased.

'Well if you wanted to come, I wouldn't complain.'

I smiled. 'Well it's probably one of the better offers I've had, but I'm afraid the answer's no. We had our moment Alex, but it's in the past now.'

He looked crestfallen.

'Come on, you. I'll tuck you up at least.'

With Alex safely in bed and snoring gently, I decided to have a quick dip in the pool. Changing into my swimsuit in the bathroom, I grabbed a towel and went out into the garden. The sun still wasn't quite strong enough to heat up the pool and I gasped as I lowered myself into the chilly water. Turning over onto my back and floating, I felt the sun warm my stomach.

Seeing Alex had upset my equilibrium. Whatever I might have tried to suggest to him, life here, although definitely on the up, was still far from perfect. It was honestly as hard as life in London, just in a different way. London was physically tiring, but France was wringing me out emotionally. I missed the easy friendship of people I had known, in some cases, for most of my life. I missed working, even dealing with the likes of Shitty Kitty. The money worries were fairly constant now and I wasn't nearly as confident as he was that I could make it here. But on the other hand, I had all this. My little cottage, the beautiful scenery, sunshine and the start, I hoped, of a new relationship. I just prayed it was enough.

Turning on my stomach, I ducked my head under the water, then swam a few lengths, a token attempt at taming the croissant top. I pulled myself out of the pool and lay down on a sun lounger to dry off. Looking at my watch, I was surprised to see an hour had passed already. Alex would be awake soon so I picked up my towel, wrapped it round my head and went inside to take a shower.

Standing under the hot stream of water and feeling it run down my body, I decided Nick might have made a huge mistake with the toilet, but I was pretty sure I had one of the best showers in the area.

Through the noise of the running water, I became aware of someone knocking on the bathroom door. It must be Alex, awake at last. I turned off the water and wrapped myself in a towel.

'You OK?' I called through the door.

'There's someone here to see you, some country bumpkin type.'

Now that was much more like the old Alex. 'OK, I'll be out in a minute. And Alex...'

'Yes?'

'... don't call them bumpkins.'

It was probably Laure collecting her arnica I thought, as I slipped my clothes back on. I'd better go and rescue them. I could just imagine poor, sweet Laure left alone with Alex eyeing her suspiciously.

Out in the hallway, a pair of work boots drew me up short. Unless Laure had taken to wearing size twelve boots, it had to be...

'Julien. What are you doing here?'

He was standing by the window looking as if someone had stolen his favourite tractor. I noticed that Alex, who was standing in the kitchen doorway, bare-chested in a pair of shorts, had left the bedroom door ajar, with the rumpled bed on show. The two men were eyeing each other up like a pair of rutting stags on a Scottish moor and I realised with horror how this must look to Julien. The bed that had clearly been recently used, Alex in his boxers and me in a dressing gown. Shit, shit, shit, I thought.

'Hello,' he said turning to me. A flicker of hurt flashed across his face. 'I just came to see how you were. I'm sorry, I didn't know you have a visitor.'

'Oh, that's OK,' I said faux-breezily. 'This is...'

'Yes, he has already introduced himself.'

I wondered exactly what Alex had said.

God, this is agony I thought, but I smiled at him, hoping to defuse the situation.

'Coffee, Julien? I was just going to put some on.'

'Oh, I'm sure that Julien doesn't have time for coffee. It must be a busy life being a farmer. He was telling me all about it. He's probably got a field that needs ploughing. I'm sure he's got to get off. Haven't you Julien?' Alex's look was little short of a challenge.

'No, he's staying for coffee,' I answered quickly. 'I'll just go and put it on.'

'Really, I have to go. I just came to see if you were OK after what happened yesterday.'

'Yes, Alex, it was Julien who pulled the mad Tarrant woman off me. I might have had more than a black eye and a split lip if he hadn't been there.'

'Quite the hero, eh?' Alex looked at Julien as if he was something unpleasant he had stepped in, then came and stood by me, slipping his arm around me in a proprietary manner. I shrugged him off.

'As long as you are fine. That's all I wanted to know.'

Julien glared at Alex, then at me, before marching out of the room. I caught up with him at the front door, angrily ramming his feet in his work boots.

'Julien. Look, it's not what you think...'

He held up his hands. 'No, I have nothing to say to you. Go back to your *plan cul*.'

'Look, this is no time to blind me with French,' I said, trying to lighten the situation. He leaned in towards me, anger etched in his face.

'Fuck buddy. Really, I thought you were a better person than this.'

'But Julien, he isn't... we didn't...'

He pushed roughly past me and out of the door. I sank against the door post and watched him go. In the bedroom, I could hear Alex banging around. My past and my present, but which one was my future?

'Julien, Julien, wait...'

Without even bothering to put my shoes on, I sprinted up the drive after him. The sharp gravel wasn't really conducive to chasing after your lover. In my mind I was Cathy chasing Heathcliffe across a windy moor but the reality was a half-crazed English woman in a dressing gown looking like she was walking on hot coals, hobbling along to the accompaniment of a chorus of 'ouch' and 'shit'.

'Julien, wait...' His long-legged six-foot four frame was no match for my five-foot five one and it was like a seaside donkey going head to head with a racehorse. In a spectacular display of selective deafness, he ignored me and continued up the drive towards his car.

'Julien, please wait. *Attends.*'

Well, there was an outside chance he'd suddenly forgotten how to speak English. He jumped into his car, slammed it into gear and roared off down the road in a cloud of dust.

'OK. Fine. Just bloody run off like a typical man,' I shouted down the road after him. 'You're all the bloody same, no matter where you come from...'

A small cough came from the within the dust cloud that the car had thrown up, like a hamster trying to clear its throat. As it started to clear, I was rewarded with the sight of Madame Brunel, hair looking like a bad advert for dry shampoo, with the all too familiar glare on her face. She looked me up and down distastefully. Instinctively, I drew my dressing gown tighter round me. This woman was like a harbinger of doom. Whenever she was around, I was in trouble and, more often than not, suffering from some sort of wardrobe malfunction. I was in no mood for neighbourliness.

'What? What do you want?' I shouted. 'Come to have another gloat at the *anglaise* making a fool of herself? Well here you go. Glad that I haven't disappointed.'

Madame Brunel looked at me as if I was on a day pass from some local institution. A little whimper escaped from her lips and she turned and scurried away leaving me feeling dreadful. It wasn't her fault that my life was so complicated.

'Not having a good day then?' I turned to see Tracey Tarrant standing by the gates to her house.

'And you can sod off too,' I shouted.

'Ooooooh,' Tracey sing-songed, 'a bit touchy today are we?'

'Touchy? I should be bloody touching my hands around your neck after the trouble you've caused me. If it wasn't for you behaving like Lady Gaga on testosterone I wouldn't be in this mess.'

'Yeah, well, maybe I over-reacted…'

'Over-reacted?' I pointed to my black eye. 'Over-reacted? You should be locked up. You're bloody mad, you are!'

'Yeah, well I'm not the one standing in my dressing gown screaming at old ladies am I?'

She turned and disappeared back behind the high walls of her house leaving me seething at the injustice of the whole situation.

Maybe Alex was right. Maybe I couldn't make a life for myself here. It was always one step forward and two back. Well, if you counted the events of the last few days it was probably a good 200 steps back. I turned and went back to the house to face him.

He was sitting on the edge of the bed, his head in his hands so I sat down beside him, not quite sure what to say.

'Look, I'm so sorry about all this, Alex.' I took his hand but he pulled it away. 'I really do appreciate you coming out to see me but I have to see if I can make it work here.'

He didn't answer.

'Alex, please, talk to me,' I rested my head on his shoulder. After a few moments he, in turn, rested his head on mine and we both sat there quietly, deep in thought.

I turned to look up at him.

'Does it hurt?' he asked, touching my bruised eye with his fingertips.

'Oh, it's OK. I'll live. She's got a pretty good right hook on her though.'

Alex smiled and kissed my forehead. 'I've called a taxi. It will be here any moment.'

'What? You managed to get a signal? That's a miracle in itself around here.' I smiled at him and he smiled back. It was the best I could hope for. At least we could leave as friends.

Outside, a car horn tooted twice.

'That'll be my taxi. Goodbye.'

He picked up his bag and left. The front door bang shut and I exhaled. I felt like I'd been holding my breath since Alex arrived. At the window, I watched him put his bag in the boot of the car that looked vaguely familiar, then stand back to let the driver shut it.

'Oh no! Gérard.'

I ran for the door but not quickly enough to stop them and the car bumped and jolted up the drive.

'Watch out for the *fosses*,' I called as the car, still bearing some signs of earlier ditch-damage, sped away.

Chapter Thirteen

A full week had passed with no sign of Julien. I had spent inordinate amounts of time loitering in the village, at the café, in the shop, even *La Poste*. It was just as well that France hadn't got into the ASBO habit or I'd surely have one by now.

Since my verbal decapitation of Madame Brunel, my neighbours gave me a wide berth, although quite how wide you could get in our tiny hamlet was a moot point. My most regular companion was a glass of cheap *rosé*. I'd worked out that buying the 10-litre wine boxes made it practically as cheap as water, if not cheaper. It didn't take much to persuade myself that it was just in the interests of economy and not because of a fug of depression that I was struggling to shift, rather like my muffin top which was starting to overhang my waistband. I'd renamed it a 'croissant top' and vowed to get rid of it, but still those buttery crescents of delight kept calling to me.

The previous day, a lorry had pulled up next door and started removing furniture. I'd read on the Internet that Warren Hartson was heading off to Los Angeles for an emotional reunion with his wife, so I guessed that Tracey was gone too. It had certainly been very quiet.

Right, I said to myself one lunchtime, this won't do. Get off your sorry arse and pull yourself together. First things first: no booze till sundown, and we're not talking sundown in Sydney either.

I poured the remains of my glass of *rosé* down the sink, all except the last drop which I quickly swigged, checking to left and right before I did so, like some sort of lush.

'Next, return that editor's call and get some work sorted out.'

I took the business card off the fridge where it was pinned behind a magnet which said 'Wine: how classy people get funny'. I wasn't feeling either classy or funny at this moment in my life.

Picking up the phone, I dialled the number.

'Yes, hello, I'm calling for Mr Maxwell.' I loved the fact that the editor was called Robert Maxwell and wondered whether the real Robert Maxwell hadn't secretly faked his own death so he could hide out in rural France. From what I'd heard, he wouldn't be the only one. Whispered rumours abounded among the expats about this person who was on the run from a cuckolded husband, to one who had been in prison for murder. What was a supposedly dead former newspaper editor among friends?

'Oh yes, hello, yes, that's right. I'm just returning your call… Yes, about the feature you want me to write. A cat? The oldest Persian cat in France? Um, yes, sounds fascinating. OK, I'll wait for you to email me all the details. Thanks, goodbye.'

Christ, how the mighty are fallen, I thought. One day supermodels, the next supermoggies.

A few moments later, my laptop pinged to tell me I had an email. Sitting down, I opened it and read the details. My heart sank. How I was supposed to make an interesting piece about the oldest Persian cat in France was anyone's guess. The cat was, apparently, a twenty-six-year old white Persian and belonged to an elderly English lady. It was called Snoopy and was the father of at least thirty champion cats. I suddenly saw the headline: 'Snoop Mogg – Doing it Moggy Style'. I sniggered. No, that wouldn't do, even if the readership of *The Expat Times* were to get the reference to an American rapper.

Aha, I thought, as I read on. This could be the hook. The French didn't recognise it as the oldest cat in France because it was registered in the UK. Was there a racism angle? Could you even be racist about cats? I picked up the phone to ring the owner, a Mrs Violet Merriman. Maybe I'd have to do the interview then work out the hook later.

After a few rings, a thin, reedy voice answered.

'Hello, Mrs Merriman, I'm calling from *The Expat Times*. Mr Maxwell told you I'd be calling. Yes, about the feature on your cat. Today? Well, yes, I probably could. In half an hour? I think that might be cutting it a bit fine. Oh, I see, well yes, if you are going away for a fortnight then we'd best get it done today. What's your address?'

I noted down the details and agreed to be there at two o'clock.

Not wanting my wine breath to put Mrs Merriman off, I dashed into the bathroom to brush my teeth, She had sounded quite an upright sort of person. Then it was into the bedroom to find something decent to wear. The problem with living in the sun and having an expanding waistline was that these days I favoured floaty dresses with no bra, but for this I felt I needed to be a little more corporate.

Twenty minutes later I was in my trusty Renault winding my way through the lanes on the short journey to see Mrs Merriman and the aged Snoopy, with my directions on a piece of paper on the passenger seat. It was another beautiful day with a vast blue sky and cotton wool clouds and I felt the depression of the previous week start to lift.

I didn't need a man in my life. I had a job (hopefully) and that would bring me enough money to lead a simple life here. The air conditioning in the car wasn't working, so I wound down the window and let the wind blow through my hair, cooling my face and turned on the radio for a bit of company. The French radio stations were a bit dire, although in fairness it wasn't the radio stations that were dire, the problem was the regulations. As Louis had told me, they were only allowed to devote a small portion of their airtime to foreign songs and French music, to be completely frank, was mostly on par with a bad Eurovision entry from the 1970s.

Still, I was nearly there – only a few more minutes of listening to some dreary song that seemed to be about a smoky chimney in a village. I looked down to consult my directions, not noticing something moving on the verge at the side of the road. Suddenly, there was a bumping sound that rolled and thudded along the underside of the car.

'Shit,' I said out loud. 'What the hell was that?'

I stopped the car and got out. Behind it, lying in the road, was a very white and clearly very dead cat.

Oh my God! It couldn't be, could it?

I tiptoed up to the cat and nudged it with my shoe. Maybe it was just knocked out or something. It didn't move. Glassy eyes stared up accusingly at me. Perhaps it was just in a coma and would come round in a while. Poor little thing. I bent down and stroked its fur. Then I noticed a collar lying in the road a few feet from the cat. Filled with dread, I picked it up and read the name tag, 'Snoopy', followed by a telephone number that I recognised as belonging to Mrs Merriman.

Shit, shit, shit! I was one swearword from blind panic. My first proper job, a feature about the oldest cat in France, and I'd run the damned thing over. I walked round in ever decreasing circles, muttering to myself, trying to decide what to do, not just with the newly-deceased cat, but with Mrs Merriman too. What the hell was I going to say to her? Tears started to prick the back of my eyes as I thought of her grieving over her cat.

The sound of a car coming up the lane spurred me into action. Opening the boot, I picked the cat up and flung it in, muttering an apology before slamming it shut, then jumped in the car and carried on towards Mrs Merriman's house. My hands were shaking on the steering wheel as I turned into the drive. Parking the car, I sat for a moment to gather my thoughts. Maybe I should just drive off and have done with it? How could I face Mrs Merriman, knowing that her beloved moggy had come to a violent end under the wheels of my car?

There was a tap on the window and an elderly lady with long, grey hair wound up into a tight bun was peering through at me.

'Are you all right, dear? You look a little pale.'

I got out. I'd have to tell her what had happened. How could I not? The old lady grasped my hand and shook it firmly.

'Hello, I'm Violet Merriman, nice to meet you. You will call me Violet, won't you?'

'Hello Violent... sorry, Violet. Lovely to meet you.'

'Come on in dear, I've got a nice pot of tea brewing for us. I was just looking for Snoopy. I can't seem to find him anywhere.'

I blanched. 'I'm so sorry Mrs Merriman...' I began, but my courage failed me and I stopped mid-sentence.

'Oh don't worry, dear, he'll show up. He always does.'

But not this time, I thought, guilt gnawing at my stomach. My throat filled with bile and for a moment I thought I might gag.

'So, where shall we sit for this interview? Snoopy and I are very excited about it.'

'Let me just get my things.'

I turned to the car, remembering my bag was in the boot. I stopped short. How was I going to get my bag out without Mrs Merriman seeing the body of her dear, departed Snoopy?

'Er, Mrs Merriman, Violet, why don't you go on ahead and pour the tea. I'm gasping. I'll be with you in a few minutes.'

'All right, dear. If you see Snoopy, do chivvy him along, won't you?'

I smiled weakly and, waiting until Mrs Merriman was safely out of the way, went to open the boot. My hand paused on the boot catch.

'Please God,' I said out loud, 'if ever there was a time for a miracle, this is it.'

I opened the boot but Snoopy was still there, lifeless. I stared hard at his little body, looking for any signs he may be breathing, still holding on to the vain hope that he was just unconscious. There was nothing. I grabbed my bag and shut the boot, taking a deep breath, before turning to face the worst interview of my life.

In the coolness of the house, Mrs Merriman was sitting in the lounge, a tray of tea and biscuits on a little table beside me.

'I've got out the best china in your honour. It's not every day that Snoopy and I become celebrities.'

I smiled at her and began. 'Mrs Merriman...'

'Please dear, call me Violet.'

'Violet...'

'Milk and sugar?'

'Milk, no sugar, thank you. Mrs Merriman...'

'Snoopy loves a bit of milk. I know they say you shouldn't give cats milk, only that evaporated stuff, but it's never done him any harm. He's going to be twenty-seven next week you know. I don't know what I'd do without Snoopy. He's been my best friend since Archie, my husband, died.'

I couldn't do it. I knew I should, but I couldn't face breaking this poor, sweet woman's heart. I'd find a way to let her know that Snoopy had gone to that great cat's home in the sky but for now, I'd let her carry on in blissful ignorance. Of all the things that had happened since I had arrived in France, this was by far the worst.

I sipped at my tea. 'Now, tell me all about you and Snoopy.'

An hour and a half later, I said goodbye to Mrs Merriman, my notebook full of plenty of material to write a really good feature. The only thing missing was the cat.

I opened the boot just on the off chance that the miracle I was hoping for had somehow taken place, but Snoopy was now not only very dead, but also very stiff. What's more, he seemed to be leaking a bit. The summer heat seemed to be hastening the decomposition process. Fortunately, I had a collection of plastic bags in the boot left over from my last trip to the supermarket. I took one and shook it out, checking over my shoulder that I was far enough from the house that Mrs Merriman couldn't see what was going on.

If I'd thought ahead, I could have arranged poor Snoopy so that he was easy to fit into a standard carrier bag once rigor mortis set in. As it was, he had died outstretched and was proving to be a bit awkward. Putting him in head first left his legs waving over the top; putting him in feet first left him peering out with lifeless eyes in a pretty freaky fashion. I opted for head first and pushed gently on his hind legs but they were rigid.

'My dear…'

Mrs Merriman's voice behind me made me jump.

'You left your… what's that?' She pointed to the bag.

'Oh, nothing.' I hastily slammed the boot shut. Mrs Merriman looked at me doubtfully. I could feel a crimson blush starting on my neck and creeping slowly up towards my face.

'You forgot your pen.' Mrs Merriman handed it to me. 'Snoopy's still not back. You haven't seen him have you?'

Was it me, or did she look suspicious?

'Me? No,' I laughed nervously. 'Thanks for the pen. Right, I'd better be going. It was lovely to meet you. I'm sure Snoopy will come back soon and when he does I'll make a special point of coming out to meet him.'

Shut *up*, I thought. Getting into my car, I drove off, waving gaily to Mrs Merriman who watched me go through narrowed eyes. I was quite sure I hadn't heard the last of this.

I was still rattled by the time I reached the road up to St Amans and with the only link to me and the crime lying (sort of) in a carrier bag in the boot, I knew I had to get rid of the evidence. That was the next problem. The ground was baked hard by the sun so that the chances of digging a grave for a hamster, never mind poor Snoopy, were remote. I could dump his body in the woods and let nature take its course, but what if someone found him? As I drove past the little pond on the hill up to St Amans, an idea started to form. Checking that no one was around, I pulled in and opened the boot. This gave a whole new meaning to letting the cat out of the bag. If I chucked Snoopy in, he'd sink to the bottom and no one would be any the wiser. I just hoped that the pond was far enough back from the road so that we wouldn't be seen.

Making my way stealthily towards the pond, I gently took the cat out of the bag and laid him on the bank. It was only right to say a few words. Who knows if cats went to heaven, but I'd always felt it best to hedge your bets where religion was concerned.

'Dear Snoopy, faithful friend, loyal servant, I commend your body to the water.'

It sounded a bit like a second-rate black and white war film. I made the sign of the cross over him just for good measure and threw his body into the pond, expecting it to sink in a halo of bubbles. The trouble was, it didn't. Instead, Snoopy floated on the surface; the gentle eddies of the waterfall propelling him round the pond in a leisurely fashion.

'Oh shit,' I said feeling the panic starting to rise. 'Oh *shit*!'

I grabbed a long branch from the bank and tried to reach him but with insufficient length, all it did was tickle Snoopy and send him careering round in tight little circles.

'Well, I've seen a few things in me life...'

I screamed in surprise. A figure was standing in the shadows watching me.

I peered into the gloom. 'Oh my God, Tracey, where did you spring up from? I thought you'd gone.'

'Nah, that was all Warren's stuff being carted off.'

'Give me a hand would you?'

'To do what, exactly?'

'Sink the cat.'

'Do what?'

'Look, it's a long story. I'll tell you later. Just grab a branch, anything that's long enough, and help me will you?'

'Blimey, you really are completely certifiable, aren't you?'

'Look, it's not what it seems...'

'What? You mean you aren't trying to sink a dead cat in a pond?'

'Well, yes, but there's a good reason for it.'

'I can't wait to hear this one.'

'Look, please, just give me a hand will you?' I pleaded.

Tracey scoured the edge of the woods for a branch and finding one that was suitable set about helping me, while I in turn, explained the events of the afternoon.

Between the two of us, we pushed and prodded at the inert form with little effect.

'Oh for God's sake! What does it take to sink a dead cat?'

Tracey snorted. I looked at her and started to giggle at the ridiculousness of the situation. Soon the two of us were laughing raucously.

'Come on girl, give it some welly,' Tracey said. 'It's no good pushing it around, we've got to get it under the water or it won't sink.'

Between us, we managed to get the cat positioned under the branches so we could push it down.

'One... two... three... push,' I shouted. 'Keep the pressure on, I think we're there.'

With much bubbling, the poor unfortunate cat finally disappeared under the surface.

'Right, now don't let go of your branch. We need to get it waterlogged,' said Tracey.

'You seem to know an awful lot about dead bodies in water,' I laughed.

'Yeah, well, you don't come from where I do and not know one or two things about getting rid of the evidence. And next time, weight the bloody thing! Oops, look out, we got company.'

I looked up to see Madame Brunel and her husband watching us in horror.

'Bloody hell, how long have they been there?'

'Dunno, I only just noticed them.'

'Do you think they saw?'

'From the looks on their faces I'd say there's a fair chance.'

'It was already dead, *déjà mort, le chat, mort*.' I called out. I moved towards them but they backed away. Madame Brunel nestled into her husband's chest as if I was a mad axe-murderer. As I got closer, she visibly shrank back then turned and high-tailed it past me back to the road, calling to Monsieur Brunel as she went.

I sank down on the bank and watched the last few ripples spread across the pond.

'Poor Snoopy.' Without warning, I started to cry. Gentle sniffs at first, then it rapidly descended into full-on sobbing. Tracey came and sat beside me.

'I'm not going to ask you what's the matter,' said Tracey. 'I beat you up, you ended up on national telly with your arse hanging out, your Frenchie's done a bunk, and you killed a cat you were supposed to be writing a story about. I know it wasn't you who tipped off the paps by the way. I'm sorry.'

'I'd never have done that, Tracey. Don't think it didn't cross my mind, but in the end, I couldn't do it.'

'Yeah well, you did me a favour in the end. Warren's gone.'

'I heard. I'm sorry.'

'Me too, I really loved him. Thought he loved me too but he could never get that wife of his out of his mind.' She sniffed loudly, her eyes starting to glisten.

'The clue's in the name, Tracey, "wife". I read on the Internet they're having a big reunion in LA.'

'Thanks for reminding me.'

'Sorry.' I put my arm round her shoulder and we sat, snivelling, by the pond. Snoopy had finally gone to his watery grave and the water was still again.

'How about we start again? Hi, I'm Mel, walking disaster, killer of celebrity cats and disposer of the evidence. I think we're neighbours.'

'Hello, I'm Tracey, talent show runner-up, marriage-wrecker, most likely a one-hit wonder.'

'Come on, don't be too hard on yourself. Like I've always said, if you can't be a good example, be a terrible warning and thanks to you, I'm *never* going to go out with a married premiership footballer. Job done.' I nudged Tracey with my shoulder.

'Come on, let's get back to mine and drown our sorrows. The sun's bound to be over the yardarm somewhere in the world.'

'Deal. Do you fancy roughing it in my old jalopy?'

'Well, I'm not bloody well walking back up, am I? Let's go.'

We drove back up to Les Tuileries in silence.

'I've got a box of *rosé*. Shall I bring it?' I asked.

'Stuff your cheap plonk, I've got a fridge full of Cristal that Ryan left and a wicked thirst. Give me ten minutes then come on over.'

I went in to the cottage to freshen up and change into something more comfortable. The light on my answer phone was flashing so I pressed the button on the machine to listen to the message.

'Hello, it's Sam here. Look, we've just had a strange call from Mrs Merriman. Can you ring me, soon as?'

Well, that's going to be the shortest journalistic career in the modern world, I thought, picking up the phone to dial her number.

Chapter Fourteen

'So, how much longer are you going to wait until you go round and see Julien?'

I was lazing on a lilo in the middle of Tracey's beautiful free-form swimming pool. Every now and again, when the heat got too much, I'd paddle under the waterfall that flowed down some faux-rocks at the end of the pool.

Since I had made my peace with Tracey, the two of us had been almost inseparable. Well, it was really the three of us if you counted the constant supply of Cristal champagne that soaked our days. Tracey turned out to have a heart of gold, a far cry from the foul-mouthed, promiscuous tart that the media portrayed. She'd had a rough life, dragged up by an abusive father who'd spent more time drunk than sober, and a stepmother who couldn't give a damn about her. Singing with a hairbrush in the sanctuary of her bedroom had been the only thing that kept her sane.

In her teens, Tracey had put together a girl band, which she had unwisely called 'Premenstrual Tension' and, needless to say, they got exactly nowhere; but her aunt entered her for a national television talent show and the rest, as they say, is history. She hadn't won, but historically the runners-up had done better than the winners, although Tracey looked set to reverse that trend. The trouble was, the public just hadn't engaged with her, according to her former manager, and the affair with Warren was not a Good Thing.

I thought about her question.

'Oh, I don't know. Is it even worth the bother? He was pretty quick to jump to conclusions and flounce off in a temper.'

'That's 'cause he likes you, innit?'

'Yes well, he's got a funny way of showing it. I don't know, Trace, he blows hot and cold all the time. One minute he's coming on to me, the next he's pulling away.'

'Well, you're not his cousin are you? This is probably uncharted territory for him.'

'Stop it will you, bad girl. They don't all marry their cousins.'

'Nah, for the rest of them, there's always line dancing.'

'So that's our choice is it? Cousin marriage or line dancing? Better get our cowboys hats on,' I said. 'There's a class starting in Bussières next week.'

'Watch my lips. N.O. No, not now, not ever.'

'Oh come on, it will be a laugh,' I giggled.

'No, people only line dance because they have a defective gene.'

'Oooh, hark at you, I didn't know they had such long words in Essex.'

'Yeah, well that's the only one I know. Apart from that, nothing in my vocabulary's got more than four letters.'

'Apart from vocabulary, of course.' I ducked as a flip-flop winged past my ear, narrowly avoiding spilling my champagne.

'Seriously though, you need to go and have it out with him. You can't hang around here forever swilling Cristal and comfort-eating croissants. You've got an arse the size of the Mississippi Delta already.'

'Which is only slightly smaller than your mouth,' I quipped. 'Where's that bloody flip-flop? And while you're at it, more champagne.'

Tracey dropped the bottle of Cristal into a floating cooler and sent it across the pool to me.

'God, this is the life isn't it? Just a pity it isn't sustainable without a job. I've got to find something Trace, seeing as my budding journalistic career has gone pear-shaped after the cat affair.'

'No luck with the estate agents?'

The previous week I had dropped in to talk to the Belgian man who ran a property company in the square in Bussières. His website was very basic and I'd offered to redo it for him.

'It's all about your brand these days, and you need to build yours. You need an Internet presence, a social media profile...'

He'd looked at me as if I was speaking a foreign language, which I was, of course, although it was one he'd understood perfectly.

'In a declining market you need to be more proactive.'

He'd eyed me suspiciously but agreed for me to come up with a proposal for his consideration.

'Oh my God, Trace, didn't you hear?'

'Hear what? I don't leave here unless I need to eat these days.'

'He was arrested the next day. Apparently he was selling properties that he didn't have any right to. Some poor English people were working on the roof of the barn they'd bought from him when a farmer came past and asked what they were doing. When they told him they had bought it and were planning to turn it into a house, he pointed out that the barn was his and no one was turning it into anything. It turns out that he'd never sold it. There was a hell of a row and the *gendarmes* were called. Apparently it's not the first time the Belgian's done it but they still let him trade.'

'Bloody hell. Poor sods.'

'They lost their life savings apparently.'

'You've got to see the funny side though,' said Tracey, snorting champagne.

'Oh, you would.'

'Seriously though, do yourself a favour and go round and see Julien. Much as I enjoy your company, at the moment you make Posh Spice look like the Laughing Policeman.'

'D'you think?'

'Oh for God's sake, stop pre… prevar…'

'Prevaricating?'

'Smart arse.'

'Fat arse. Oh no, that's me isn't it? OK. You win. I'll go this afternoon.'

I looked at my reflection in the mirror, turning to left and right to check it from all angles.

I'd chosen a strappy sundress and a floppy straw hat that I hoped made me look a bit ethereal. My black eye was now just a faint smudge that was barely noticeable and I'd smothered my sun-kissed skin in a scented moisturiser.

Letting my imagination run away with me, I saw myself walking through the fields of sunflowers to his farm where he'd be fixing a tractor or something, preferably bare-chested. He'd see me, drop everything and run through the fields to sweep me up in his arms. What happened next I was going to keep to myself.

Half an hour later, I was discovering that my dream was slightly less romantic in practice. Pollen from the sunflowers was lightly coating my skin, stuck to the scented moisturiser that had seemed such a good idea at the time, and the local bee population seemed to have trouble discerning me from a flower head. The ground underfoot was baked hard and rutted, so rather than floating delicately through the field, I was stumbling and tripping like a drunk whilst batting away angry bees. The farm hadn't seemed far away from the cottage, but now I was walking, it just didn't seem to get any closer. And it was bloody hot.

Eventually I reached the farmyard and stopped to lean on the gate, catching my breath and straightening myself up a bit. The farm looked quite run down, not what I had imagined at all. It was littered with rusting farm equipment and here and there, mangy-looking dogs were snoozing in the sunshine, tethered to long chains. The yard was dominated by a large barn, which seemed to be in an advanced stage of decrepitude, tilting drunkenly to one side. From the barn I could hear the assorted lowing and snorting of cattle and pigs.

Between me and the farmhouse was a very oozy-looking yard. Next time I'd make sure to visit before milking. Hitching up my dress, I started to make my way towards the house, dodging the cowpats as I went. With my innate ability to trip over a matchstick, I could only hope I would make it safely to the other side. The dogs opened lazy eyes and scratched, but took little notice of me before returning to their slumbers in the heat.

I knocked on the door. After a few minutes it was opened by a small, round man dressed in shorts and little else.

'*Bonjour*, er, Julien? Julien d'Aubeville? *Ici?*' With my still-limited French it was the closest I could get to asking if he lived there. I pointed to myself. '*Amie*'

The man beamed at me.

'Philippe d'Aubeville,' he said and stood back, beckoning at me to come in. He led me into the house and down the hallway, which curiously had a toilet cubicle in the middle of it. In the kitchen, he swiped a fat tabby cat off a chair and motioned me to sit down before disappearing off, I presumed, to find Julien. On the stove, a large pan was bubbling away filling the kitchen with steam that made the windows run with condensation.

I studied my surroundings. In my mind, I imagined a French farmhouse kitchen to be full of old copper pans and jars of preserved fruits, with definitely a dresser at the very least. This looked like something from the unfashionable part of the 1970s. The cat sat at my feet, staring up at me, clearly annoyed at being so unceremoniously removed from its sleeping place.

'Hello kitty,' I said, leaning down to stroke it. It hissed and went back to staring at me with unblinking eyes.

'OK, so we won't be friends then. Well to be fair I don't have a good record with cats so you're probably doing the right thing.'

I sat back and waited, feeling slightly unnerved, and waited for Julien. Without warning, the cat jumped on my lap, making me jump and for a brief moment I remembered the lifeless body of poor Snoopy lying in the road. It still made me feel ill.

'So now you want to be my friend, eh?' I said, tickling it under the chin.

It settled down on my lap, curling up into a ball to resume its afternoon siesta and I stroked it absent-mindedly while I waited. Out of the corner of my eye I thought I saw a movement, then another. Looking down at the cat, I saw my lap was speckled with little black dots. Little black moving dots. Fleas! I leapt up, sending the cat flying and yowling onto the floor.

'Jesus Christ,' I muttered shaking out my dress and brushing off my arms and legs.

'*Bonjour, mademoiselle,*' said a voice behind me. I turned to find Philippe standing in the doorway with a similarly small, round woman with the trademark vivid orange hair, although hers had the added attraction of a sort of tiger-striping effect. It clashed with her fuchsia-pink floral housecoat and the concertina'd stockings set the whole ensemble off beautifully.

'*Bonjour monsieur, madame,*' I said, standing up to greet them.

Philippe pointed to his wife, 'Madeleine'. The woman gave me a semi-toothless smile, motioning at me to sit down again. They joined me at the table, Monsieur d'Aubeville next to me, Madame opposite, then sat in silence staring at me, smiles fixed to their faces.

I wracked my brains for something to say, but I had still barely progressed beyond a running commentary on the weather and a request for the location of the toilet, and I already knew where that was. This place really wasn't what I expected. Julien seemed quite cosmopolitan but this was just on the decent side of feral.

'Speak little English,' said Philippe, when it became obvious that we couldn't just sit there smiling at each other for much longer.

'Speak little French,' I laughed.

'Drink?' he said, pointing to his mouth with his thumb.

'*Oui,* yes please. My mouth is very dry after my walk.'

Madame d'Aubeville got up to switch on the kettle but her husband had other ideas.

'No, we have *bière.*'

'Oh no, really, I don't like to drink in the afternoon,' I said thinking of the liberal amounts of champagne I had already downed.

But Monsieur d'Aubeville was having none of it. Before you could say *la plume de ma tante* he was prising the caps off two bottles of beer, one of which he placed in front of me.

'*Santé,*' he said, raising his bottle to me.

'Cheers.'

'Cheese? You want cheese?'

'Oh, no, I said cheers. It's what we say for *santé* in England. Cheers,' I said again, over-enunciating the word.

'Cheese,' replied Monsieur d'Aubeville, saluting me with his drink. Madame d'Aubeville sat impassively at the table, hands folded in her lap. I wondered what was keeping Julien.

'You live London?' he asked

'Yes. Have you been?'

'No London. Algeria.'

'Oh, right.' I wasn't sure I entirely got the connection.

A flea jumped onto the table and, without thinking, my hand flew out to squash it.

Monsieur d'Aubeville laughed. 'Everywhere, *les puces*, everywhere.'

I smiled weakly. 'So, Algeria? What did you do?'

'War. Civil War.'

'Ah.' As conversation stoppers went, that was up there with 'I put kittens in wheelie bins for my own amusement', but Monsieur d'Aubeville was not put off.

'I soldier. Fight. Kill many men.' He mimed shooting a gun with his two fingers.

'Right, er, good.'

Madame d'Aubeville continued to sit impassively.

'So your farm. Animals? Wheat?'

'Cows, pigs, for food. I kill them.'

There was a bit of a theme going on here.

'And...' he cast around for the right word then opted just to make a quacking sound.

'Ducks?' I offered.

'Yes, for *foie gras*. My wife, she make *pâté* out of anything.'

I was a little bit concerned about the 'anything', especially bearing in mind the number of dogs outside in the yard.

He turned and babbled to his wife who got up and disappeared off, before shortly returning with a large slab of *pâté*. With great ceremony, she cut a large slice then placed it reverently on a plate before rummaging in a drawer for a knife and fork. Honestly, you'd think the French would know how to serve *pâté*. It needed a nice oatcake or a Bath Oliver, but here they just seemed to eat it on its own. To be polite, I tucked in, even though I wasn't terribly hungry.

'Mmm, delicious,' I said, smiling at Madame d'Aubeville.

'*Museau de porc*,' she said shyly. I had no idea what that was so I shrugged helplessly at her.

Madame d'Aubeville took my arm and led me over to the saucepan, which was still bubbling furiously on the stove. Lifting the lid she let me look inside. As the steam cleared, half a pig's head appeared, its one eye staring reproachfully at me. I screamed and jumped backwards, nearly overturning the pan.

Monsieur d'Aubeville laughed a deep, rumbling laugh that was totally out of proportion to his size and slapped his thigh. Even the silent Madame d'Aubeville cracked the slightest of smiles.

'*Désolée*, sorry, sorry,' I laughed. 'It just made me jump.'

I went back and sat down at the table, comedy-fanning myself. On top of the pig's colon sausage, I now had the pleasure of pig's head *pâté*. Was there no part of an animal the French didn't eat?

Still chortling, Monsieur d'Aubeville got up and went to a cupboard, returning with a deep scarlet liquid in a wax-topped bottle. It looked dangerous.

'*Non*, really. No more.' I put my hands up to him. 'Too much.'

'For the *choc*,' he said, pouring several fingers into a glass that he'd found on the draining board. It looked none too clean but I was sure that whatever was in the bottle could kill salmonella at thirty paces.

I took a sip and gasped as the heat of the liquid trickled down my throat and into my stomach. It brought to mind the one and only time I'd tried Polish Pure Spirit. That was about 80 per cent proof and this didn't taste that far behind. It made my eyes water.

'*Bon*, very good,' I croaked.

'*Eau de vie*,' said Monsieur d'Aubeville, saluting me with the bottle.

Water of life, I thought. A very romantic name for high-octane paint stripper. It was more likely to kill you.

'*Santé*.' Monsieur d'Aubeville tipped his head backwards and downed his shot, bringing the glass down with a bang on the table.

'*Oh là là, c'est bon ça,*' he said, shaking his head and flapping his cheeks.

'Very good,' I agreed sipping mine a bit more decorously.

'No, not like that. You drink like me.'

The alcohol was already starting its inexorable march to my head but in the interests of *entente cordiale*, I followed suit, downing the rest of my drink in one and banging the glass down on the table.

I wondered where Julien was. I'd been there a good while and there was no sign of him. Probably busy milking a goat or something.

Monsieur d'Aubeville was already pouring himself a second glass. Just my luck to be stuck with an elderly French binge-drinker. I looked across at Madame d'Aubeville. Surely she'd say something. It was only early afternoon and he was already power drinking, but she just sat impassively, with an expression that gave nothing away.

Reaching across he took my glass and refilled it.

'No, really, no more.'

'No policemen. We drink.'

He stood up and started to sing 'La Marseillaise'. What was it about inebriated Frenchmen and their national anthem? He motioned at me to join him. I'd only ever managed to crack the first verse of my own one, never mind this, but Monsieur d'Aubeville was determined to educate me.

'*Allons enfants de la Patrie...*' he sang tunelessly. '*Le jour de gloire est arrivé.*'

He translated it as best he could as we went. It was all a bit politically incorrect to my London point of view, all about bloody standards and fields running with the blood of our enemies. Considering all the fuss that was made over 'Land of Hope and Glory' for its colonial overtones, it was surprising that a national anthem should be so triumphalist. Gradually I started to pick up the words and, aided by another glass of Monsieur d'Aubeville's ruby nectar, I was starting to enjoy myself a bit.

When I managed to get all the way to the part about 'impure blood' all by myself, Monsieur d'Aubeville cheered and even *madame* looked faintly amused.

'Phew, enough,' I told them, my head starting to reel a bit. I curtseyed to Monsieur d'Aubeville, who bowed back to me with a drunken flourish before sitting down to pour himself another drink.

I sat down, pulling my glass out of the reach of Monsieur d'Aubeville and his deadly bottle before he could pour me another.

A meaty hand descended on my thigh. I sat very still as it started to stroke my leg.

'So, Monsieur,' I said, jumping up from the table and away from his wandering hand, 'Julien is here?'

'Julien, no,' he said and got up to led me unsteadily to the window. Further down the lane, hidden behind the barn, was another farmhouse. 'There Julien. Next door.'

'So... so he doesn't live here?'

'Here? *Non.*' Monsieur d'Aubeville smiled drunkenly.

'And you are... ?'

'His *oncle.*'

Chapter Fifteen

Madame d'Aubeville opened the door to let me out. Her husband, now very much the worse for wear, was slumped forward with his head on the table, still singing 'La Marseillaise' off-key.

'*Merci, madame.*' I put my hand out to shake Madame d'Aubeville's. She took it and smiled the tiniest of smiles before turning back into the house and closing the door.

I looked round the run-down farm, the rusting machinery and the mangy dogs and thought that it couldn't be much of a life for the poor woman. Underneath the careworn, unsmiling face, there showed the remnants of the very pretty girl she had once been. I wondered what dreams she'd had when she was young. Was this how she thought she'd end up? More importantly, if I pursued my feelings for Julien, was this actually how *I* would end up? Whenever I'd let my imagination run away with me, I'd thought of myself throwing corn to the hens with a couple of rosy-cheeked, cherubic children at my feet. Julien would come back from the fields (always clean, of course) and rush to kiss me and we would walk through our immaculate farm to our equally immaculate house. Was Philippe d'Aubeville's ramshackle farm and downtrodden wife closer to reality?

Pushing away the unwelcome thought, I wobbled my way down the lane to the right house. It hadn't seemed so bad when I was sitting down but now I was standing up (and trying to walk), I realised that I was pretty plastered. The road seemed to buck and sway as I walked along. Closing one eye didn't make it any easier. Having not seen Julien for a couple of weeks this really wasn't how I wanted to be for The Big Reunion.

'Bums,' I said out loud. 'Bums, bums, bums!'

Maybe it would be better to head home and try again another day, but I'd come so far and to be honest, I didn't really fancy walking all the way home, the way I was feeling. The *eau de vie* seemed to be having a slow-burn effect. The fresh air was making me feel more drunk, instead of sobering me up. In fact, I felt pretty awful. I was hot and sticky in the heat and a headache was starting behind my eyes. I was sure that I was sweating alcohol.

The sound of a tractor coming down the lane brought me out of my thoughts. I squinted into the sun to see who was driving but it was too bright, and despite shading my eyes with my forearm, all I could see was a black outline against the brilliant white light. The tractor slowed down as it reached me.

'*Ma belle?*' asked the one voice I'd been longing to hear. 'What the hell are you doing here?' Not the words I'd hoped would be spoken.

'I came to find you,' I slurred, 'to talk.'

He turned off the tractor and climbed down to me.

'Are you drunk?'

'Not zhrunk, jusht a bit tipsy.' I smiled, doing my best to focus on him. He looked bloody lush, I thought. His damp T-shirt clung to his body, outlining the contours of his muscles, the sweat throwing off a musky fragrance that I found ridiculously sexy. Must be all those phenomones... phemonomes... phero. Oh, what the hell, never mind what they were called, I just wanted him. Right there, right then, there. Bloody hell, what was in that stuff I'd drunk?

'Why do you keep moving?' I said, swaying gently.

'I'm not, it's you.'

'Oh. So, sit down with me.' I plonked myself down in the middle of the road.

'Maybe not there.' He pulled me up and helped me to the verge at the side of the road.

'Not more of your bloody dizhes there, I hope.'

'No, you're quite safe,' he replied, sitting down next to me.

I turned to look at him. 'Hmm, I can see two of you. Which one is the real you and which one is the imposter?' I said, swinging my arm wide and nearly hitting him square in the face.

'Ooops, sorry,' I giggled and put my hands up to my cover my mouth like a naughty schoolgirl.

'I think I should get you home. Can you manage to get in the tractor?'

'You think I'm drunk, don't you? Well I'm not. I'm a little bit tipsy maybe, but I'm most definitely not drunk. Look.'

I stood up and made my way unsteadily to the middle of the lane. 'You know how they do it in the American movies? I'm going to walk down the white line in the middle of the road.'

'There aren't any white lines.'

'Hmm. Well I'll pretend. Here's the white line.' I pointed out an imaginary white line in the road. Then, carefully putting one foot in front of the other, I made little fairy steps down it, wobbling like a tightrope walker.

'See. Now, I'm going to shut my eyes, put my finger on my nose and stand on one leg. Oooh…' I crashed painfully to the ground. 'It's nothing,' I said, seeing the concern on Julien's face.

'I think, maybe, I should get you home,' he offered, helping me up.

'Your home or mine?' I put on my best provocative face but with the addition of Philippe's *eau de vie* the effect was probably more drag queen than seductress.

Julien smiled benignly. 'Yours I think.'

'But yours is nearer. Look, it's only down the lane.' He didn't answer.

'What? Are you hiding a wife there or something?'

He just smiled and tried to steer me towards the tractor.

'So,' he asked, 'where have you been to get like this?'

'At your Uncle Philippe's.'

'Oh *mon Dieu*, that would explain it. You didn't have any of his *eau de vie* did you?'

'Jusht a little, teeny, tiny one,' I said holding up my thumb and index finger to show him just how tiny, 'or two. Maybe even three.'

'Well if you managed three, I salute you. One is enough, two is too much and three will probably kill you.' He smiled at me. I smiled back.

'Fancy a shag?' I slapped my hand over my mouth and looked at him in horror. What was in that *eau de vie*? Some sort of truth drug?

'Sorry?'

'Er, nothing,' I said, my face colouring.

'OK, it's just I thought you asked if I fancied a shag.' He smiled at me. 'Come on, let's get you home. Your carriage awaits you.' He bowed deeply and gestured towards the tractor. I didn't fancy my chances of getting in it very much.

'OK,' I said, rolling up my sleeves and squaring up to the tractor as if I was getting ready to scale Everest.

'Just put your foot here,' he said pointing to the footplate, 'and take hold of this handle here.'

It took a few tries to co-ordinate my hands and feet but eventually I seemed to be in the right position.

'OK, one, two, three…' I tried to haul myself up but the alcohol in my body seemed to sap the strength in my arms and I barely managed more than a little hop.

Julien laughed. 'OK, try again.'

The second attempt was hardly much better than the first but on the third, I managed to get myself up onto the footplate with a bit of manhandling from Julien.

'Julien,' I said, turning round on the tiny step to face him.

Without warning, he wrapped his arms round my waist and buried his face in my neck, murmuring softly in French.

'Yes?' he asked.

'Forget it,' I said. Our mouths grazed and I nibbled his lower lip. He nipped me back and then it happened. The moment I'd been waiting for since I first met him. He kissed me, slowly at first, then with more passion until we were buried in each other, kissing as if the world would end. He pushed his hands through my hair, pulling my head towards him. It was everything and more than I had hoped for. I pulled away to catch my breath.

'Julien…'

'Yes?'

'I think I'm going to throw up.'

He let go of me unceremoniously and I rushed for the verge, only just getting there in time before I emptied the entire contents of my stomach. I felt too awful to feel mortified, even when Julien came over and started to rub my back gently as I dry heaved into the wild flowers.

'I'm so sorry,' I whispered, in between retches.

'Don't worry. If I had known you'd go to Philippe's, I would have warned you not to touch that stuff. It's deadly.' He went back to the cab of the tractor and came back with a bottle of water.

'It's a bit warm but it will do to rinse your mouth.'

I took it, drinking deeply and swilling out my mouth. Well, that's blown it, I thought. Again.

When I couldn't be sick any more, he helped me up into the cab of the tractor and turned it back up the lane towards the fields and on to Les Tuileries. I sat in the tractor ashen-faced, every jolt churning my stomach, and breathed a sigh of relief when we finally pulled up outside my cottage.

'Allez, hop,' said Julien, helping me down. I felt distinctly unsteady as I made contact with solid ground again.

'Keys?'

I got them out of my bag and he unlocked the door, helping me in with an arm around my waist.

'I need to go to the bathroom. Make yourself at home,' I said waving in the vague direction of the lounge.

I looked at myself in the bathroom mirror. A pale face with red-ringed eyes stared back at me.

'You look like shit, girl,' I told my reflection, before squeezing some toothpaste onto my toothbrush and brushing away the sick taste from my mouth.

I splashed my face with water and raked my fingers through my hair before pouting at myself in the mirror.

'Julien d'Aubeville, I fully intend to have you.'

I rummaged through the laundry basket for my push-up bra which I was pretty sure I'd put in there a couple of days previously, at the same time pulling out a pair of minute denim shorts that erred just on the wrong side of decency and a tiny camisole top. They were a bit scrunched up so I shook them out, after all, I wasn't planning on keeping them on for very long. A quick squirt of perfume to freshen everything up and I was ready for the next part in my seduction plan. Well, it wasn't so much a plan as I was just making it up as I went along. Could I get him into the pool to practise the lifts like in *Dirty Dancing*? Unlikely. Maybe Kim

Basinger in 9½ *Weeks*. My girlfriends and I had often had 9½ *Weeks* movie nights, even though most of us hadn't even been born when the film came out. Our other favourite was *Sing-a-long-a Sound of Music*, but I was prepared to concede that, even if I did have a convenient nun's habit lying around, it would probably be a bit too weird. But 9½ *Weeks*, now that was a classic seduction scene and all I needed was a chair and Tom Jones singing 'You Can Leave Your Hat On'.

On second thoughts, the chair was a bad idea bearing in mind the problems I was already having with co-ordination. I'd have to manage without it.

I bent over – bad move – and shook out my hair. The months without a hairdresser had left me with a full head of pre-Raphaelite curls and I wanted a tousled, bed-hair look. I stood up, staggering slightly and checked my reflection again. Not bad, I thought. A bit pale though. I applied a bit of blusher, forgetting the key rule about never putting your make-up on in artificial light. I was so pale that I decided a second layer was necessary.

'Right,' I said to myself. 'Let's go.'

I opened the door, wincing slightly as I walked out into the sunny hallway.

'Da, nah, nah, nah, nah, nah...' I sang as I slid round the door frame into the lounge.

Julien looked slightly alarmed.

'Do, do, do, do, do, dooo...'

I started to gyrate against the wall. The look I was aiming for was vampish, the one that I achieved was Eastern European soft porn, especially with my over-made up face.

'Baby take off your coat...' I sang tunelessly, wiggling my bottom at Julien, whose chin was now in his lap, but not in a good way.

'... real slow.' I turned towards him, pulling out the straps on my camisole to reveal the very impressive cleavage that my push-up bra had produced, then leaned forward, thrusting my breasts towards him. He looked like a startled rabbit. Clearly *9½ Weeks* movie nights were not big in rural France.

'What the hell are you doing?'

'You can take off your shoes...' A few more hip gyrations and he was mine, my drunken self told me. I threw my head forward so my hair tumbled down in front of me then flicked it backwards. With an alarming *thwack* I cracked my head on the stone wall behind me and collapsed on the floor.

I slowly became aware of a voice calling my name. It seemed a million miles away. I concentrated hard then opened my eyes.

'Thank God, don't move. The ambulance is on its way.' Julien's concerned face swum into view, a bloodied tea towel in his hand. I tried to sit up but he pushed me gently back down onto the floor. 'Stay where you are until the *pompiers* get here. You are bleeding.'

'The *pompiers*? Why is the fire brigade coming? Are we on fire?'

'Well you certainly were,' he smiled gently. 'The *pompiers* always come out first then we will decide if you need to go to hospital.'

'What happened?'

'I'm not really sure to be honest. You were being very, er, entertaining.'

'Shit. I remember now.'

There was a knock at the door and Julien got up to answer it. Five burly men suddenly appeared in the living room, all talking away rapidly in French to Julien. I recognised the man from the paper shop, the young guy who worked at the petrol station in Bussières and another who worked in the local supermarket. Suddenly the downside of living in a small rural community became apparent. There was a sudden burst of laughter and they all looked over at me.

Now was probably a good time to be unconscious, I thought. Either that, or a giant fissure in the earth's crust, previously unknown to man, could open and swallow me right up.

An older man came over with Julien and knelt down next to me. Julien introduced him as *le chef,* the chief rather than the cook.

'He doesn't speak English so I'll translate for you. He wants to know your name.'

'Well can't you tell him that?'

'No, he's asking you so he can see if you remember what it is.'

I reeled off my full name, including middle ones.

'He wants to know if you remember how you had your accident.'

'Tell him, unfortunately yes.'

Julien chuckled quietly and turned to the *chef* who spoke to him for several minutes.

'OK, he needs to do a thorough check over. Can you take your top off?'

'What? No!'

'Come on, *ma belle.* He needs to check your heart.'

'Oh ho, does he indeed. I banged my head. You're not getting me like that.'

'*Chérie*, please be reasonable.' The *chef* reached over and started to try and remove my top. I hung on to it for all I was worth.

'I'm not taking it off in front of this lot. I have to see them at least once a week.'

'Look, they are all professionals. There is nothing they haven't seen before.'

'Maybe not, but they haven't seen mine and they are not going to.'

The *chef* took hold of my top again.

'*Mademoiselle, s'il vous plait,*' he said gently, prising my fingers off my top. Realising that resistance was futile, I let him carefully pull it over my head.

'*Et votre soutien-gorge*,' he said.

'*Soutien-gorge?* What's that?'

'He wants you to take your bra off.'

'Hang on, so what's a *brassière* then? I thought that was French for bra?'

'Look, I'm not going to have a discussion about the origins of French words. Just take it off.'

'Oh God,' I moaned quietly. All these months of dreaming of getting naked with Julien d'Aubeville and now I was going to have to do it in a room full of firemen.

I unhooked my bra and lay there, mortified, as the chef connected me up to a heart monitor.

Suddenly the door burst open and two doctors in white coats, who had clearly been watching too much *ER*, ran in. One actually jumped astride me and started listening to my chest, while the other drew a syringe from his bag, filled it with some clear liquid and squirted a bit into the air.

'Julien, what the...' So this was how it was going to end? Drugged and sold into white slavery. In *la France profonde*, no one can hear you scream.

'OK, he's just giving you a shot in case you have a blood clot in your brain from the knock.'

'Owww,' I cried as he jabbed it into my arm.

The doctors conferred with the *chef* and with Julien while I lay there, in just a pair of tiny shorts, wishing that the day would end, or better still, that it had never started.

'We are going to take you to hospital.'

'But I'm fine, really.' I hated hospitals and the thought of one where I couldn't even speak the language was too much. I wanted to cry.

'You were unconscious. We have no choice just in case you have injured your brain.'

The chef summoned the other *pompiers* and gave them some instructions. They quickly returned with a stretcher and tucked me up with a blanket.

'Julien, where are they taking me? Will you come too?'

'They are taking you to the clinic in Villeneuve but I can't go. I have to get back to the farm. Take your phone and call me later.'

They bundled me onto the stretcher and took me out to the waiting ambulance. Julien motioned to me with his thumb and forefinger to call him and that was the last I saw as the doctors climbed in the back and the doors closed.

Chapter Sixteen

The sun slanting through the blinds at the window nudged me gently from a dreamless, drug-induced slumber. I sat up, momentarily disorientated, but the pounding in my head was too much and I lay back down, staring up at the ceiling.

'Oh God,' I said out loud, remembering the events of the previous day. There was no way I could show my face in Bussières after half the town had seen me naked. I was pretty sure that in such a small place, word of my hopeless seduction of Julien would have got around. I put my hand to my head, feeling a lump the size of Jupiter. It had taken eight stitches to patch me up.

Outside the room, I could hear the nursing staff whispering. All I could catch was *l'anglaise*, the English woman, so clearly they were talking about me. I strained my ears to hear but then, even if I could, it was unlikely I would understand it. I'd been lucky the previous day in the Emergency Room that they had managed to find a Moroccan doctor who spoke reasonable English otherwise I would have been sunk. The French doctors could barely conceal their impatience at my lack of language skills and I knew they had a point. I still hadn't managed a single French lesson since my arrival. The only word I had picked up in the ER was *le bassin*, the bedpan, as I'd suddenly developed a bladder the size of a gnat, necessitating the need to use it several times. The doctor told me it was the shock but I thought it was more likely that the *eau de vie* had some sort of diuretic properties. While on the one hand it was good that I had picked up a new word, 'bedpan' was hardly likely to be something I would be using in everyday speech. Oh, and there was another thing I had learnt. *'Portable interdit'*, no mobile phones. They had told me in no uncertain terms, as I'd tried to phone Tracey to tell her where I was. I had a quick look round but there was no sign of my mobile. Perhaps it was in the drawer by my bed? I sat up gingerly and pulled it open and there it was – my lifeline to the outside world. I took it out and turned it on, hoping the battery wasn't flat and joy of joys, it sprang to life. I quickly glanced towards the door. No one seemed to be around so I quickly tapped in a text to Julien.

'At the clinic in Villeneuve. Please send rescue party.
Will pay for liberation! Xxx'

'Bonjour, mademoiselle,' said a young, fresh-faced nurse wheeling in some sort of giant instrument of torture. I quickly shoved my phone under my pillow, hoping I hadn't been caught.

'We need X-ray your head.' She fussed around with the machine as she moved it towards the bed.

'Bon,' said the nurse, repositioning my head gently. When she was happy, she told me to keep very still then went out of the room, taking a handset on a long wire which snaked out behind her. Once she was safely outside, she pressed a button and the machine whirred to life, moving around me to X-ray my head from several angles.

Very *Star Wars*, I thought as it buzzed and clicked away.

After a few minutes, the nurse came back in, turned the machine off and wheeled it away. 'The consultant come later,' she said as she left the room.

I gave it a few minutes to make sure that no one else was coming then slipped my phone out from under the pillow. There was nothing from Julien. Hiding my phone back under the bedclothes, I stared at the ceiling, huffing with boredom. I looked out of the window but the view across the back of Castorama, a big DIY store, was hardly inspiring. Julien had told me that a *castor* was French for a beaver. 'Beaverama,' I said out loud, giggling.

A po-faced older nurse with hair scraped back into a French version of a Croydon facelift walked in and glared at me, banging down a tray of food.

'*Petit déjeuner.*'

'Breakfast, thanks, *merci beaucoup*,' I said, smiling broadly. The nurse barely acknowledged me before stalking out, the rubber soles of her shoes squeaking as she went.

Breakfast wasn't bad. A croissant but no butter or jam. The French didn't quite get the English custom for slathering them with even more butter and a dollop of *confiture*. It was like putting cheese on bread or crackers; in France, both co-existed side by side and never the twain would ever meet except on the plate of an expat. There was a little pot of orange juice and some water. Starvation rations. No wonder they say the French don't get fat, although of course the truth was that I had seen plenty of evidence that they did. Despite my pounding head, I had a ferocious hunger and devoured the croissant in two bites, washing it down with the thimbleful of orange juice. I wondered if there was any chance of a skinny latte. Probably not. The French weren't really into foreign stuff.

Under the bedclothes, my phone vibrated. I grabbed it quickly, hoping it would be Julien. It was a text from Tracey.

'OMG! What the bloody hell did you do? Everyone talking about you. Totes hilare.'
'Great! Can u come? Bored. No hot doctors just grumpy nurse. In Clinique St Victor in Villeneuve.'

My phone was silent for a few minutes and I felt my heart start to sink, but then it vibrated again.

'Sure. There in hour.'
'Not sure what time visiting is.'
'Visiting hours is for the riff-raff. Don't they know who I am?'
'Prob not!'
'Har-de-bloody-ha-ha. *Vache.*'

I smiled to myself. Whatever her faults, Tracey always cheered me up. I slipped my phone back under the covers, waiting for Julien to reply.

The po-faced nurse returned holding a kidney bowl covered with a paper towel. A wave of disquiet swept over me when I saw the look on the her face, a mixture of twisted evil and grim delight. She put the tray down on the bedside cabinet then took some latex gloves from her pocket, snapping them as she put them on. Turning to the tray, she took off the paper towel and revealed a large bullet-shaped object and a tube of lubricating jelly. With a smile, the nurse held them up, one in each hand.

Shit, I thought, backing up the bed away from the nurse. No wonder she was looking so happy. It was a suppository. I'd heard about the French penchant for shoving stuff up your bum, not in a small, furry animal kind of way, but for pain relief. No way was this woman going anywhere near my rear end. I pulled my knees up to my chest and my hospital gown tight round my knees.

'Non,' I said firmly.

The nurse advanced towards me, gesturing at me to turn over.

'Not bloody likely,' I exclaimed but the nurse clearly didn't understand.

She pointed to my bottom. 'You feel better. For bad head.'

'In England you take tablets through your mouth for a bad head, not up your arse!'

'This is France. You must. Doctor say so.'

'No, *non*, never, *jamais*.' I was almost shouting now.

The nurse offered the suppository and lubricant to me. 'You do yourself?'

Well this certainly brought a new meaning to DIY but seeing an escape route, I took them from the nurse and swung my legs onto the floor. As I stood up, a rush of light-headedness made me stumble slightly, but determined to get myself to the bathroom with the suppository, which, incidentally, was going nowhere other than down the toilet, I straightened up, taking the tray from Nurse Po-Face with a smile.

In the bathroom, I slumped down on the toilet, wondering how long it normally took to insert a suppository. Well, better make this sound authentic. I made a few oohs and aahs, of the sort I thought someone shoving a bullet-sized lump of wax up their bum might make while, at the same time, breaking it up into small pieces and wrapping the bits in toilet paper. After a few minutes, I dropped them into the toilet bowl, loaded on more toilet paper, pressed the flush and watch the dreaded thing disappear into the eddying water and away into the French sewage system. My bum would live to fight another day and I'd have to put up with the cracking headache.

I squirted some soap from the dispenser onto my hands and washed them, looking at myself in the mirror over the sink. I looked like shit, again, turning my head from side to side to see the full extent of the damage. The back of my hair was matted where the blood had dried even though they had tried their best to clean it up. I'd had more injuries, bruises and black eyes in the few months I'd been in France than in the rest of my life put together. I always considered myself a fairly lucky person but anyone hearing of my recent adventures would probably beg to differ. Ho hum, I thought. All part of life's rich tapestry or something like that.

Outside the door, Nurse Po-Face coughed to get my attention.

'*J'arrive, j'arrive*,' I called. 'I won't be a moment.' I dried my hands on some disposable paper towels, dropped them in the bin and went out, taking care to walk a bit awkwardly for added authenticity.

I pulled a face, motioning towards my bottom. 'Ooooh, *pas bon*.'

The nurse smiled the sort of smile you'd have just before you pulled the wings off a butterfly. She clearly had issues, I thought. Directing me back to the bed, she informed me, '*Docteur* come soon.'

I snuggled back under the covers, waiting for her to leave before I took a sneaky peek at my mobile. The message icon was indicating a new text. I opened it, smiling to see it was from Julien. The smile faded quickly.

> '*Chérie*, I am so sorry but I can't come. I have a problem
> on the farm that I need to sort out. Biz, JuJu.'

JuJu? The French certainly loved to shorten a name. I'd heard Martine called Mo-Mo, even McDonald's (them of the Golden Arches fame, McDonald not being a terribly popular French name) was shortened to McDo. Bummer, I thought, smiling slightly at the irony, but at least Tracey was coming.

'*Bonjour mademoiselle*.' A deep, throaty voice breezed through my thoughts and into the room. 'I am *Docteur* Ahmadi, your consultant.'

'Oh, hello, you speak English! There's more English-speaking doctors here than back in the UK,' I joked taking in his medium build, dark wavy hair, and sparkly, mischievous-looking eyes.

'Yes, we North Africans are generally brought up speaking French and English, luckily for you British, who seem not to want to learn the lovely French language.'

He winked at me, then sat on the edge of the bed, gently lifting my hand to take the pulse in my wrist. 'So, how is your head this morning?'

'Not bad, all things considered. It's a bit painful but nothing I can't handle.'

He bent my head forward and gently felt the area around the stitches.

'Well, it all looks very clean. It should heal well. Now,' he said, standing up and taking some X-rays out of the large envelope he had been carrying. 'I'm afraid we found something when we X-rayed your head.' He looked at me seriously. 'It's not something I've ever come across before.'

I suddenly knew the meaning of the expression about your blood running cold. I felt like I had iced water coursing round my veins and without warning, tears began to prick the backs of my eyelids. I took a deep breath, wishing I wasn't alone to hear the news that, undoubtedly, they had found some sort of brain tumour. He held up the X-ray to the light, so I could see it.

'Look, you have a mobile phone embedded in your brain. No wonder your head hurts,' he smiled.

There, in glorious monochrome was the clear outline of my phone, which I had hidden under the pillow when the nurse came in to do the X-ray. It appeared to be stuck in my brain. I flushed a deep scarlet.

'I'm, I'm sorry, it's just that...' I stuttered.

'Don't worry,' he said sliding the X-ray back in the envelope, 'I'm sure you are not the first to smuggle your phone into the clinic and we are all grateful for the laugh you gave us.'

'Yes, well I seem to be doing rather a lot of that these days.' I gave him a wry smile.

'Da nah nah nah nah naaaaah!' From nowhere, Tracey oozed around the door, in a mocking imitation of my 9½ *Weeks* dance, grinding her hips against the door frame in a classic porn star manner before turning and shimmying her well-endowed chest.

'Ooops, sorry mate, didn't know there was anyone else in here.' Tracey laughed a deep, sexy laugh that made Dr Ahmadi squirm. He looked as if all his Eid al-Adhas had come true at once. 'No, please, don't stop on my account,' he smiled, half joking.

She swaggered over to him, swaying her hips suggestively. Dressed in leather shorts, red killer heels and a sprayed-on top, she looked every bit the dominatrix. His look was a mixture of lust and sheer terror.

'I'm sorry, mate,' she said running a long, red fingernail under his chin as beads of sweat appeared on his brow, 'but I don't do private shows.'

'*Docteur* Ahmadi!'

Nurse Po-Face was standing at the door, mouth open in shock. Dr Ahmadi jumped up, grabbing the large envelope with the X-ray, which he held in front of the bulge in his trousers. A brief but fiery exchange in rapid French took place with disgusted looks being thrown in the direction of Tracey and me.

'Cor, I'd love to know what that frigid old bat's saying,' whispered Tracey into my ear.

'Actually, for once I'm glad I can't speak the language.'

After giving the poor doctor a tongue-lashing, Nurse Po-Face turned on her heel and stalked off, no doubt to tell her friends about the loose-moraled English girls and was it any wonder they had the highest teenage pregnancy rate in Europe if this was how they behaved in front of decent, respectable people.

Sheepishly, Dr Ahmadi turned to us and told me I was free to leave and that he would leave a prescription for painkillers at the nurse's station. Then he left.

'Do you think I'm being thrown out?' I asked.

'Ah, who cares? Don't want to stay here any longer, do you?'

'Well, no, but...'

'Well nothing, grab your stuff and let's hit the road. I'll be Thelma and you can be Louise.'

'We don't have to drive off any cliffs though do we? I've had enough adventure for one day.'

Chapter Seventeen

I sat on the edge of the pool, swirling the water around with my feet. It was only ten o'clock but I could already feel the heat of the morning sun beating down on my back. I had come home from the hospital over a week ago and there was still no sign of Julien. I flushed with humiliation at the thought of how I'd made a fool of myself in front of him. Just when a bit of alcohol-induced oblivion would be a welcome relief, I found I could remember exactly what I'd done. Even the rocket fuel that Philippe had given me hadn't erased my memory. It would serve me right if Julien never spoke to me again. I'd certainly confirmed any suspicions that he might have had that British women drink far too much. I'd made myself into a tabloid cliché.

Those bloody 'make a new life abroad' programmes should be banned, I thought. Where did it say that you'd be beaten up by a mad, D-list celebrity, run over a record-breaking cat and hospitalise yourself trying to recreate an iconic Hollywood seduction scene? Come to think of it, where did it say that you wouldn't be able to find a job, the locals would treat you with a profound suspicion and that the average age of the expat population was about a hundred and three?

Sighing, which I seemed to do an awful lot of lately, I slipped into the pool to start my daily regimen of lengths. The 'croissant-top' that hung over my jeans was in danger of settling in for the long run and, with the hope that some of my glamorous London friends might visit soon, I wanted to swim it into submission. I had built up to forty lengths, which sounded impressive, until you took into account how small the pool was. Three strokes and you were across it.

The good thing about swimming was that it was fairly mindless. Once I got going, it was just one stroke after another and I could just let my thoughts wander. And invariably they wandered to Julien. He was quite an enigma. Although he was clearly interested, if that kiss was anything to go by, it was as if something was preventing him from having a full-on relationship with me. Certainly Louis didn't seem too happy about it, but mind you, he didn't seem to be too happy about anything.

I turned over onto my back to do a few more lengths. The sky was so blue it looked Photo-Shopped and there wasn't a cloud to be seen anywhere. I stopped swimming and just floated on my back, arms and legs spread, feeling the warmth of the sun along the length of my body. It was quite sensual and I wished Julien were there, in a bad, wicked way.

'OK girl, back to the swimming. Enough of your filthy thoughts,' I said out loud, and turning over onto my front, I swam as if I was in an Olympic final, trying to wipe out the mental picture that had been building of me and Julien and...

'Oh look, it's The Little Mermaid!'

Tracey's flat estuary vowels broke through my thoughts. It was probably just as well.

'Ah, Trace, ever the comedian. You should actually try swimming yourself but it would probably wash your fake tan off.'

'Cheeky bitch. This is me, all me, this lot. None of your spray tans, thanks very much.'

I swam to the ladder and pulled myself up and out of the water. I hated that moment when you went from almost weightless to very weighty. It was an unwelcome reminder that I was heading towards being twice the woman I used to be.

'Chuck me a towel would you? There's one on the sun lounger.'

Tracey threw the towel, hitting me square in the face. 'There you go.'

'Take my eye out, why don't you?' I smiled.

'Where's the wine then? Got a nice chilled glass of *rosé* hidden somewhere?'

'You've got to be kidding. It's not even ten-thirty, you old lush. I'll go and get us some sparkling water.'

'With a shot of something?'

'Orange juice if you play your cards right.'

I dried off my hair then wrapped the towel round myself.

'Back in a minute, unless you want to come and keep me company in the kitchen.'

'Fack off, and miss all this sun? I've got a tan to work on. A real one.'

In the cool of the cottage, I stripped off my bikini and slid a sundress over my head. It was almost too hot for underwear, but taking into account my recent form, I pulled on a pair of cotton knickers. I ran a brush through my hair and twisted it up onto my head, securing it with some hairpins, then went into the kitchen to sort out the drinks. It was shaping up to be a scorcher of a day.

'Here you go,' I said, putting the tall glass full of ice-cold water down on the little table between the sun loungers.

'Blimey, it's hot.' Tracey took the glass and pressed it to her forehead. 'What's it going to be like in August, eh?' I took a long gulp of my drink. 'Hey, do you fancy going to the Fourteenth of July *fête* next week? I've heard it's a good night.'

'Yeah, why not? It's not like I've got anything else planned.'

We sat in silence for a while, sipping on our drinks, both deep in thought.

'So, any news from lover-boy?' asked Tracey, interrupting my thoughts.

'No. Not a whisper. I think I may have blown my chance there.'

Tracey was silent for a while.

'Well, at least you did it in style. God, I'd love to have seen it. It must have been priceless, especially the bit when you knocked yourself out.' Tracey laughed so much she snorted water out of her nose.

'Thanks. Didn't you have somewhere you needed to be?' I said.

'Ooooooh, hark at you. Yep, got to go. Things to do, people to see and all that.'

'Yeah, right. You're about as much of a pariah as I am around here.'

'Oh for God's sake, stop mooning around and go see him if it bothers you that much.'

'Oh yeah, marvellous idea. Look what happened last time.'

'Yeah well, it's up to you; you're a big girl now.' Tracey got up, gathering up her bag and sunglasses.

'You should keep those on,' I said motioning to her shades. 'You're getting crow's feet.'

'Bitch,' Tracey smiled

'Cow.'

'See you later.' She air-kissed me on both cheeks then headed back next door.

I lay on the sun lounger clutching my glass, deep in thought about life, the universe and Julien d'Aubeville. Mainly about Julien d'Aubeville. Maybe it was for the best if I'd scared him off.

I'd been in France for three months now without the whisper of a job. Well, there had been the one with the newspaper but the less said about that the better. I still dreaded running into poor Mrs Merriman. I'd heard on the grapevine that she had taken the disappearance of Snoopy very badly. I had intended to go over and explain, but every time I got in the car to go and face her, my nerves had failed me.

If I was being really honest with myself, I was even a little bit bored. All the sunshine and cheap plonk was lovely, but I needed more than that in my life. When I was bogged down with work and celebrities in rainy, cold London, the whole France thing seemed like the answer, but now I was here, I was actually missing it: the impossibility of getting a cab when it was raining, elbowing my way up Oxford Street, alcohol-soaked men falling asleep and dribbling on my shoulder on the last Tube home. I was even missing Zane and his lecherous comments and developing a nostalgic fondness for Shitty Kitty. I looked down at my feet, which seemed to be spreading now I spent my life in flip-flops, saw the chipped nail varnish on my toes, and longed for a new pair of shoes. You could take the girl out of Louboutins but it seemed you couldn't take Louboutins out of the girl.

Draining the rest of my drink, I took the empty glasses back to the kitchen. As I washed them up, the sight of the arnica cream that Laure had bought round, and which I had forgotten to return, caught my eye. Well, at least that would give me something to do. I put the glasses on the side to drain, picked up the cream and set off for her house at the other end of the hamlet.

I pushed open the old iron gate and let myself into Martine and Laure's garden. It was a mass of flowers and, on the far side, two raised beds were bursting with summer vegetables. Purple and green lettuces grew in neat lines, and tomatoes in a kaleidoscope of colours tumbled off plants growing up curly metal poles. There were tiny yellow ones, enormous black ones and ruby-red plum-shaped ones.

'You want to try some?' A voice behind me made me jump a little.

'Oh, hello. Um, thanks, um, they do look lovely,' I said, turning to face Martine who was a vision in a pink nylon housecoat set off with lime-green rubber clogs. As usual, a couple of hens were following behind her.

'I have more than I can eat so I would be happy for you to take some.'

'Thanks, that would be really nice. I've just bought back the arnica cream that Laure brought round. I'm sorry it's taken me so long... wait a minute, you're speaking English.'

She smiled warmly at me. 'Yes, I can speak it a little,' she said, taking the tube of cream from me. 'I'm very rusty but I manage.'

'More than a little from the sound of it. Where did you learn?'

'Come inside. Would you like a drink? A little *tisane* maybe?'

'I'm sorry. A what?' After my experiences with Philippe d'Aubeville there was no way I was going to say yes to anything I wasn't totally sure about.

Martine smiled at me. 'Don't worry, it has no alcohol. I won't do what Philippe did.'

I groaned. 'You heard then.'

'I think most people have.'

Martine opened the door and indicated for me to go through. 'The kitchen is at the end of the hallway.'

She pulled out a chair from beneath an old pine table. 'I shall make you one of my special *tisanes*. It's full of fruit and herbs from my garden and is perfect for all sorts of bruising. Heads... hearts...'

Inexplicably, I felt tears start to well up in my eyes and I looked away for fear that Martine would notice. 'Is it that obvious?'

Martine smiled. 'Love is complicated but you must take care. Sometimes, things are not what they seem.'

I swallowed hard and had the uncomfortable feeling that she was giving me a warning. 'What do you mean?'

'Oh, don't take any notice of me. I'm just rambling on.'

Martine pottered around the kitchen, pouring scoops of dried herbs and fruit into an old china teapot.

'There,' she said finally, 'we will just leave that to draw.'

She sat down across the table from me.

'So Martine, oh, is it OK to call you Martine? I don't actually know your surname.'

'It's OK, Martine is fine.'

'So where did you learn to speak English so well? I mean, it's a bit more than managing.'

'Many years ago I lived in Paris. I shared a *chambre de bonne* with an English girl.'

'What's a *chambre de bonne*?' I asked.

'It is the cheapest way to live in Paris. They are the old servants' quarters at the top of their masters' houses. They are usually very small so you get to know each other well,' Martine laughed. 'She taught me English and I taught her to dance. It is a long time since I have spoken it though.'

'Well you're pretty amazing, if you don't mind me saying. So were you a dancer?'

Martine suddenly looked coy. 'Yes, I was. Not that you would think so now.'

She got up from the table to pour the *tisanes* into two glass cups and put one down in front of me. 'Let me know what you think of it.'

'So what sort of dancer were you? Ballet?' I asked, sipping my hot *tisane*.

'No, burlesque...'

I spat out my tea in shock. 'Oh my God, I'm so sorry. It's just I wasn't expecting you to say that.'

I was worried that I had offended her but the twinkle in Martine's eye told me otherwise. Without commenting, she took a cloth from the sink and mopped up the table.

'So, burlesque?'

'Yes, I danced at the Moulin Rouge.'

'No way! Really?'

'Just a moment.'

Martine got up from the table and went to the room next door where I heard her rummaging around. She returned with an old black and white photo in her hand and gave it to me.

'That's me.' She pointed to a beautiful young girl with thick waves of dark hair cascading down her back and dressed in a sequinned outfit with a huge pink feather fan. She had a figure to absolutely die for. 'And that is your Queen. It was in 1981 when she came to visit the Moulin Rouge.'

'Oh wow, you were so beautiful.'

Martine blushed. 'It was a long time ago, a lot has changed since then.'

'How amazing though. You must have some stories to tell.'

'Yes, dancing took me to Paris but love kept me there.'

Martine smiled mysteriously and sipped on her *tisane*, her eyes averted.

'So how did you end up here?' I asked.

'Oh, I come from here originally. I was born in the big house next door. It was our family home for many years. You can imagine the *scandale* when I left here to dance half-naked in Paris. My father never spoke to me again. He thought I had been bewitched by the Parisian side of the family.'

'And what made you come back?'

'Oh, I don't know. After my husband died I didn't really want to stay in Paris. I wanted a simpler life back here in the country. There was also Laure. She is my niece. She suffered brain damage in a car accident which killed her parents, so there is only me to look after her.'

'Oh my goodness, that's terrible. Poor thing.'

It all made sense now; her slightly strange behaviour, her crippling shyness, the way she always seemed to be off somewhere else. I felt a wave of sympathy for them both.

'Well I'm not really sure that she is very aware of what is going on in her life. That is one small mercy, and she has her little pony, have you seen him? He's in the field on the hill. He was the last present from her parents so he's very precious.'

'The white one? Yes, we met on my first day here. He's very sweet.'

Martine got up to put the photograph on the side. There was a certain grace about her that I had never noticed before. 'It must have been hard, with your Dad, I mean.'

'Well, yes, but French families are funny things. There is so much animosity between the country people and the city ones so when his sister married a teacher from Paris who was working down here, she was treated like a traitor. I knew what I was letting myself in for but my desire to dance was too strong and I couldn't just stay here and work on the farm. My father used to own all the land around Les Tuileries and it was expected that we would stay here and work with him. He was a difficult man though. In the end, both of my brothers left to go somewhere else and he had to sell off the farm. All that is left is this house.'

For all her bravado, I could see that the rift with her father had been painful. Time to change the subject, I thought.

'This is lovely, this *tisane*. Is that what it's called? It's so refreshing.'

'Thank you. I'm glad you like it. You can come round any time and have another. We don't get many guests these days.'

'So, if you've come from here, you must know the d'Aubevilles well,' I said, just a bit too brightly. I was almost sure I saw Martine's face cloud over briefly.

'Well yes, I went to school with their father and I've known the twins all their lives.' She picked up her cup and sipped the *tisane*, giving me the feeling that that particular conversation was over.

'I don't suppose...' I started, 'no, never mind.'

'What?'

'Well, the thing is, I need to learn French. You couldn't teach me could you? I went down to the Club in Bussières but, well, it wasn't for me really.'

'Oh dear, the Club. I don't think many of them really speak French although they like to think they do. I think it's just an excuse to suck you into their expatriate world.'

'That's the feeling I had too. So would you?'

'Well, why not? How about if I teach you French and you let me practice my English with you?'

'Perfect,' I said, smiling brightly at her.

She smiled back and I knew straight away that we would be friends.

Chapter Eighteen

'Come on, Trace. At this rate it will be over before we even get there.'

It was seven o'clock and I was leaning on the door frame outside Tracey's bedroom waiting for her to finish getting ready for the Bastille Day party in the village. I'd been there for a good twenty minutes and was itching to go.

My first French lesson with Martine had gone really well that morning and I'd casually asked who was going to be there from the hamlet. Martine was a wise old bird and had realised straightaway what I really wanted to know. She had put her head to one side, regarding me with a look that I couldn't quite make out.

'Love is a funny thing,' she had said. 'It makes us forget the rules we normally live by, throw caution to the wind. Be careful. Don't get your heart broken.'

I had laughed. 'Oh don't worry about me. My heart is made of reinforced steel. It takes an awful lot to break it.'

Secretly though, I had been unsettled by Martine's comment. Were they just the wise words of someone who had been there before, or was there something else I should know? I had pushed it to the back of my mind, determined that tonight it was make or break with Julien d'Aubeville. Maybe I would be a little bit more subtle this time. Never mind my heart, I didn't want to break any bones.

'Oh, shaddup moaning. I'll be out in a minute.'

When the door finally opened, Tracey came out wearing possibly the shortest skirt in the Northern Hemisphere with a tight-laced gold basque which created a *décolletage* that you could balance a tray of drinks on. She'd teamed it up with a pair of towering gold platforms. The shoes had probably cost more than the monthly wage of many of the people in the village.

'What do you think?' she asked, giving me a twirl.

'Er, well, um, it's, well it's… not really suitable for this sort of thing if you want me to be totally honest.'

'Perfect. That's just the reaction I wanted.'

As we drove down the hill in darkness, the glow from the festivities was visible on the other side of the valley and the gentle hum of music could just be heard. It was a beautiful, star-filled, balmy night and for once, I couldn't even be bothered to pull Tracey up on her driving as we careered down the winding hill.

The village was decorated in red, white and blue bunting with open-sided marquees dotting the grassy area by the *salle des fêtes*. A stage had been set up at one side with a dance floor in front and fairy lights woven through all the trees; it looked quite magical. I had run into Chummy during the week who told me good things about the celebrations. Apparently no less than twenty-one *maires* or mayors from neighbouring villages were attending. The number who attended, Chummy told me, was a barometer for how successful your Bastille Day celebrations were. I guessed that the high *maire* count meant that Rocamour's was a triumph.

We parked in the village square, which was uncharacteristically busy with cars vying for the remaining parking spaces, amid hooting horns and light-hearted banter from the drivers.

'Got the tickets?' Tracey asked.

'Yes,' I replied, patting my handbag as we walked through the village to the festivities. 'Wow, doesn't it look great?'

Outside the *salle des fêtes*, a pyramid-shaped metal contraption with hooks round it sat atop a blazing wood fire. From each hook hung a huge joint of meat.

'How good does that smell?' I commented to Tracey.

A wine stall and bar were already doing a roaring trade, people weaving between the tables weighed down with bottles of red and *rosé*, and in the far corner, a band was playing. I spotted Martine sitting at a small reception table with Madame Brunel, swapping tickets for plates and cutlery. She smiled warmly when I saw her, offsetting the scowl that Madame Brunel threw at me.

'Hey, Martine, how are you?'

'*Rebonjour*,' she said, taking my ticket. 'There is a table plan over there so you can see where you are sitting. We have put all the British together so you can be with your compatriots. Have a nice evening.'

'I think I'd rather be sitting with my French neighbours than a bunch of expats,' I whispered to Tracey. 'Still I expect they think they are doing what we want.'

I ran my finger down the list, looking for our names. 'Ah, here we are. Oh joy, we're on the same table as the Blythe-Cholmondeley-Walkers and their lot.'

'Oh shit, just what I need. The snotty triple-barrelled BCWs.'

'Now don't you start anything. Come on, let's go and get it over with.'

Ours was a long table, seating about twenty people, some of whom I recognised from the village café. Holding court in the middle was Chummy, bedecked in a giant tent-like floral affair, while everyone hung on her every word. She certainly knew how to command an audience. Sitting next to her was Roddy, then a scowling CeeCee, who clearly wanted to be anywhere but there.

'Ah, hello my dear. And, er...' Chummy's voice died away as she saw Tracey, or rather what Tracey was wearing. Roddy, on the other hand, brightened considerably.

'Awright, missus,' Tracey said, working the Essex accent for all it was worth. 'I'm Tracey. You might recognise me off the telly. I was in that talent show fing. Bet you watched it, didn't yer? Yer look like the sort of girl that likes a good bit of reality telly.'

'Er, yes, I, er... Well, let's see, I'm not quite sure...' she blustered. 'Who don't you know?' she said, quickly changing the subject. 'This is Steve and Ginny,' pointing out a middle-aged couple, 'and their children, Fanny...'

Tracey snorted loudly.

'It's very popular in France,' said the teenager sullenly.

'I bet it is!'

'... and Heston...'

'What? Like the chef?' she laughed. I nudged her sharply.

'Lucinda and Andrew...'

Another couple smiled at them.

'Pamela and Monty. Pam is on the village council.'

Apparently that was supposed to impress us.

'Nick and Libby and their children.'

I groaned inwardly as Nick raised his glass to me and Libby smiled shyly. The children barely even looked up and continued to squabble over a toy. It was going to be a long night.

'Hello everyone. Shall we sit there?' I asked indicating two empty seats halfway down the table.

Roddy's eyes lit up as he realised that Tracey and her superlative *décolletage* would be sitting opposite him.

'So, what's on the menu?' I asked

'Patagonian Beef,' said Roddy. '*Très* French. Chap doing it is from some South American country apparently.'

'Looks great anyway. Well, shall we get some wine in, Trace?' I motioned to Tracey with my head to follow me.

'This is going to be a nightmare,' I said as we made our way to the bar.

'Just drink loads. People like that always seem so much better when you're pissed. So, red or *rosé*?' I asked as we stood in line at the bar.

'*Rosé* for me any time. I don't drink red, it plays havoc with me teeth whitener.'

Clutching two bottles of *rosé* we walked back to the table, like prisoners heading to the gallows.

'So,' said Pamela, looking at us like a lioness who had just found her next prey. She was a pinched-looking Scottish woman with the demeanour of someone who had spent her life sucking lemons. 'You look familiar,' she said to me, 'have I seen you in the papers recently?'

'Bloody Nora!' said Tracey, springing to my defence. 'Didn't have you down as a *Sun* reader. Like a bit of tits and arse do you? Oww!'

My kick under the table caught Tracey squarely in the ankle.

'So tell me about the village council. What's that all about?' I said, avoiding her question. Pamela visibly puffed herself up, clearly very full of her own self-importance. 'I'm the liaison between the English-speaking community and the *maire*. I speak fluent French you see and so many of the others don't.'

'Never quite understood this whole marie business,' said Tracey, taking a slug of wine and deliberately mispronouncing the word.

'I mean, I've hardly even seen him and everyone tells you you've got to go and introduce yourself as soon as you arrive. He couldn't even be arsed to look up from his desk when I went in.'

'It's *"maire"* not marie. Do you speak much French?' asked Pamela pointedly.

'Hardly a word,' interjected Tracey. 'I never got much further than *putain* myself. It's the only French word you really need. "I've lost my dog. *Putain*!", "I'm going to be late. *Putain*!" "*Putain*! You are such pain in the arse." It means whore, literally, you know.' She smiled sweetly.

'I'm well aware of its meaning,' Pamela replied briskly.

'So what's he like that marie bloke?' Tracey asked.

'*Maire*. He's very pleasant.'

'He seems a bit of an old misery to me. Heard he doesn't much like the Brits neither. Still, it can't be much fun being the marie of this place.'

I tried to stifle a giggle. '*Maire*,' Pamela corrected her again.

'Yeah, whatever. So what did you do before you moved out here? I'm sure I've seen your husband before. He's not that bloke that was up in court last year for fraud is he? Changed his hair though.' Tracey looked at her with mock sympathy.

Pamela visibly shrunk in front of us. 'It was all mistaken identity. Monty was completely innocent,' she hissed.

Tracey looked taken aback. 'Bleedin' 'ell, I was only joking. So you're in hiding here then are you? Does the marie bloke know that he's got the wife of a fugitive on his council?'

The table went quiet and Monty studied his napkin in great detail.

'It's *maire*,' she replied through gritted teeth.

'Ha ha ha,' I laughed. 'She's only joking, aren't you, Trace?'

A nervous laugh moved round the table like a Mexican wave, stopping at Monty, who still looked miserable.

'Yeah, only joking. Not even a good joke either.'

After a brief moment, everyone went back to their conversations, leaving Tracey and me smiling conspiratorially at each other.

'You are so bad, winding her up like that,' I whispered.

'So, Happy Bastille Day, ladies,' said Nick, sidling up on my blindside before I had a chance to make a run for it. 'Nice to see you here.'

He squatted down next to Tracey, making little attempt to hide the fact that he was more interested in her cleavage than anything she had to say.

'Yeah well, there's not much choice round here really, is there? Personally I'd rather be at the Ice Bar.' Tracey smiled sweetly. 'Only the French would celebrate the liberation of four forgers, two lunatics and a deviant aristocrat. That's all what was in the Bastille when they stormed it. Any case, they were after the gunpowder because they'd just stolen thirty thousand muskets from Hôtel des Invalides and hadn't noticed they didn't have anything to fire. Bloody wallies!'

I looked at Tracey, taken aback at the depth of her historical knowledge. 'I'm impressed.'

'Don't be. It was a project I did in secondary school. Me and Snotty Bates of the permanently runny nose. He did all the work and I took the credit. Got an "A" for it too.'

Tracey turned her back on Nick in the hope that he would go away.

'Bloody hell Trace, check out the one in the newsprint trousers,' I said, nodding towards the dance floor.

Jigging from side to side in the tightest pair of spray-on trousers made from a decidedly tacky newsprint fabric and an off-the-shoulder top was a lady of a certain age, with nut-brown skin and cropped, peroxide blonde hair.

'Ungulate alert!' I whispered.

'You what?'

'Ungulate. Animal with hooves.'

Tracey looked at me as if I'd lost my mind.

'Like a camel. Camel toe?'

'Aahh, right. Blimey, that's an impressive one and I've seen a few in my time.'

'She's certainly getting a lot of attention.'

We watched as a stream of men made their way towards the woman, flirting outrageously. She fended them all off with a sneer and a wave of her well-manicured hand until a particularly unattractive, gap-toothed man approached her, two bottles of wine in his hands. Her face lit up and she threw her arms round him, kissing him deeply.

We looked at each other, eyebrows raised.

'That's the Comte de Saint-Simon,' said Nick, making us both jump. 'He's minted.'

'Bloody hell, you still here?' said Tracey. 'Don't you need to be getting back to your wife?'

Nick smiled weakly and sidled back down the table to where Libby sat, picking at her finger nails.

'So, what is it about the millionaire Comte that first attracted her, do you think?' I said

'There's some places I just wouldn't go, even for money and he's one of them.'

I poured us both a generous glass of wine. '*Santé*,' I said raising my glass to Tracey, took a sip, swallowed and grimaced.

'God, that could strip the enamel off your teeth. They should be giving it away.'

We sat back, watching the *fête* unfold, lulled by the gentle swell of chatter around us. The band was a Franco-British affair with a keyboard player who seemed to be constantly one bar behind the rest of them. The lady in the newsprint trousers was sitting down with her Comte and the dance floor was being monopolised by a single woman who moved to the same beat, whatever was being played, while a small group of elderly ladies danced together in couples, their husbands clearly more interested in the liquid refreshment than the entertainment.

'Uh oh, look out.'

Armand, the village drunk, who I had saved from the road on the day of Alex's visit, was wobbling his way to the dance floor, smiling a red wine-coated smile. When he reached the centre of the floor, he unleashed a dance that would have impressed St Vitus. In a frenetic whirl of arms and legs, he twitched and thrashed, even trying a spot of break dancing. It was fair to say it didn't go well. Another couple, with the tanned blondness of the Dutch, dosey-doed around him, enthusiastically egging him on.

'He's going to have a heart attack if he keeps that up,' I said as I watched his dance reach a crescendo. To my surprise, Madame Brunel appeared at the edge of the dance floor. She watched Armand nervously before walking up to him, carefully avoiding the thrashing limbs, and putting a hand on his shoulder. He stopped almost instantly and placing her arm around him, she led him off the dance floor and back into the crowd.

'Wonder what all that was about,' commented Tracey as we watched them go. 'Come on, the floor's free now, let's go and bust a few shapes.'

She pulled me up from my seat, dragging me onto the dance floor, where we both shook our respective booty for all it was worth, much to the delight of our fellow dancers, until the starter was served and we had to go back to our table.

As I tucked into my melon and Parma ham, having worked up an appetite on the dance floor, loud, raucous laughter came from a table at the far end. Following the sound, I noticed Julien sitting with a crowd of young French people, enjoying the jokes that someone was clearly telling. My heart skipped a beat as I watched him, my fork poised in mid-air.

'What are you gawping at, as if I didn't know?' teased Tracey.

'He's just so bloody gorgeous, Trace, and that accent and the abs...'

'So do something about it. What's the matter with you? You like him, he clearly likes you. Jeez, after your 9½ Weeks fiasco, there's no way he couldn't have got the message.'

'I know, but I made such a prat of myself, didn't I? I'm not sure he's interested anymore.'

'Well you won't know if you don't try and find out, will you?'

'I know, I know. If he comes over tonight then I'm going in for the kill.'

'So,' boomed the unmistakeable voice of Chummy from further down the table breaking into the conversation, 'what have you been up to?'

'Oh, you know, not much. Still on the lookout for a job, that sort of stuff,' I told her. 'I didn't realise it would be so difficult.'

'Oh, are you looking for work?' piped up Lucinda, who had barely said a word since our arrival. She was a small, mousy-haired woman, pale-skinned despite a life in the sun, who kept looking across nervously at her husband, Andrew. He was a big, bearded man, with the bulbous purple nose and slightly glazed expression of a serious drinker.

'Yes, I am. Do you know of anything?'

'Well Andrew and I run a property management business, doing gîte changeovers in the summer, that sort of thing. We could do with another pair of hands. It's only until October but if you are interested, it might tide you over until you find something more permanent.'

'Oh yes, that would be amazing. Yes, I'm definitely interested.'

'Let me have your phone number and I'll give you a call.'

I fished in my bag for a piece of paper and a pen and scribbled the number, then passed it down the table to Lucinda.

'Please do give me a call. Not that I'm desperate or anything. No, actually, I am desperate,' I joked.

Lucinda smiled at me. 'Don't worry. I'll call. It's hard work though, especially when the weather gets really hot.'

'No problems. I can handle it. Thanks so much.'

I felt my spirits lift. It was unlikely to be well paid, but anything would be good at this stage. I felt a hand on my shoulder and looked round. It was Julien. Things were definitely looking up. He leaned down to kiss me on both cheeks.

'Hello, I hoped you would be here. How are you?'

'Yeah, good. You?'

'Good too. Look, I'm sorry I couldn't get to the hospital to see you.'

I put my hand up to stop him. 'No apologies necessary, really.' To be honest, I didn't want to have to relive that particular moment of my life.

'I'm over there with some friends.'

'Yes, I noticed.' No point in being coy, I thought.

'Maybe we could have a dance later? Why don't you come over when you are finished?'

'I will. See you later.'

I watched him walk back to his table, pausing several times to greet people from the village.

'Those blasted d'Aubeville boys,' said Pamela. 'You watch them, young lady. Mark my words. There's nothing but trouble around those two.'

Before I could reply, any further conversation was cut short by the arrival of the main course of beef with rice and *ratatouille* delivered by some of the teenagers from the village on old doors carried between them like enormous antique trays.

With the promise of the rest of the evening with Julien, I was suddenly too nervous to eat. My earlier hunger had disappeared and I pushed the food around my plate listlessly.

'Lost your appetite then?' Tracey winked at me. 'Hand it over if you don't want it.'

By the time the dessert arrived, I was positively twitchy.

'You won't make it any better by getting all stressy, you know,' Tracey warned.

'I know, but why do the French have to take so bloody long to do anything?'

After what seemed like an age, the dessert, cheese and coffee was served and cleared away. Tracey and I wended our way through the crowd, a knot slowly forming in my stomach. Julien saw us coming over and got up, putting his arm round both of us as he introduced us to the others at the table.

'Hello everyone, I'm sorry but I won't remember any of your names in a few minutes.' I smiled brightly at them but only got a blank look in return. Shit, I thought. They don't speak English. This should be fun.

'Don't worry, I'll translate for you. In any case, I want you to myself tonight.' He whispered the last bit close to my ear. A little shiver ran down my spine and I felt my cheeks reddening.

'But there is Tracey too and she doesn't speak French either.'

'Don't you worry about me. I've got a plan,' said Tracey. 'Back in a minute.'

Julien and I watched her go over to where the band were taking a quick break from their set. Soon she was laughing with the lead singer who looked slightly overwhelmed with the attention. She chatted for a few moments, gesticulating and laughing, then turned and came back to the table.

'Well?'

'Well what?'

The band were back on stage and the lead singer was calling for a bit of quiet so he could make an announcement.

'So, ladies and gentlemen,' he said, first in English, then in French, 'we have a real singing superstar here tonight, apart from me of course.'

A polite burst of laughter broke out.

'And she's agreed to join me on stage for a few numbers. I am pleased and indeed honoured, to welcome to the stage of our little village *fête*, the British singing sensation, Miss Tracey Tarrant!'

There was enthusiastic applause and cheering from the British, who clearly recognised Tracey, while the French clapped politely, not entirely sure who she was.

'See you later,' she smiled, making her way to the stage and into the outstretched arms of the lead singer. Taking a microphone from him, she introduced herself.

'Hello Wembley…' she shouted, 'sorry, Rocamour.'

The audience cheered.

'So, for those of you who don't know me, I'm Tracey Tarrant. I've had two Number One records in the British charts and a Top Ten in the US Billboard charts.'

The French remained quiet.

'And I love Johnny Hallidaaaaayyy!'

The French people around me erupted in cheers.

I had never seen Tracey on stage and it was clear that it was where she belonged. Watching her work the audience was a delight to behold and by the second song, she even had the French audience eating out of her hand. I hadn't really followed the talent show she'd been in and had forgotten what a great singer she was. She had a rich, soulful voice that was perfect for belting out power ballads.

'She's pretty amazing, isn't she?' I said to Julien as Tracey launched into yet another soft rock standard that had everyone on their feet.

'She really is. Come on, let's dance.' He took my hand and led me to the dance floor, holding me close as we swayed slowly until the end of the song.

'And now, here's something especially for my lovely friend. That's her, down there at the front.' She waved at me and I smiled and waved back.

Wrapped in Julien's arms, with the warm breeze gently ruffling my hair and a star-filled night sky above, I felt a calm descend on me. Julien sang softly into my ear, his hands running up and down my back. I pulled him closer to me and we danced, oblivious to everyone around us. The wait for this moment made it all the more special and I smiled to myself. After so long, I had finally got my man.

Chapter Nineteen

I stretched languorously, like a cat in the sunshine, and turned to look at Julien as he slept beside me. Smiling to myself, I ran my finger down the side of his face then leant forward and kissed him gently on the lips. His eyelids flickered open and he returned my smile with one of his own, as dazzling as the morning sunshine.

'*Chérie*,' he said pulling me towards him. I snuggled down into the dip in his shoulder and traced patterns on his chest.

'So, good night last night then?' I asked.

'Yes, I think the Fourteenth of July celebrations were another triumph for the village.'

I nudged him. 'That's not exactly what I meant.'

His fingers ran up and down my back, making my toes tingle, and I could feel myself starting to come alive again. My hand started to circle slowly down his chest to where I could see he was enjoying the moment just as much. He let out a long groan.

'I have to go, *chérie*, my cows will not feed themselves.'

'Just a few more minutes?' I said, running my fingers across the hard muscles of his stomach. 'One more for the road, as we say in England?' I suggested, nipping his neck playfully.

'One more? Weren't the four last night enough?' he joked.

'Picky, picky. Come on, you know you want to.'

'Of course I want to. I've wanted to for months. I wish we didn't have to move from this bed until the end of next week... but I am a farmer with responsibilities.'

'OK, OK, I know, in a straight fight between me and those big brown-eyed cows of yours they'll win every time.'

'Welcome to my world,' he said, kissing the tip of my nose. 'Anyway, your eyes aren't so bad.'

'Thank you... I think.'

'Listen, there's a concert on tonight at the lake in Bussières. Would you like to go?'

'What sort of concert? I'm not really an accordion and *béret* sort of girl.'

'No, it's country rock with a Celtic flair, according to the posters.'

'Well, that covers most bases doesn't it? OK, why not. It could be fun.'

'*Bon*, I will pick you up at seven.'

'I'll be here.'

'OK,' said Julien, sitting up and gently pushing me away. 'Where are my clothes?'

'Well, I think you'll find them in the lounge, the bathroom and the kitchen.'

He swung his legs onto the floor then stopped, leant back and kissed me again.

'Oh God, I don't want to go.'

'But you must. Your ladies are waiting.'

Getting up, he walked to the door to go and find the clothes that had been discarded with such abandon.

Now that's a view I could never tire of, I thought, admiring his rock-hard buttocks and long, muscled legs. I lay back in bed, luxuriating in my memories of the previous night. It was true what they said about French men making good lovers.

'*Merde!*'

I was startled out of my daydream by Julien swearing, followed by a loud crash and a rich, dirty laugh that could only belong to Tracey. Grabbing my dressing gown from the chair by my bed, I ran into the lounge to find Julien in a heap on the floor, his jeans round his ankles and his hands cupped over his crown jewels, or whatever the Republican version was.

'*Ooh là là!* Good night then?' she laughed, her eyes blatantly running up and down Julien's naked body while he stared at her like a rabbit caught in headlights.

'Oh, Tracey. For goodness sake, give the man a break. What are you doing creeping round here at this time of the morning anyway? You're never usually up before midday.'

'I needed to borrow a cup of sugar,' she said archly.

I smiled, knowing that there was as much likelihood of Tracey needing a cup of sugar as there was of her going out without her false lashes on. 'OK, where's your cup then?'

'Ah, well…'

'Etiquette, that's good manners to your lot, dictates that when you come to borrow a cup of sugar you bring the cup.'

'You are so rude, girl,' Tracey answered, pretending to be annoyed.

'Come on, I'll make you coffee. Let this poor boy get his boxers on.'

'Oh, must we?' she said raising her eyebrows.

I grabbed her arm and pushed her towards the kitchen, saying to Julien over my shoulder, 'Right, make a run for it while I've got her distracted.'

He scrambled to his feet trying to pull up his jeans, grabbed his boxers and headed back to the bedroom.

'OK you, coffee?' I said to Tracey, once we were safely in the kitchen.

'Well, I guess it's too early for a glass of wine, even though the sun must be over the yardarm somewhere in the world.'

'Isn't it always over the yardarm in your part of the world?'

'Oh, ha ha. Actually, my mouth feels like the inside of a boxer's jockstrap this morning so if you've got any water that'll do fine. That wine last night wasn't half rough. A bit of rehydration is needed before I take on the day.'

Julien, now fully dressed, walked into the kitchen.

'*Bon, chérie*, I must go now. See you later.' He bent and kissed me on the lips and I kissed him back hard.

'See you later when you've finished with all the other girls in your life.'

'Oooh, *chérie* is it?' joked Tracey as Julien left, closing the front door behind him.

'Come on,' I said, 'let's go and lie by the pool.'

'Shagged to death, eh?'

'*Moi?* I'll never tell!'

'Oh go on, I want all the dirty bits too.'

We flopped down on the sun loungers and lay in silence for a while. It was going to be another scorching day. I pressed the glass to my forehead, enjoying its coolness against my hot skin and felt that warm tingly feeling in my stomach that you get when you know you are on the verge of falling in love. I smiled to myself, Julien was gorgeous and kind and in bed... wow! I could feel myself blushing as I remembered our wild night.

'Penny for them?'

'Nothing. Just wondering if this is a turning point. I've got the man, I've even got a job of sorts. So, anything from Warren?'

'Nah, he's all loved up with his missus in La La Land. That bloke she was seeing has been kicked to the kerb and there's talk in *Heat* of a big, blingy party to renew their wedding vows. Don't suppose they'll be inviting me.'

'I'm sorry, Trace. I know you really liked him.'

'Yeah well, don't mess with another woman's man. That's all I can say. To be fair I always knew I was just a pawn in his headfucks with her. I guess I just hoped that in time he might see something in me. Guess not.'

'Well if he didn't then he's stupid, Trace. I wish I had half your talent. Don't be so hard on yourself.'

'Yeah? Like what? My great left hook?'

'No, you're honest, down to earth, loyal.'

'Great. Like a Labrador.'

'Those are great qualities so don't knock them *and* you are an amazing singer.'

'Yeah, well...' Tracey went back to drinking her water, lost in contemplation.

'Julien's taking me to a concert tonight. It's at the lake in Bussières. Fancy it? It's a Franco-Celtic country rock band, apparently.'

'Sounds unmissable. I dunno if I want to be a gooseberry to love's young dream. I'll see. Anyway, about last night?'

'Good *fête*. I quite enjoyed it.'

'Oh stop being so thick. You know what I meant, and stop smiling like some lovesick cow,' Tracey teased.

'Oy, enough of the cows. If it wasn't for them I'd still be in there shagging his brains out.'

'Maybe you can apply for an EU subsidy. There must be something you can get for helping a farmer sow his seed.'

'Oh very droll. Don't give up the day job. Oh sorry, you don't have one do you?'

Tracey looked at me with a hurt expression in her eyes.

'God, Trace, I didn't mean that quite how it came out. Anyway, you don't need a job. You've had a hit record. You'll be living the life of Riley on the residuals for years to come.'

'Yeah, but don't forget I also had a shyster for a manager. If he'd been any good I wouldn't be here now, I'd be in some recording studio making my next album – nice though it is to be sitting here with you.'

'You do miss it, don't you?'

'It's all I know, all I've ever done since I was ten years old. I don't know how to do anything else. When I got to the final of that competition I thought I'd made it. You know how everyone jokes that it's the act in second place that always does well, so I didn't even mind about winning. Mind you, losing out to that horrible little stage school brat was a bit harsh. And then I got offered a contract, released a couple of records and then made the biggest mistake of my life.'

'Warren?'

'Spot on. His missus got the knives out and stuck them in me at every opportunity. Her agent pulled in some favours and had me dropped from playlists, got me taken off the line up at the V Festival. She may be five foot nothing with a toothy grin but trust me, you don't want to get on the wrong side of her. A decent manager might have defended me but mine just hung me out to dry. Apparently she made it known she was interested in working with him in return for him selling out on me. It was him that tipped the press off that I was here.'

'But I thought it was CeeCee. I was convinced it was her.'

'Nah, it was him all along. You have no idea what a lot of messed-up people work in the music business. Sometimes I think I'm better off out of it. So anyway...'

A ringing in her bag had Tracey diving for her phone. She looked at the number on the screen. 'Effing hell! I've got to take this. See you later.'

She jumped up from the sun lounger and headed back to her house, talking into her phone in a hushed voice.

I lay back for a few more minutes, listening to the birdsong and the far-off puttering of a tractor. A slow smile crept across my face.

Chapter Twenty

'Oh my goodness, I had no idea this place was here. I mean, I've seen the signs on the road but I didn't realise it would be like this.'

I stopped to admire the huge lake surrounded on all sides by a wide sandy beach.

'It's not at all what I was expecting.'

The lake nestled in a valley in the middle of a pine forest. Log cabins were scattered around the shore interspersed with colourful tents, dotted like confetti. Children were paddling in the shallows while the more adventurous older ones were diving off a pontoon moored in the deeper part.

'Let's go and get a drink shall we?' He placed a hand gently on my back and led me up some steps to a terraced area with tables and chairs beneath huge blue and white parasols.

Choosing a table overlooking the lake, we sat down to order a bottle of *rosé*. With the sun starting to set on the horizon, casting a vivid orange stain across the water, I could almost believe I was down on the Mediterranean.

'This is really lovely,' I said raising my glass to him. '*Santé*. Thanks for bringing me.'

We sat quietly watching the last few children playing in the water. A lifeguard was tying up a flotilla of bright yellow canoes that visitors could hire for a few hours, and the water on the big waterslide was gradually reducing to a trickle.

Julien reached across the table and took my hand. I smiled, marvelling again at my luck to have found him. He gently stroked the back of my hand before lifting it to his lips.

'*Chérie*, you look beautiful tonight.'

I blushed slightly. 'Thank you, you don't look so bad yourself.'

'You English girls,' he smiled, 'you can never take a compliment.'

I smiled back. 'You French boys, always so smooth.'

He poured me some more wine. 'Trying to get me drunk now, are you?' I leaned across the table and kissed him. 'So where is the concert then?'

'At the cultural centre on the other side of the lake.'

'A cultural centre? That's so French! What do you have there? Poetry readings? A bit of Molière?' I teased him gently.

'Ah, we French like a bit of culture.'

'And add in a bit of philosophical navel-gazing and you are happy.'

'A bit like you British are with vodka, eh?'

'Oh Julien, you've got us so wrong,' I paused, 'it's gin!'

'You need something to save you from the London fog,' he laughed. 'You know, when I first went to England I thought that everyone stopped working at four o'clock to have tea and cucumber sandwiches and went everywhere in red double-decker buses. That's what we were taught in English lessons at school. Prince Charles went to Rugby School and it rains all the time.'

'Rugby? It was Gordonstoun. Well, I suppose it's no different to the British believing that the French are all rude and never speak English.'

'And that we are all cheese-eating surrender monkeys.'

'Well, I wasn't going to mention that.'

'Come on, drink up. The concert starts in ten minutes.'

I downed the last of my glass of wine and let Julien lead me down the steps and round the lake, linking my arm through his and leaning on his shoulder. The sun had gone down and a sprinkling of stars was beginning to appear in the sky. The gentle lapping of the water on the shore, mingling with the soft chatter of voices in the distance, created a sublime effect and I felt a rush of love for my adopted country, and for the man next to me. I looked up at him, feeling suddenly quite emotional. He smiled at me and bent to kiss me gently, looking perplexed at my misty eyes.

'What is it, *chérie*?' has asked anxiously.

'Oh, nothing. Don't mind me. I just feel so ridiculously happy.'

'I'm glad. Me too.'

The cultural centre turned out to be a large hall with a semi-circle of plastic chairs occupied by a motley collection of local people, campers and holidaymakers with an average age of sixty. The younger ones had obviously found something better to do.

We took two chairs in the back row and sat down. Julien recognised a few people and chatted to them while I listened, pleased that I was actually starting to understand a bit of what was said, although the local accent was proving hard to crack. Anything that ended with a short 'a' sound, like *bien* or *pain* or *vin* had an extra 'g' so it became 'bieng', 'peng' and 'veng'. It was very unlike the Parisian French I had learned at school and was now relearning from Martine. I pondered whether it was the French equivalent of a rolling West Country burr or the harsh sound of a Black Country accent. If Julien and I were to have children would they sound like French yokels? I smiled at the thought, watching him as he talked animatedly to some friends.

A few more people started to arrive, some older, some younger, swelling the crowd to about fifty. A bunch of young French people with hair in dreadlocks and clothes that came from Army Surplus sat down behind us. The unmistakeable aroma of marijuana started to waft across the room. No one else seemed to take any notice. It wasn't the first time since I'd moved here that I had come across people smoking dope in public. They seemed to have a much more liberal attitude to it here.

After a while, the lights went down and the band appeared: a lead singer, two guitarists and a drummer. They were clearly oblivious to the fact that they were playing the cultural centre in Bussières and were so hyped up that you would have thought they were playing a stadium.

Julien's armed slipped around my shoulder as they launched into their opening number, a strange mix that sounded like French country and western mixed with whale song. It was a dreadful noise that actually hurt my eardrums. I noticed an elderly French lady in front of me surreptitiously turn down her hearing aid.

If only, I thought, grimacing at the cacophony. The lead singer was like a demented Mick Jagger, gurning and curling his lips as he sang. He seemed to have an inordinately long tongue that flicked in and out like a lizard. It was faintly repellent.

Polite applause greeted the end of the song, followed by a virtual stampede for the door which reduced the crowd by half. The band looked crestfallen.

'That was terrible,' Julien whispered. 'Are you sure you want to stay?'

I looked across at the band, who were all droopy shouldered and sad looking and I didn't have it in me to join the exodus.

'It's OK. I'm sure it will get better.'

It didn't. The next song, which went on for a full fourteen minutes, was about fishing for cockles in St Malo. My hopes that it would get better were fading fast. After that, they livened things up a bit with a rendition of Billy Ray Cyrus's country classic 'Achy Breaky Heart' or 'ecky brecky art' as it came out. The deaf lady in front seemed to have dozed off.

Just as I thought it couldn't get any worse the door swung open and in breezed Chummy in a 10-gallon hat and cowboy boots, her vast behind squashed into a pair of very tight jeans.

'Hello chaps,' she boomed across the room as all eyes turned to her. An assorted group of people, some of whom I recognised from the café and the village *fête*, were filing in behind her looking like they had got lost on the way to the OK Corral.

'Hello Chummy, you look, er, great,' I called back.

The band looked relieved that they wouldn't be playing to a half-empty room and immediately decided to capitalise on their change of fortune by playing a string of country classics that I couldn't quite name. Before you could say 'step, hitch, kick', Chummy and her friends had formed themselves into lines and were stepping, hopping and lassoing imaginary steers to their hearts' content. So line dancing really was alive and well in here. It was a sight to behold, this motley bunch of women (and the odd man) decked out in their sparkly, cowboy finery in the middle of south west France.

'Come and join in,' shouted Chummy to me, a broad smile splitting her red, sweat-dampened face.

'Oh, really, no thanks. Two left feet, me.'

'Doesn't matter, I'm no Darcy Bussell myself,' Chummy replied, stating the patently obvious.

'Go on,' whispered Julien, amused at my discomfort.

'Shut up or I'll take you with me,' I replied under my breath.

'Come on, don't be shy, girl,' Chummy was advancing on me waving her imaginary lasso above her head.

'No, really, I'm quite happy to watch.'

Just as her meaty hand was about to descend on my arm the band struck up another tune that was vaguely familiar.

'Ooh,' squealed Chummy like an excited teenager, 'The Tush Push! I just love this one.'

She turned on her cowboy heel and rushed back to join the other dancers and what happened next would haunt me for years. The sight of Chummy pushing her extremely large and wobbly tush was like a study in Einstein's Theory of Perpetual Motion or possibly a jelly on a vibration plate. I could hardly bear to look, unlike some others in the audience who sat with their chins in their laps.

'Never mind *"Rhinestone Cowboy"*, this is more like Twenty-Stone Cowboy.' I whispered to Julien.

'Be nice,' he chided gently. 'she's having fun. She's not doing any harm.'

Feeling chastened, I went back to watching the band. They were thoroughly enjoying the attentions of the line dancers who were shouting out requests and having the time of their lives. They had probably never had such an expressive audience before.

Julien had a point. It was a dreadful concert and the band should have been arrested for crimes against music. Chummy and her friends should just have been arrested. There was something inherently embarrassing about a bunch of out-of-shape Brits in France pushing their tushes. My London friends and I would have been laughing and poking fun, but here it didn't really seem to matter as long as people were enjoying themselves. I didn't have to show off or prove anything to anyone here. I could just be myself. And maybe I was also learning to be a little bit more tolerant in the process.

Chapter Twenty-one

'Living the bloody dream,' I muttered to myself as I scrubbed the toilet bowl. I straightened up, stretching out my aching back. This was my fourth week of helping Lucinda with her *gîte* cleaning and I had developed a new respect for the chambermaids who had cleaned my room on my last drunken holiday to Ibiza. On paper, cleaning wasn't rocket science but the reality was that holidaymakers seemed to be hard-wired to notice every missed cobweb and speck of dust. I had also discovered that even the nicest people seemed to leave their normal standards of behaviour firmly behind them at the airport.

Last week I'd had the guests from hell, the Weevils. Well, they were called the Keevils really but I nicknamed them the Weevils because they were irritating and got everywhere. I had spent most of the previous week driving back and forth at the whim of Mrs Keevil who claimed the property was damp and dusty. She had stood at the door, for all intents and purposes as if she had a nasty case of the Black Lung, coughing like a poodle choking on a dog biscuit. I wasn't sure how somewhere could be damp in 35-degree heat but in the service industry, as Lucinda had told me, the customer is king so all their demands had to be responded to, however ridiculous. I had worked very hard to hold my tongue when Mrs Keevil had called me up to the house for a third time to complain about a dusty curtain rail. I was on the verge of telling the bloody woman to just get a duster and do it herself. Fortunately, Lucinda was familiar with guests' little games.

'She's just a professional complainer. She's after a discount on her holiday, mark my words. She'll send in a letter of complaint the moment she gets home. We see them all the time. Don't take it personally. It's not you, it's her.'

In the few weeks I'd worked with her, I'd developed a real respect for Lucinda, She may have seemed quiet and reserved on the outside but she was one tough cookie underneath – and an astute businesswoman to boot. Her husband, Andrew, was a different matter. He drank too much and talked loudly about how successful his business was to anyone who would listen. But Lucinda was the real power behind the throne. Without her, he'd have drunk the business into the ground long before.

That week I had a bunch of public school brats called Cosmo and Bunty and other such ridiculous names, who had left the house littered with empty beer cans and vodka bottles and a lingering smell of vomit. They looked down their noses at me, something I was well used to from home. My comprehensive had shared the same road as a second-rate public school for the not-very-bright offspring of minor aristocracy and small-time Russian oligarchs, who considered themselves infinitely superior to the other school kids in the town. Even walking down the street was like a game of chicken with the 'rich kids' refusing to move over to allow the 'comp kids' to pass. As soon as Cosmo and crew realised I wasn't going to be impressed by the mentions of polo and 'that night in Raffles with Harry', though, they pretty much left me alone.

I had got the cleaning down to a fine art and could do a full clean and changeover for the four-bed house in three hours; but when I had arrived that morning, one look at the scene of devastation told me it was going to be a long one. Three hours in and with the temperature hitting the forties outside, I was only halfway through and running horribly behind. Bending down, I went back to scrubbing the toilet.

'How can people be so filthy?' I muttered, blowing a strand of hair out of my face.

'I don't know, how can they?'

I looked up to see Julien leaning on the door frame smiling that dimply smile of his at me. He still made my heart jump every time I saw him and I got that funny fluttery feeling in my stomach.

'Honestly Julien, these people are supposed to be the elite. You wouldn't believe what I've found. Used condoms under the beds, half-eaten food behind the sofa. Their parents might have paid a fortune to send them to the best schools but clearly they didn't learn any manners while they were there. They treat us like their bloody servants...'

His mouth closed over mine, cutting me off mid-flow.

'Well hello you,' I said smiling up at him when we came up for air.

'Hello you, too. I like a woman in rubber; did I ever tell you that?'

I snapped my gloves like a dominatrix and pushed him gently away.

'I'm not touching you while I've got these yucky things on,' I said, peeling off my gloves and dropping them into the sink. 'I prefer my rubberwear without E. coli.'

He wrapped his arms round me and pulled me tightly to his chest. It felt like it was the safest place in the world and I turned my face to his as he kissed me deeply, sending tingles right down to my toes and a few places in between. He lifted me up and I wrapped my legs around his waist as he carried me, lips and tongues still connected, into the lounge and placed me gently down on the sofa.

'Oh Julien, I'd love to, really I would, but we can't. Not here and I've still got the garden to do. This lot were a right bunch of pigs and I'm way behind.'

He looked into my eyes and groaned. 'Later then?'

'You're on. Definitely.'

Julien stood up and offered me his hand to help me up. I straightened up my dress and kissed him quickly on the lips.

'Go on, get out of here before I change my mind. I'll call you when I'm finished. Can you come round to mine? I'll make us some dinner.'

I watched him leave, smiling rather smugly to myself.

My phone dinged, announcing an incoming text. It was from Charlotte.

'How's life in French France today? Still with that hunky French farmer? Xx'

I quickly texted back.

'Head down toilet. Not being sick, cleaning! French farmer still hunky and still mine. Will text you later xx'

Charlotte and I had been friends since primary school. Every memory I had featured Charlotte. First school play, my winning goal for the school netball team, my first boyfriend, my first break up. Charlotte had been through it all with me. We had even gone to uni together and I was ridiculously excited that she was hoping to come out for a visit soon. I couldn't wait. She'd recently landed a new job as assistant to a film producer and had spent the last few months rushing round Europe working on an action film. We had hardly had a moment to text, never mind talk. I folded clean towels on each of the beds then took a last look round, checking all the bins were empty and the duvet covers straightened out.

'Hellooooo,' called a woman's voice.

I went into the hallway to find an elderly, grey-haired woman standing there clutching a sheaf of papers.

'Hello, can I help you?'

'Oh I do hope so, you see, I've lost my cat. He's a big ginger tom.'

She shoved a poster at me showing a ginger and white cat wearing a bow tie.

'It was Christmas,' she said, seeing my look of surprise. 'He loves to dress up a bit. He went missing a few days ago and I was wondering if you might have seen him? I just live up the road and I know he sometimes comes down here. I wondered if he might have got shut in the barn or something.'

'Oh dear, well, you're welcome to go and have a look. It's open.'

'Thank you so much. I'll pop back and let you know if I find him. Don't I recognise you?'

'Er, well I don't know. From the café maybe?'

A fleeting look of horror passed across the woman's face. 'I know who you are,' she said accusingly, 'you're that woman, aren't you? Violet Merriman's cat.'

There was no point in denying it. 'Yes, I interviewed her the day he disappeared.'

I hoped she'd leave it at that. Although I knew there was a certain amount of gossip and conjecture surrounding poor Snoopy's disappearance, so far no one had come right out and asked. If they did I would have to admit my culpability.

The woman backed away as if she was in the presence of a mass murderer.

'We were just talking about you the other day at the meeting of the Feline Friends in France...'

She left the comment hanging in the air but I could imagine what they had said.

'Look, I'm sorry about your cat but I can promise you, I know absolutely nothing about it. Please feel free to have a look in the barn in case he's there but if you don't mind, I'm running a bit behind and I need to get on.'

The woman scuttled out with hardly a backward glance leaving me to finish off my cleaning.

A few minutes later she was back. 'There's no sign of him. Would you mind leaving this in the house just in case any of the guests see him?' She thrust a poster at me.

'No problem. I'm sure he'll be back soon.'

The woman smiled weakly and wished me goodbye.

'Right, next stop the garden and the pool, then I'm finished,' I said aloud.

The grass needed mowing thanks to a few nights of summer thunderstorms with some heavy downpours of rain. It was the bit I hated most about looking after the *gîte*. I liked the fact it was just down the road from Les Tuileries, but it also had the most temperamental lawnmower in the Northern Hemisphere. Opening the barn door, I wheeled my nemesis out.

'Right you. Behave or I'll... I'll... well I don't know what I'll do but it won't be pleasant.'

I primed the engine as Lucinda had shown me, switched on the choke and pulled hard on the pull start. It coughed asthmatically.

'So much for a bloody one-pull start,' I said, scowling at it.

I pulled a few more times but the engine just spluttered a bit then fell silent. I checked the fuel and quietly cursed myself for not getting Julien to start it while he was here. Taking a deep breath, I pulled the cord again. Still nothing. I started to pull it frantically.

'I. Hate. You. I. Hate. You,' I muttered in time with each pull. It puttered a bit then stopped. 'Right! This is your last chance. If you don't start I'm going to give you the biggest kicking of your life. Understand?'

Bracing myself for another round, I pulled the cord sharply and to my relief it started.

'A wise move, if I might say so,' I said to it, reaching for my iPod which I had left on the garden table. I put in my earphones, engaged the engine and set off down the garden to the sound of Coldplay singing 'Paradise'. Quite appropriate, I thought to myself.

Fortunately it wasn't a very big garden but in the heat, even a reasonably small, flat one like this was hard work. Within a few minutes, I was feeling the full force of the August sun and sweating like a carthorse. I stopped for a minute, running the back of my hand across my forehead, and let the mower fall silent, grateful that Julien couldn't see me now, hair plastered to my face and my dress clinging to my body. My throat was dry and scratchy so I went into the kitchen and filled a large glass with water from the tap to slake my thirst. I drank it down in one go and then went to the bathroom to splash some water on my face. Catching sight of myself in the mirror above the sink I sighed. No point trying to be glamorous in this weather unless all you had to do was laze by a pool. Living in a hot country, when you had to try and earn a living as well, was nothing like going on holiday and I smiled ruefully at the thought that all my London friends thought this was one big, long jolly.

When I had got on that plane all those months ago, I hadn't expected to be earning a living cleaning toilets and mowing lawns. Even I could laugh at my naivety now. This was the bit they didn't show on those daft television programmes. Everyone had to earn their money somehow, but in rural France the options were limited. Making a new life here definitely required a certain amount of lateral thinking. I wandered to the door and looked out. The view across the valley was still just as stunning. I could never tire of the undulating fields criss-crossed with streams and orchards. Yes, life might be very different but it had its advantages and now I had Julien, it seemed pretty much perfect.

Smiling that slightly smug smile of someone who has taken a risk and seen it pay off, I went back outside to finish the garden. Checking my watch, I saw there were still a couple of hours before the next guests arrived. Maybe if I whipped off my dress and carried on in my underwear it would feel a little cooler. It was so stuck to me that I felt constricted and it would be a good opportunity to top up the tan. I wriggled out of it then spread it over a bush by the pool to dry off.

Mowing in my underwear felt strangely liberating and definitely much cooler so I soon built up a cracking pace. Part of that was undoubtedly due to the certainty in my mind that, based on previous history, the next guests would arrive early and find me mowing in my knickers. The mower had a mind of its own and when I put it up to full speed, I practically had to jog to keep up. I didn't have much experience with mowers, there not being much call for one in my little courtyard garden in London, and part of my rental deal was that a gardener came to Les Tuileries once a fortnight to garden, although he seemed to operate a bit of a scorched earth policy. My lawn had been mowed to within an inch of its life and was now pretty much dead and brown and with every drop of water metered, there was no way I was going to put a sprinkler on. I had been told by some of my fellow expats at the café that the thing to do was to get to know a local farmer and use his water as they didn't have meters. Well, I'd certainly got to know one very intimately but sadly his fields were too far away and his irrigation hoses wouldn't get anywhere near my garden. I grinned to myself at the double entendre.

Another half hour of semi-naked mowing and I was finished. Hands on hips, I admired my handiwork. The garden looked lovely and the stripes I had managed to mow into the lawn were almost dead straight. Funny the things that pleased me now. In the 'old days' it would be a successful PR campaign. Now it was a well-mown lawn.

I put on my now dry dress and pushed the mower back to the barn, having a quick look for Mrs Chamberlain's cat at the same time, then shut the barn doors and locked them. Just the pool to go and I was finished. It was at the bottom of the sloping garden, set slightly into the ground with decking around it and big pots of geraniums at each corner. I lifted up the flap in the decking to get to the skimmer and put in some chlorine tablets. It was a job I hated because the strong smell of chlorine caught in the back of your throat and made your eyes water; but despite that I could just make out an underlying odour of something a bit rotten.

'Bloody guests,' I murmured. It wouldn't be the first time that someone had chucked the remains from their barbeque under the decking and with the filthy lot who had just left, nothing would surprise me. A quick look around revealed nothing out of the ordinary and I closed up the flap. The smell would subside in a few days and it wasn't so bad that you noticed it around the pool.

I did one final check of the house and garden, locked up, put the key in the key box for the guests and headed home. Another day's work successfully completed and a few more euros in the bank. Now it was back home for a long, cool dip in my own pool.

Chapter Twenty-two

Sunday morning was my lie in, especially when Julien was by my side, so I was seriously annoyed to hear my mobile ringing at seven in the morning. The display showed Lucinda's number which could only mean one thing – a problem at one of the properties.

'Hi Lucinda, what's up?' I said, a bit over-brightly and trying hard to hide my annoyance.

'I'm so sorry, I know it's Sunday and it's early, but I've just picked up a message from the guests at Grandes Vignes about a nasty smell round the pool. They left the message last night but I was out so I didn't get it until this morning. Did you notice anything yesterday?'

'Well, there was a bit of a smell when I put the chlorine tablets in the skimmer. I expect that one of the guests has chucked an old burger under there. It wouldn't be the first time.'

Lucinda sighed. 'Honestly, what's wrong with these people? You know what I'm going to ask, don't you? It's just that I have twenty people for lunch today.'

'Sure, no problem. I'll get there as soon as I can.'

'You're a star. Thank you. I really appreciate it.'

I went back to the bedroom and flopped down on the bed next to Julien.

'Duty calls, I'm afraid. Unidentified pong at Grandes Vignes. Will you stay here and keep the bed warm?'

'If you like I'll come with you. Two noses might be better than one.'

'Oh would you? Thanks so much.' I planted a big kiss on his lips. 'I'll just get dressed then we can go.'

Twenty minutes later we were in my car.

'Don't pull into the drive, just in case they aren't up yet,' I told him as we arrived at the house. 'I'd rather sort this out without their help.'

Julien parked in the lane leading to the house and we walked quietly round to the garden. There was no sign of life in the house.

'Great, they're still asleep. Let's see what we can find.'

As we got nearer to the pool the distinct smell of something rotten became stronger.

'God, it's much worse than yesterday,' I exclaimed.

'It is probably just a rat that has died under the decking. How can we see underneath?' said Julien.

'There's a flap where I put the chemicals in, then there's a gap at the far side where you get to the pipework under the pool.'

'OK. I'll take the side, you take the top.'

I lifted up the flap but slammed it down quickly as a putrid smell assaulted my nostrils.

'Oh my God! What *is* that?'

'It is decomposing flesh. I'd recognise it anywhere,' said Julien as he knelt down to look through the gap and under the decking.

'I can't see anything but it smells really bad. Can you look down the opening at the top?'

'If I must.' Taking a deep breath and holding my nose, I opened the flap and leant down as far as I could to peer into the gloom. The smell was revolting.

'Can't keep my head down here any longer,' I said in a strangled voice, sitting back up and taking a deep gulp of fresh air. 'OK, I'm going in again.'

Like a deep-sea diver going underwater, I took a deep breath, held it and dipped my head back under the decking. Right in the far corner, I caught a glimpse of red fur.

'Oh shit!' I sat up quickly, banging my head as I went.

'What is it?'

'It's only Mrs Chamberlain's bloody cat. I can't believe it. Another dead cat and I'm in the vicinity. I'll have a fatwa on my head from the Feline Friends in France at this rate.'

Julien laughed.

'What's so bloody funny?' I said crossly.

'You. If you could see the look on your face.'

'Well I'm sorry, but I don't think this is a laughing matter. More to the point though, how are we going to get the damned thing out? It's right up in the corner. I can't reach it from here.'

'OK. Now I know where it is I'll try to get to it from this side. Have you got anything long we can use to try and pull it out?'

'There's a net for the swimming pool. We can use that.'

I went and got it from the pool house, checking quickly that there was no sign of movement from the guests. The coast was clear.

'*Bon,* you are going to have to crawl as far underneath as you can.'

'Me? Why do I have to do it?'

'You are smaller. I won't fit. *C'est clair,*' Julien reasonably pointed out.

'Thanks a million. Surely dealing with dead animals is a man's job?'

'You seemed to have managed with Snoopy quite well on your own.'

'Oh ha-de-ha-ha. Very funny. Well, if the smell makes me sick you'll be to blame.'

Kneeling down, I tried to wiggle my way through the small gap in the decking. It was no easy job and the smell was much worse.

'Pass me the net, will you?'

Taking it from Julien I reached forward to hook the dead animal. 'Almost… just a little bit further… got it! I'm coming out.'

I started to wriggle backwards. With a little help from Julien, I was quickly back out in the fresh air. He knelt down to have a look in the net.

'You are saved,' he said. 'It's a *renard*, a fox, a young one, not a cat. No fatwa for you. Not this week at least.'

He emptied out the dead fox onto the ground and we bent down to look at it.

'Hello there,' called a voice, catching us unawares. I froze. This wasn't the time to be making the acquaintance of the guests.

'You must be from the *gîte* company. Have you come to get to the bottom of this terrible smell?'

I looked up to see a heavyset, balding man in a very small pair of swimming trunks walking down the garden. I was so transfixed (in a bad way) by the sight, that I was momentarily struck dumb. There was nothing like a man in Speedos to really upset your equilibrium.

Coming to my senses, I realised that the guests, who had paid a not inconsiderable amount for their holiday, were unlikely to see the funny side of a dead fox under the swimming pool. With my foot I tried to push it back under the pool, all the while chatting gaily to the guest.

'Oh hello, nice to meet you. Yes, I'm Mel. I look after the house. It's lovely isn't it? And this is my friend, Julien. You must be Mr Wright. Hasn't the weather been superb? I hope you're having a wonderful holiday.' I stopped to draw breath.

'Er, we only arrived yesterday,' he replied, momentarily wrong-footed by my verbal incontinence. 'So, have you found anything?'

I glanced down briefly. The fox was pretty much hidden back under the pool with just its tail sticking out.

'Look,' I said, rushing towards him in an attempt to distract him from the pool, 'a green woodpecker. We see lots of them around here.' I pointed into the canopy of the trees.

'A green woodpecker?'

'Yes, look, up there. Can you see it?'

Whilst he was momentarily distracted, I gesticulated wildly at Julien to hide the fox's tail. He looked at my blankly. I pointed down to his feet, then waved my hand behind me like a tail. The *centime* dropped and he quickly pushed the errant tail under the pool with his foot.

'Are you sure?' The guest wasn't looking convinced.

'It's just that green woodpeckers are ground feeders so you wouldn't normally be looking for them in the trees.'

'Oh, if there's one thing I know about, its birds,' I blustered, 'I have a wonderful book at home called *An Anthology of Birds in Europe*. Do you know it?'

'Yes,' he answered tartly, 'I wrote it.'

'Goodness, then you probably *do* know a bit more about birds than me.'

'I dare say. Now, what's going on with the pool? Did you find the source of the smell?'

He turned towards Julien, who was trying to suppress a grin. I glared at him.

'Yes, I believe we have. It was just some meat that had been left over from someone's barbeque.'

'But how did it get under the pool?'

'Oh, I expect somebody just dropped it.' Even to my ears, I knew this sounded unfeasible. 'People do the strangest things sometimes. Anyway, Julien is going to sort it out, aren't you?' I said pointedly in his direction.

'Why don't we go back up to the house for a few minutes?' I suggested.

I linked my arm through Mr Wright's.

'Now did you know that in France some people put fresh meat in their septic tanks? It helps to keep the good bacteria at a healthy level...'

Chapter Twenty-three

'*Glissez, scouff, glissez,*' called the instructor enthusiastically.

'What did she say?' I whispered to Tracey.

'Oh, like I speak French!'

'It's like this,' whispered a woman next to us. 'Slide, scuff your heel, then slide again.' She showed us how to do the step.

'Chuffin' hell, it's not as easy as it looks is it?' Tracey pulled a face at me.

'I promise I will never scoff at line dancers again.'

'Scoff or *scouff*?'

'Oh you are so funny, Ms Tarrant.'

I looked around me at the assembled throng of line dancers. They were a motley bunch, some dressed in cowboy boots and fringed shirts and some with 10-gallon hats, but all with their fingers hooked into their pockets. I wondered how I'd got there, doing the one thing I swore I would never do.

The truth was that Chummy had been on something of a charm offensive since the concert at the lake, bombarding me with phone calls, texts and emails begging me to join the new *danse country* classes in Bussières.

'It will be so much fun,' she promised, but so far, it was not living up to expectations. I had two left feet and spent most of the time apologising to my classmates as I kicked their ankles and trod on their feet. Tracey on the other hand, was definitely trying to channel Beyoncé and every step she took was wildly exaggerated, with much pelvic thrusting and shaking of her booty.

Chummy was there, up in the front row, squashed into a pair of jeans and a sparkly top. She reminded me of an oversized glitter ball. You had to love her though. She threw herself into 'Achy Breaky Heart' and the 'Cowboy Shuffle' with the gusto of a woman half her age and a quarter of her size. I smiled to myself. I had developed a grudging fondness for this strident, overbearing woman. Next to her was Muffy, who had dragged her poor unsuspecting husband along. He was looking thoroughly miserable and proclaiming loudly his preference for entertainment that included round balls rather than imaginary lassoes. I wondered if Muffy had withdrawn sexual favours to make sure he came along. He certainly looked as if he'd rather be lying down on the TGV train line to Paris than be here.

I tried to keep up with the dance moves, hopping to the right as everyone else went to the left and struggling to separate my '*step, itch*' from my '*step, pull shaynge*'.

'Don't worry,' a younger English woman whispered to me. 'It gets easier when her husband takes over. He's American so there's no problem with the accent. Well, not much of one anyway.'

'Thanks. It couldn't be any worse!'

Eventually, half a sweaty hour later, I left the floor to allow the advanced dancers to do some more complicated routines. Tracey, always one for a challenge, stayed put.

'It's not as easy as it looks is it?' said a voice next to me. I looked round to find the same woman who had spoken to me earlier, pulling up a chair to sit down. She was a similar age to me but as dark-haired as I was blonde.

'You know, it really isn't, is it? I've always been so disparaging about line dancing but my calves are as tight as iron rods. I'm Mel by the way. I'm here with my friend, Tracey. She's the one who think she's Beyoncé in a cowboy hat.'

'Hello, I'm Jo.'

'Are you new here? I don't remember seeing you before. Not that I get out that much, mind.'

'I'm a returner really. I have a house here but I've been working in Guyane...' she cast around for the right word, 'French Guiana I think you call it, it's in South America.'

'Gosh, that sounds wonderful.' I said

'Well, it's actually on the edge of the Amazon rainforest so the climate can be hell but the way it works is that each year you spend in one of the French territories counts as two years towards your pension, so it's worth doing. I'll be able to retire a bit earlier.'

I looked confused.

'Oh, I'm French. I know,' she said, seeing the look on my face, 'I don't sound it do I? I was brought up in London. My mum is French but my dad is British, so I'm one of the lucky ones that can speak English without sounding like someone out of a second-rate comedy.'

'So do you speak French with a bit of an English accent?'

'Well, to be honest, the local accent is so strong that anyone who doesn't speak like that has an accent, if you know what I mean. I think they mostly assume I'm from Paris.'

'Which is a bit like being from Mars, but slightly less acceptable by all accounts.'

'You've noticed! Yes, it can be a bit closed around here but my grandmother lived in the village and I spent most of my summers here so they've pretty much let me in.'

'So what's brought you back, if you don't mind me asking?'

'The usual thing. Love. Cheesy but sadly true. When I was here in the summer, I became friends with a local boy. We used to hang out and do kids' stuff, then as we got older we moved up to the village dances and *fêtes*. In the end I went off to university, he stayed here and we drifted apart. But when my grandmother died, she left me her house and I came back here for a while. We met up again and we've been more or less together ever since.'

'Oh wow, that's so romantic. I love a good love story. So are you back for good?'

'No, just for a month unfortunately, then I have to go back to Guyane and finish my final year. After that, we plan to get married and have lots of babies. What about you? What brought you here?'

'Oh you know, the usual. Escape,' I said, smiling at her.

'Oh, very British! You watched those programme too, did you? My mum hates them. She says they give such a false picture of life here.'

'Well you know what they say, mothers are always right. I do love it, though it hasn't been an easy ride. Long story for another time! I've met someone here though so that's helped.'

'Really? That's lovely. Who is it? Anyone I...' She stopped as her mobile rang in her pocket. 'Oh, it's the man,' she said smiling as she looked at the screen, 'excuse me. I'll catch you later.'

She moved off to the corner of the room and I couldn't help noticing how Jo's face had lit up when the call came in and I could see her now, giggling and laughing into her phone, oblivious to the world.

I smiled to myself and thought of Julien. That was how I felt when he called. That wonderful warm, fuzzy feeling you get when you are in love.

'Come on girl, gee up!' Chummy's braying voice cut through my daydreams. 'Doc's on now. It's the Texas Two Step.'

I looked up to see a young man in very tight jeans taking the floor while Céline, the instructor, looked on smugly.

'It's her husband,' whispered Chummy loudly. 'Who'd have thought eh? She's no spring chicken either.'

Céline clapped her hands to call the room to order. I couldn't quite catch what she was saying in full but the word '*mari*', which I knew meant husband, kept cropping up with alarming regularity. Probably just making sure that we all know he's taken, I thought. Mind you, if I were a middle-aged woman with a hot young husband, I'd probably be the same.

'Hey guys, I'm Doc. Nice to meet y'all,' he shouted with a heavy southern American twang. 'Y'all ready for some line dancing?' He pronounced 'line' like 'laaaaahn'. The French looked foxed.

'Sorry guys, I meant *la danse country*.' Country came out like 'coon tree'.

'OK, I want y'all to laahn up behind me.'

He turned round and presented a very well constructed rear to the class. I was sure I caught him smiling as a bunfight, so to speak, developed among the *femmes d'un certain age* who were all pushing and shoving each other to get the prime spot directly behind him.

The music started and Doc slowly went through the steps, taking it in good spirits when he was called from the front to give a bit of personal attention to one of the women who 'simply can't seem to get it right.'

Across the room, Jo smiled at me and rolled her eyes.

'Cougars,' I mouthed back to her and she laughed.

It was the most bizarre sight. Suddenly, all these matrons had become giggling schoolgirls in the presence of a taut bum in tight jeans, fiddling with their hair and making some fairly overt double entendres.

I stumbled my way through the last few routines and breathed a sigh of relief when the clock hit eight and it was time to finish.

'Blimey, I'm so unfit,' puffed Tracey, red in the face and breathless. 'I'm just going outside for a bit of fresh air. Back in a mo.'

'OK, I'll go and get the licence forms we need to fill in.' The French government had recently decreed, in its wisdom, that line dancing was a sport and as such, you needed to have a licence to two-step and the instructors had to be registered. The French really could take bureaucracy to a whole new level.

'Never mind a licence, you should come with a health warning – "Line dancing next to this person can seriously damage your ankles", I'll be bruised for weeks!'

I gave her a comedy glare. 'Seriously, forget singing and go for stand-up. You'd be a riot. Or cause one at least. Go on, I'll catch you in a minute.'

'Bloody marvellous fun, eh?' boomed Chummy, doing an impromptu little dance in front of me.

'Well I wasn't sure at first but in the end, actually it was, even if I was totally crap at it. Thanks for making me come along.'

'Don't worry gal, I've been at this for nearly five years now and only just starting to put my hooves in the right place. Well, must dash. Rodders is waiting for me up at the bar in Rocamour. Fancy a snifter?'

'Maybe. I'll see what Tracey wants to do.' It was harvest season and I had barely seen Julien, who seemed to spend all of his time out on the combine. He told me there were a few more weeks to go and then life would be back to normal. I was really missing him so it was good to have something else to focus on, even if it was only line dancing.

Standing in line, waiting to collect the forms, I watched Céline and Doc. Despite the age difference and everything else, they were clearly in love. As he chatted to everyone, he would inadvertently touch her back or rub her arm and she just oozed adoration. When I got to the head of the queue, I couldn't help myself.

'So, how did you two meet then?' I asked Doc.

'Well, ah was working on detachment at the US Embassy in Paris. Ahm from the Midwest so we just lurve to lahn dance and ah found a bar that had dancin' every week. It was a liddle diff'rent from back home…'

'You mean the Achy Breaky thing,' I laughed.

'Yeah, you noticed then. The French think that Billy Ray Cyrus is the only country singer to come out of the US. Ah had to re-educate them. Céline was the teacher so ah got to know her real well and we just sorta fell in love really. When it was time to go home ah couldn't leave her so ah bought mah way out of the military and we got married. Got two lil' ones now as well.'

'That's a lovely story. You're both very lucky people.'

'Ah think so too.'

I wished him goodnight then went to collect my bag and Tracey's jacket. Céline and Doc had obviously found their soul mates and I wondered if I had too.

I had hoped to catch up with Jo at the end of the class but she had left pretty quickly. I was just about to leave the hall when Tracey rushed in looking flustered and uncomfortable. She grabbed my arm, pulling me back inside.

'Right, let's get this licence thing sorted now shall we? Strike while the iron's hot and all that.'

'No, it's fine. We can bring them back next week.'

'Nah, come on. I know what a lazy cow I am. If we don't do it now we'll be back to our old ways, eating too much and necking Cristal, and your new man will be leaving you for a thinner model.'

I unconsciously pulled in my stomach. 'Well, if you really want to. Are you all right? You look like you've seen a ghost.'

'Nah, I'm fine. Still a bit puffed. That's all.'

With the forms duly filled in and handed back to Doc and Céline, who were pleased at our enthusiasm, we left the hall and decided to go to the bar for a quick drink.

As we walked to Tracey's car, I couldn't help but notice her glancing around nervously.

'Are you sure you're all right?'

'Yeah, I'm fine. Don't worry. Let's go and get a drink. I think I need one.'

After a quick drink up at the bar with Chummy and Rodders, I arrived home and went straight to lay on a sun lounger in the garden to gaze at the stars and mull over the evening's events. Despite my initial reservations, they were both turning out to be really good fun. Rodders had tried to ply us with *rosé* but Tracey had still been a bit distracted and didn't want to stay long. I wondered what had happened to upset her, but whatever it was, she wasn't telling. The phone dinged to let me know a text had come in.

> 'Chérie, I miss you so much. Can I see you tonight? I won't finish until late, maybe after midnight. Can I come over then? Xxx'

I texted back.

> 'Yes, yes, yes, any time, day or night. I miss you.'

I lay back on the sun lounger and continued my stargazing. It had been a fun night in the end and I was glad I had given line dancing a go. It amused me to think that for all this time, I had carried around that defective line dancing gene and it just needed a move to south west France to set it free. I got up and went inside to get ready for Julien's arrival. It was the perfect end to my day.

Chapter Twenty-four

The long, hot summer slipped seamlessly into a rich, blue-skied autumn with a definite nip in the air. My morning coffee and croissant, a habit I just hadn't managed to ditch, was still taken on the terrace but in a warm jumper rather than a summer top. Around me, the landscape changed as the fields were ploughed ready for winter crops and the leaves on the trees turned from greens to red, burnt umber and gold. I never tired of the view from my terrace. Julien was still in the midst of harvesting and ploughing and time together was rare and precious – and more often than not, in the middle of the night. The lot of a farmer's partner was a hard one, I thought to myself.

'*Coucou*, you out there?' called Tracey, who had taken to using the French version of 'coo-eee', the nearest she had ever quite managed to integration – if you don't count line dancing.

'On the terrace. Grab yourself a coffee. It's in the pot.'

A few minutes later, she sat down next to me, hands wrapped round a streaming mug. 'Bloody brassic out here today. Is it nearly summer again?'

'I wish. We've got winter to get through yet. Mind you, loads of people have told me that you can eat Christmas dinner in your shorts here, so maybe it won't be so bad.'

'Yeah well, you could eat Christmas dinner in your shorts in Siberia too. It just might kill you.'

I smiled. It was a fair comment. Quite a lot of what I had been told about life in France had proved to be a figment of someone's overactive imagination, or one too many glasses of *rosé*.

We sat in silence, lost in our own thoughts, gazing out across the valley. After a few moments, Tracey broke the silence.

'Look, there's something I need to say. Don't interrupt me or I'll lose my nerve.'

I turned to her, a worried feeling growing in my stomach. Tracey had been a bit distant for the past few days, as if something was playing on her mind.

'You know the other night, at line dancing, when I went outside… the thing is…' she struggled to find the right words.

'Come on, Trace, Whatever it is can't be that bad, surely.'

'Don't bet on it,' she muttered. 'OK.'

She took a deep breath but before she had a chance to say what was on her mind, a deafening volley of shots rang out across the valley, followed by shouts and the baying of dogs.

'Bloody effin' hell,' shouted Tracey, flinging herself to the floor. 'Get down!'

She pulled me off my chair and on to the floor next to her. 'Keep down. It must be some loony going on a shooting spree. What? What is it?'

I was convulsed with laughter, tears streaming down my face. I could barely breathe, let alone talk.

'What?'

'*La chasse*, hunters,' I choked.

'What hunters?'

I pulled myself together, wiping my eyes on the back of my hand.

'It's the hunting season. It starts today. Julien was telling me about it.'

'Hunting what?'

'Boar, deer, partridge, wood pigeon.'

'Wood pigeon? What the bloody hell do they do with a wood pigeon? Is there nothing that these people don't eat?'

I stood up, putting my hand out to pull Tracey up too. From the end of the garden we could see the hunters crossing the valley, the dogs on the scent of some poor, unfortunate animal.

'Don't worry Trace, it only goes on until February.'

'You're kidding. We have to put up with this bloody racket for five months?'

'Apparently it's mainly weekends and they still take the long French lunch break,' I told her.

'Bleedin' hell! Geezers with guns and a bellyful of red wine. A perfect combination.'

'Julien says we shouldn't go out walking in the woods without a high visibility jacket on.'

'That'll go nicely with me gold platforms.'

I laughed. 'Like you ever go walking in the woods.'

'Yeah, well I might want to one day. You never know.'

'Well, I suppose stranger things have happened. So, what was it you wanted to say?'

She looked uncomfortable. 'Nothing. It's OK.'

'It didn't sound like nothing.'

'Nah, honest. It's fine. Another time, eh?'

I shrugged my shoulders, 'OK, if you don't want to say. Listen, do you fancy coming to Beauville with me? There's a chicken sale on. I fancy getting a few hens for the garden.'

'You?' she exclaimed in disbelief. 'I thought you hated them.'

'Well, that was before I knew any,' I said, smiling. 'Did you see the henhouse that Julien brought round for me when you came in?'

'Er, no, can't say I did but then I wasn't really looking, to be fair.'

'So, will you?'

'Oh, go on then. I haven't got anything else to do. Let me go and get my bag.'

I downed my coffee and picked up her empty mug to take back to the kitchen.

'See you in a few minutes. We'll take my car.'

'Too right. You're not putting any filthy birds in my Merc.'

Whilst I waited for Tracey to come back, I went to have a look at the place I had chosen to put my chickens. It was a perfect corner, too shady for anything to grow and with some good strong fencing on two sides. With Julien's help, I had managed to fence the other two sides and a gate had been fashioned out of an old pallet. The henhouse was a higgledy-piggledy affair, cobbled together out of some old tongue-and-groove cladding, but quite adequate. I had painted it a fetching shade of yellow but resisted the urge to put curtains up at the little windows, built to allow air and light into it. Julien had rolled his eyes when I suggested it.

Martine had told me to make sure I got laying birds and not table ones and had lent me an old cardboard pet carrier to bring them home in. To be honest, I had no idea how I would even know the difference between layers and table birds but at least I could ask now. My French lessons were going well and I enjoyed the hours I spent with Martine, getting a little slice of real French life.

'You coming?' Tracey was standing by the car, ready to go.

'Yes, I'm ready. Let's go.'

'Good grief, it's like a scene from *Deliverance*,' I whispered as we drove down the hill from St Amans de Pierrepoint.

'Just keep driving. Don't look at them.' Tracey was sitting bolt upright in the passenger side, staring straight ahead.

On either side of the road, white vans were parked a few hundred metres apart. Some had dogs in the back, barking to be let out, but each one had a man with a gun lounging against it. As we drove past, heads swivelled and followed us. The men were all dressed in camouflage gear set off with fluorescent orange caps.

'You'd think the hats would scare the wildlife off, wouldn't you?' I said.

'To be honest, I don't care. Just get me out of here. It's like the hood in LA but with less smog and uglier dogs.'

'Said the girl from Essex.' Under my breath, I started to hum the beginning of 'Duelling Banjos'. Tracey punched me hard on the arm.

'Oh come on, you townie,' I said. 'They're just out enjoying a pleasant day shooting small, furry animals.'

No sooner had I spoken than one of the hunters stepped out into the road in front of us, holding up his hand.

'Oh shit,' squealed Tracey, 'this is it. We're going to be executed.'

Recognising the round, smiling face of Monsieur Gautier, the baker from Bussières, and one of the most unthreatening people you could ever hope to meet, I stopped and wound down the window.

'*Bonjour monsieur.*'

In slow, precise French, Monsieur Gautier explained that the hunters had found a large number of boar in the woods and were in the process of flushing them out towards the road – so would we mind just waiting for a few minutes?

'*Bien sûr!*' I agreed and pulled over.

'Oooh, get you, talking like a native!'

I looked smug. 'I know. I'm getting pretty good now. Having a French boyfriend helps.'

'Yeah, but I don't suppose you're learning the sort of things you could use in polite conversation though!'

The sound of howling dogs and hunting horns broke the silence, and something crashed down the hill through the trees. The cacophony got louder and louder until suddenly three large boar broke cover and charged across the road in front of the car, quickly followed by a gaggle of piglets and some more adults. I counted about twenty-three of them. Not far behind were a ragged assortment of dogs and following them, more hunters. Orders were shouted as the boar made for the woods on the other side of the valley. I found myself caught up in the adrenalin rush of the hunt.

'Come on little pigs, come on, you can make it.'

'Blimey, don't let them hear you or they *will* use you for target practice.'

Gunshots rang out all around us as the hunters took aim and started shooting. The boar carried on galloping across the fields for the safety of the woods.

'Come on, faster,' I urged them.

The gunfire got more intense, as did the shouting and howling of the dogs. It was completely feral. Still the boar continued, seemingly unharmed by the bullets that whistled around them.

'Barn door and twenty paces springs to mind. This lot couldn't hit the *Titanic* if it floated past,' commented Tracey.

I was still too wrapped up in the hunt to answer. The first boar were nearly at the edge of the woods. 'Good piggies!' I shouted excitedly as the last of the herd reached the safety of the woods. 'You made it!'

Around them the hunters started to regroup, talking and gesticulating wildly as they worked out a new plan of action. Meanwhile the dogs milled around yelping and howling, not quite sure what to do next. Monsieur Gautier waved us through.

'Wow, that was exciting!' I exclaimed breathlessly.

'I think it's fair to say you won't be joining *la chasse*.' Tracey emphasised the last words.

'Only on the side of the animals,' I replied.

Half an hour later, we were walking through the town of Beauville looking for the poultry sale. It was market day and the town square was full to bursting with stalls and shoppers. After a few false starts, we tracked it down to a building on the edge of the town that bizarrely doubled up as the local cinema.

Inside, two rows of chairs facing each other were occupied by old men in *bérets* with a variety of birds either in cages or just sitting on the floor next to them. Some had baskets of eggs of every hue, from light blue to deep brown. Over in one corner, plastic crates of ducklings were stacked high, their inmates quacking indignantly to each other.

We walked between the two rows of chairs, every pair of eyes following us as we went, until I spotted a likely looking farmer with some rather beautifully plumed birds.

'Right. Here goes.' I marched purposefully up to the farmer.

'*Monsieur,* are your hens good layers?'

He gave me a withering look. '*Mademoiselle,* these are cockerels.'

'Ah, so not good layers then?' I laughed to cover up my embarrassment. The farmer looked at me as if I was some alien creature dropped into his world from another galaxy. Behind me Tracey was snorting in a very undignified manner while the old men continued to stare at us. I still wasn't used to the whole French staring thing – and it wasn't just a surreptitious stare, this was the full-on gape. Accustomed as I was to our English reserve, I found it very unnerving.

I grabbed Tracey's arm and pushed her towards the door.

'Come on, let's get out of here. This place is giving me the creeps.'

We made for another door at the side of the building so we wouldn't need to walk back through the line of farmers.

'Oh my God,' I breathed, leaning on the wall on the other side of the door. 'I sort of imagined big willow crates with happy hens clucking away to each other. That was like being in some sort of asylum for chicken fanciers.'

The door opened and an elderly man appeared, a chicken hanging upside down on a piece of string in his gnarled hand. The poor bird seemed resigned to its fate and just hung there like a feathery handbag with its wings outstretched, while the old man fumbled around with an ancient bicycle that was leaning up against the wall. He put his shopping bag on one side of the handlebars and the poor chicken on the other, before mounting the bike and wobbling off into the market place with the chicken slowly swinging backwards and forwards as he pedalled.

'Well I really think I've seen it all now,' Tracey shook her head slowly. 'That's Sunday lunch sorted then.'

I watched them go, my eyes starting to mist over. 'Come on, let's go and save a couple from certain death shall we?' I turned and marched resolutely back through the door.

'*Mademoiselle…*' a buxom woman dressed in the requisite nylon housecoat called as soon as we entered. I recognised the wizened old farmer next to her as the one I often bought eggs from in the market in Bussières. The woman spoke in warp-speed French but I was able to make out the words '*poules pondeuses*', laying hens. She pointed to a couple of sorry-looking birds that lay spreadeagled at her feet. I had envisaged some pretty, dark-brown speckly things but these were ginger with no feathers on their scraggy necks.

'Oh my good God,' whispered Tracey, 'they remind me of Deirdre off of *Coronation Street*.' The birds looked at us with sad, beady eyes. 'What's wrong with their necks?' she asked.

'I don't know. Hens peck each other so maybe these were at the bottom of the pecking order.'

'Pecking order? That's very funny.'

'No, it's true, that's where the saying comes from.'

'No!'

'They are very well behaved though. They aren't even trying to escape.'

The woman picked one up and it was only then that I noticed their legs were tied together with old pairs of tights. She thrust the hen at me but I backed away.

'T'as peur?'

'No, I'm not frightened,' I told the woman, putting my hands out for the hen. The woman dumped the hen in my arms and chatted on about hen husbandry, most of which I didn't understand.

'Combien?' I asked. Martine had told me the going rate was about fifteen euros for a pair.

'Quarante euros.'

'Forty euros! For these mangy birds?'

Wily woman, I thought. She knows us expats are a soft lot. I reached for my purse, to the delight of the woman.

'Oui, I'll take them.' I handed over my box.

'Sucker,' Tracey whispered in my ear.

The woman shoved them rather unceremoniously in the box, their legs still tied so they wouldn't escape.

'Un moment.' Holding a finger in the air as if she had just had a brainwave, she disappeared out through the door. The old farmer continued to watch us benignly. She returned a few minutes later with a dishevelled, ratty-looking cockerel that was probably half the size of the hens. How on earth would he...

'Cadeau,' she said, interrupting my thoughts as she shoved it in the box before I could argue and smiling as if she had just given me a winning lottery ticket.

Some present, I thought. I really didn't want a cockerel what with all the dawn crowing.

I looked from the cockerel to the hens and back again.

'*Er, madame, il est petit, le coq, mais les poules sont grandes.*'
Was I really discussing the conjugal duties of a cockerel?

The woman winked at me. '*Il se debrouille.*'

He'll manage. The old farmer, who had remained silent throughout the whole transaction, chuckled to himself. I wasn't sure if it was because of the conversation or the fact that they had managed to comprehensively shatter the local glass ceiling for poultry prices.

With the three birds in the box and the lid firmly taped down in case of any Colditz-like tendencies, we walked the line between the old men and headed back to the car.

'I could murder a coffee.'

'Do you think they'll let us in with a box of chickens?'

'They won't know if we don't tell them.'

We chose a café with a large terrace looking out over the market square and sat down in the corner, pushing the box out of sight.

'I think we got away with it,' I whispered.

'As long as the cockerel doesn't start crowing.'

We ordered two *grand crèmes* and sat watching the noisy hubbub of the market while the odd cluck escaped from the box under the table. The café looked out over an art deco-style market *halle* with three large arches on each side, topped with a canopy of red brick tiles with an ornate central finial. Stalls were piled high with fruit and vegetables, except for one corner, where incongruously, an Asian food stall was selling spicy delicacies. Every now and again, the smell wafted over to us.

'I could murder a Thai chicken curry,' Tracey murmured.

'Quiet! They'll hear you.'

'Who? Oh, sorry hens. I could murder a Thai prawn curry. Better?'

'Much. Come on, we ought to get them home before they start to object.'

I rummaged around under the table and carefully pulled out the box. A dark brown eye peered out at me through the ventilation holes in the top. The chickens were surprisingly heavy considering that they were more feather than anything else. I had almost reached the pavement when I heard a dull thud and suddenly the box become inexplicably light. The bottom had given way and the three chickens had been dumped unceremoniously on the ground in a flutter of wings.

Chaos ensued. The proprietor ran out to berate me for bringing chickens into his café, horrified diners shook their heads and even a couple of passing *gendarmes* came over to see what the commotion was about. Meanwhile the chickens sat placidly on the ground, *madame's* American Tan tights putting an end to any hopes of a quick getaway.

In the middle of the *mêlée* we were laughing so hard we could barely breathe, never mind move. Tears streamed down our faces and I was doubled over, legs crossed. Every time I looked at Tracey the laughter started again until the whole café fell quiet and watched the two hysterical English women.

Chapter Twenty-five

'Oh for heaven's sake! What time is it?' I rolled over to look at the clock on the bedside table.

Next to me Julien stirred. 'I'm going to make coq au vin with that stupid bird,' he murmured, his voice heavy with sleep.

I had been a poultry keeper for nearly two weeks now and it was safe to say it wasn't quite as easy as I had thought. I'd released the chickens into their run, fully expecting the hens, who I'd named Deirdre and Doris, to dash around and explore their new home but they had just plopped onto the ground and looked around like a couple of surly teenagers at a family wedding. They even looked bored.

The cockerel, who I had very imaginatively called Monsieur Le Coq, had strutted around, puffing out his chest and looking very pleased with himself, but had then launched a rear-guard action on poor Deirdre, grabbing her neck in his beak until she squawked in pain, and mounting her without so much as 'what's your name?' or 'can I take you to dinner?'

'Blimey,' commented Tracey. 'I've met a few blokes like him.'

It was all over in seconds, then he hopped off and went back to his scratching and pecking, leaving Deirdre shaking her feathers in indignation.

'Yep, definitely met a few blokes like him,' Tracey laughed.

Julien's car had pulled up in the driveway as I was trying to coax the hens into some sort of action.

'Right, better get on. Places to go and people to see and all that,' said Tracey suddenly.

'Don't be daft. Who do you see apart from me?'

'Don't big yourself up, lady. I have plenty of friends.' With the briefest of nods to Julien, she waved goodbye. He looked distinctly uncomfortable. For a brief moment, a horrible thought went through my mind. The two of them? No, they wouldn't. I dismissed it instantly.

'What do you think?' I said. 'I'm a bit worried because they won't move. I dropped them in a café and I think I might have hurt them.'

'You did what? No, don't tell me. Nothing surprises me with you,' he laughed as he went into the pen.

With much umming and ahhing and the odd Gallic shrug, he tried to make the hens stand up but to no avail.

'So, what's the verdict *Monsieur le Fermier*?'

'They're too fat.'

'What do you mean?'

'These are meat birds not *poules pondeuse*. Look at the breasts on them.' He poked at the hens, who clucked at him in an irritated manner. 'They have been bred for the table and they are too fat to walk.'

'Oh great. Morbidly obese chickens. That's just marvellous. And what about the feathers on their necks? Will they grow back?'

'Oh *chérie*, you really don't know much about them do you? These are Transylvanian Naked Necks, we call them *"cou nus"*. They are genetically bred to have fewer feathers. It makes them easier to pluck.'

'So not only do I have the fattest hens around here but I also have the ugliest.' I went into the chicken run and squatted down to look at them. Deirdre rewarded my interest with a sharp peck, 'And the most bad-tempered.'

'But on the plus side...'

'There is one then?'

'*Cou nus* are good layers. Once you get some weight off them they will start to lay again. You need to put them on a *régime*.'

So the following week was spent dieting the hens, and they slowly started to move around a bit more. I had taken to standing at the front door with some corn and calling them over. The only trouble was they were still too fat to do anything but run in a straight line. As soon as they tried to turn a corner, they fell over and lay there patiently waiting for me to come and right them. A few times I had found them beached in the garden, quietly pecking at the ground around them waiting for help.

Monsieur Le Coq was insatiable and each morning started with a guerrilla defilement of each hen. They seemed to take it in their stride although so far no eggs had been forthcoming and despite his diminutive size, when sex wasn't on his mind he fussed and fretted, rounding them up if they strayed too far from him and always staying alert for danger. Sadly, he saw this in every bush, round every corner and up every tree at least every few minutes. His raspy crow was driving me slowly to the brink of madness. Every time I sat down to try and do something, his endless crowing would have my teeth on edge. Even Martine, a poultry keeper herself, had commented dryly *'il chante bien, ton coq'*. I wasn't sure why the French used the same work for crowing as they did for singing because there was certainly nothing melodic about his racket.

Worse still, he seemed to think that sunrise started around three o'clock every morning. I was in the early stages of sleep deprivation. I had spent several evenings googling 'how to stop your cock crowing' and despite much sage advice about putting a sock over his head or covering the henhouse with blankets to shut out any light, the general feeling seemed to be that the only way was to eat him and I wasn't quite ready for that... yet.

The morning that I got my first egg was on par with a 'what were you doing when Freddie Mercury died?' moment. I would remember it for the rest of my life. I lifted up the lid of the nesting box, fully expecting it to be empty, and there, lying on the straw, was one, small, perfect, oval egg. Its flawless shell was straight from a Farrow and Ball paint chart.

I had been so excited that I grabbed the egg and ran straight round to Tracey's, let myself in and jumped on her bed – a dangerous activity when clutching a fresh egg.

'Scrambled egg for breakfast?'

Half an hour later we were sitting round my table sharing a small spoonful of scrambled egg on toast. It was the colour of a high-visibility jacket.

'Is that normal?' asked Tracey, looking at it slightly suspiciously.

'Yes, apparently it's the grass that makes the yolk so yellow.'

'Yeah, but even so...' Tracey prodded it with her fork.

'Oh just eat it. I know you're more used to the ones from the supermarket that are weeks old.'

'It's not just that. I keep thinking where it came from, you know, literally.'

'Well don't, or you'll put me off too. We live in the country now so it's time to connect with our food and where it comes from.'

'Bloody hell, you're starting to sound like a party political broadcast for the Eco-Nutters.'

I took a mouthful of egg. 'It's pretty good though.'

'Pretty good? It's bloody amazing!'

From that day on, every morning I found one or two eggs, laid on the straw like the Crown Jewels on a velvet cushion. Now into my second week of a diet of omelettes, frittatas and boiled eggs I was starting to flag a bit and had the beginnings of what promised to be my very own EU egg mountain. There was no point trying to give them away either as just about everyone in St Amans had chickens themselves. My dreams of a little cottage industry selling eggs at the gate, or maybe even supplying the village shop in time had come to nothing. Eggs, it seemed, were certainly not as rare as hen's teeth in these parts. Maybe they had an off button somewhere.

Despite all that, I found myself spending more and more time just watching them as they scratched around in the garden with Monsieur Le Coq, all puffed up with pride and full of his own self-importance. I found it quite cathartic. If only the damned crowing would stop.

I put my pillow over my head and tried to block out the sound, snuggling up to Julien's warm back. After a few moments, I listened. Nothing. Halle-bloody-lujah! I wrapped my arms around Julien, pulling myself close to him and waited for sleep to claim me again.

Fat chance! The crowing started again almost immediately followed by the muffled sound of voices. Someone was stealing my hens. I leapt out of bed and shoved my feet into a pair of sandals. No wonder the cockerel was so agitated. Clever boy, I thought as I ran for the front door.

'Where are you going?' Julien, sleep-rumpled, was standing in the doorway rubbing his hands through his hair.

'Someone's outside,' I whispered urgently.

'Wait, let me go.'

But it was too late. I was already creeping across the garden towards the henhouse.

'Would you shut the bloody fack up, you stupid bird.'

'Trace??'

Standing in a pair of very short pyjamas, clutching a broom, Tracey was yelling at the henhouse like a woman possessed.

'I've had it with that sodding bird. Honestly. I'm going to bloody kill it.' She shook her broom at the henhouse.

'Come on Trace, what are you going to do? Sweep the poor thing to death?'

'I'm not in the mood for jokes. I've only just gone to bed and he starts his bloody racket. Every sodding morning. It's driving me mental.'

'Look, I know. I'm really sorry. Maybe you could try earplugs or something.'

Tracey glared at me.

'I don't mean for ever,' I continued, 'just until I can work out what to do.'

'I can't spend the whole night with cotton wool in my ears. I have phone calls to make.'

'Who on earth are you calling at three o'clock in the morning? You're not trying to get back with Warren are you?'

'Don't be daft! What would I want with that muppet?' It seemed as if I had hit a raw nerve.

'You are, aren't you?'

'No I'm bloody not. I'm going to LA to make a new album if you must know. I can finally kiss goodbye to this bloody place.'

'What? When?' I suddenly had a sick feeling in my stomach.

'Two weeks. It's all arranged. I'm going to work with Rihanna's producer.'

'Two weeks? Trace, that's fantastic, but when were you planning to tell me then?'

'I don't have to bloody tell you everything do I?' Tracey stalked off, pushing roughly past Julien who was standing there rather incongruously holding a rolling pin, the only weapon he had been able to find, there being no stale baguettes available.

'No, you're right. You don't have to tell me everything. After all, it's not like we are friends or anything is it?' I shouted after her.

Without even looking round, Tracey stuck her middle finger in the air and carried on walking. I watched her go, trying hard to hold back my tears. She was leaving. I was losing my best friend in France. Julien slipped an arm round my waist.

'Come on, let's go back to bed.'

Even the cockerel had been shocked into silence.

Chapter Twenty-six

I sat outside the Café du Midi watching the progress of an auburn leaf from the lime tree as it danced and spiralled on the wind. Autumn had arrived with a vengeance and the languid, hot days of the summer were nothing but a memory that warmed me as I sipped on a steaming mug of *chocolat chaud*. And it really was hot chocolate. Stéphane, the owner of the café, had brought out a big machine that looked a bit like a slushy maker, except that in this case it was melted chocolate watered down with milk. A chocoholic's dream.

'It is just for the winter,' he had told me, 'to keep us warm.'

There was certainly no hint of Christmas in shorts today. The village was almost deserted with many of the houses shuttered up for the winter, their summer owners and the last of the holidaymakers long since departed. The glorious displays of blood-red geraniums were gone, replaced by empty pots on empty windowsills. Even the shop was only open three days a week now. The vibrant colours of summer were gone and in their place were fields of brown earth and the half-naked skeletons of trees with their branches thrusting upwards into the leaden grey skies. There was an air of melancholy that did nothing to lift my mood.

Tracey was leaving for her new life in LA today. I hadn't spoken to her for two weeks, since the ridiculous argument at the henhouse. Every time I called round she was either out or wouldn't come to the door. In the end I gave up trying.

'Why do you look so sad?' Stéphane pulled up a chair and sat down with me. My French, thanks to Martine's lessons, was now good enough to hold a basic conversation and it was bringing me closer to my French neighbours who now only regarded me with mild suspicion. I was practically a local.

'I don't know, maybe it's because Tracey is leaving today.'

'Bof,' said Stéphane, in that particular French way that can mean anything from 'whatever' to 'that's a tragedy'.

'Oh, I know she wasn't everybody's *tasse de thé,* but underneath it all she's a really nice person, you know, quite...' I searched around for the French word for vulnerable.

'Vulnérable?' Stéphane suggested.

I smiled. When in doubt just say an English word with a French accent and you had fair chance of getting it right. 'Yes, *vulnérable.* She has the air of someone who is tough but in reality she's not.'

'So why did you fight?'

'Oh, it was nothing really, but she didn't tell me she was leaving to go to LA. I thought we were friends.'

'Well, sometimes it is not easy to tell people who are important to you that you are leaving.' Stéphane looked wistful, like a man who had something on his mind.

'Not you too?' I said as the realisation hit me.

'Yes, us too. Our family are too far away and we want to be closer to them. Also, it is warmer down on the Cote d'Azur. Claire and I find the winters here too hard.'

'So when do you go?'

'Soon. We have had the café up for sale for nearly a year now but no one wants to buy it. Times are tough.'

We sat in silence, both contemplating the future without the café. My mood, already gloomy, was now positively miserable. I had been relying on the café to be my lifeline when Tracey left. Although I didn't always feel I had that much in common with many of my compatriots, there was generally someone to have a chat and a laugh with. As Claudine had told me on my first day in France, you should never underestimate the importance of having someone who shares your sense of humour.

'What about Jack? Can't he buy it? He must know the business inside out.'

'He would love to. He has tried but he can't get a loan for the money. He is as sad as we are. He and Aurélie moved back here to be close to her family and if he can't find work anywhere else they will have to move away too.'

'I wish I had the money to buy it, Stéphane. I'd love to have a café in France.' As I said it, I realised it was true, I *would* love it. Ideas started flowing into my head, for jewellery sales and theme nights, not the sort with fancy dress but with food from different regions. What better way to satisfy my growing urge for a proper curry? And I had heard that there was a good curry chef in a village called Villette, about half an hour away. Chummy had mentioned him. Suddenly I felt energised by the whole idea.

'Stéphane, how much is it on the market for?'

'Three hundred and fifty thousand euros including all the equipment, stock, everything that you need.'

As quickly as my excitement had grown, reality drove it away. 'Three hundred and fifty? Oh dear, I don't think I could afford that.'

'Well, I'm sure we could come to some arrangement if you could get near to the asking price,' said Stéphane, throwing me a lifeline.

'Let me see what I can do.'

With a spring in my step, I went back to the car full of enthusiasm for my new idea. As I drove into Les Tuileries my heart sank. The removal van was gone and there was no sign of the Merc. Tracey must have left already. I'd hung on to the slim possibility that she might at least hang around to say goodbye. I stood at the tall, iron gates and looked pensively through them at the house where we had shared so many good times. So this is what people meant when they talked about having a heavy heart. Mine felt like a cannonball lodged in my chest. It was worse than a break-up.

I hurried back round to the cottage to see if Tracey had left a note. It had been such a stupid argument that surely she wouldn't have left without extending some sort of olive branch but there was nothing. Kicking off my boots, I sat on the sofa and stared into space, a huge feeling of loss overtaking me. After a few minutes I tried to call Julien but his phone went straight to voicemail. At least I still have him, I thought.

Powering up my laptop, I fired off a quick email to Julie, the negotiator at my local estate agents back in Wandsworth. She had sold me my house and we had stayed in touch ever since. I had no idea how much it was actually worth now but I knew she would be honest with me.

I didn't have long to wait for an answer. Julie must have been sitting in her office twiddling her thumbs when the email came through. The reply wasn't good news. Despite all the money I had spent on a new kitchen and bathroom, the flat was worth pretty much what I had paid for it. To a lot of people that would have been positive news but with a café in south west France to buy, it was nothing of the sort. My equity, after fees, would be around 150,000 euros if the exchange rate stayed the same. A nice amount but not enough to secure a deal with Stéphane, of that I was pretty sure, and I had no idea where I would find the other 200,000 euros he wanted. It clearly wasn't a goer. I rested my chin in my hands and thought, but nothing came to me. I knew my parents didn't have that sort of money and the chances of me getting a mortgage with no job were non-existent, so barring a lottery win in the near future, I was destined never to be the owner of the Café du Midi.

A knock on the door roused me from my thoughts and I perked up, thinking it might be Julien. However, my smile quickly faded as I opened the door to find Madame Mollet standing there. '*Bonjour madame, entrez,*' I said, surprised, and opening the door wide for her to come in.

'*Merci*, but it is just a quick visit. I'm afraid I have to tell you that Monsieur Marin, your landlord, has decided to sell Les Tuileries.'

My chin dropped to around knee level. Although I knew I was just a tenant, somehow I thought of Les Tuileries as mine.

'But... when?' I stuttered

'Well, it is now on the market but you know it is very different here in France than in England. It might sell tomorrow or it might not sell for years. I just wanted to warn you and let you know that the terms of your lease permit me to show prospective buyers the cottage during office hours with prior notice.'

'Well, yes of course. That's no problem.'

'Thank you. I shall always ring to give you advance warning.'

'Um, how much is Monsieur Marin asking for the cottage?'

'Two hundred thousand euros.'

I wondered if I'd understood correctly. 'Sorry, *how much*?' It seemed a little steep for something without a proper toilet.

Madame Mollet sighed, 'I agree it's quite high, but in France it is the buyer who sets the price. Monsieur Marin is just an elderly farmer who has heard lots of silly tales about the English paying half a million euros for a pile of stones. He thinks that some rich English person will come along and pay what he wants. Well, I must go. I have some viewings booked in for this Friday. One at one o'clock and one at three o'clock, but I will confirm them later. Is that all right with you?'

'Yes, fine. If you want me to show them around, please let me know. I would be happy to.'

I watched Madame Mollet go. Daft old fool, I thought rather uncharitably of my landlord. Still, at least it meant that the cottage wouldn't be snapped up by the first buyer. If I had a proper job I might even consider buying it myself, but not at that price. The chances were I would still be there the following year and quite likely the one after that as well but it left me with a sense of unease, as if the rug had been not exactly pulled from underneath me, but certainly given a hefty tug.

Chapter Twenty-seven

I'm just going to look, I'm just going to look, I chanted to myself like a mantra.

For want of something better to do, I'd agreed to go to the Open Day at the Feline Friends in France rescue centre with Lucinda, if they'd let me in. To be honest, half the reason I was going to go was to see if there was a chance of work in the spring. Despite my best efforts to find a job, the only thing I'd been offered in recent weeks was cleaning an office in Bussières. Having seen all the deductions which came off a French payslip, which included just about everything except a slush fund for the president, and by the time I had bought petrol to get there, I would be paying them for the privilege of cleaning their toilets.

Lucinda was an ardent kitty-stalker and had a whole ménagerie of waifs and strays that she'd picked up over the years. When she wasn't working she seemed to be on a constant mercy mission to rescue this cat from the rubbish tip, or that cat from an impoverished expat who was returning to the UK, but couldn't afford the apparently vast sums of money to get a pet passport. The idea of spending hundreds of euros to take Tibbles back to the UK where he would probably get run over by the first passing white van was faintly ridiculous. I shuddered as an unwelcome vision of poor, deceased Snoopy flitted across my mind.

I had asked Julien to come along but he seemed to have rather a poor view of the whole 'Save *Les Chats*' movement. To him, cats were either put to good use keeping barns and grain stores free of mice or else they served absolutely no purpose whatsoever. Difficult though it was to accept a viewpoint that went so far against the grain of my inherent English fluffiness about animals, I suppose he had a point.

We pulled up at the rescue centre and went into the house where wine (of course) and nibbles were being served. The usual crowd had arrived, a good few of whom I suspected were just there for the free drink. In one corner, a group talked loudly, their laughter revealing teeth stained slightly aubergine by the cheap wine while the host, a charming Dutch lady called Merel, flitted around chatting and pointing people in the direction of a display board with all the cats that needed a new home. On every surface cats in various shapes and sizes were dozing or enjoying impromptu petting sessions with the guests.

I was transfixed by two kittens that were running around happily. One of them looked as if he was drunk.

'Isn't he gorgeous?' said Merel, who had appeared at my shoulder with a tray of canapés.

'He is so sweet, but is there something wrong with him?' We watched as the kitten tried to take a drink from a bowl of water and succeeded only in dunking his head right in it, coming up spluttering and shaking the drips from his ears.

'Yes, unfortunately. He's been vaccine damaged. His mother was a feral cat who was brought in to us and we vaccinated her without realising she was pregnant. It's a very rare complication but sadly he has some brain damage. He finds it difficult to judge distances.'

Right on cue, the kitten shot off after its sibling who had run into another room but it totally misjudged the doorway and crashed into the wall just to one side. None the worse for its experience, it jumped up, and made the door on the second attempt. I grinned then quickly wiped the smile off my face.

'Oh don't worry,' said Merel, 'I spend a lot of time laughing at his antics but the main thing is that he is happy and he will stay with me for the rest of his life. So are you looking for a cat?'

'Well, um…' I looked around wildly for someone that I just *had* to speak to but there was no one. I knew what was coming next. The hard sell.

'Come and see who we have,' she said, taking my arm and guiding me to the display, which seemed to be one big gallery of unspeakably adorable kittens and cats. Merel talked me through each one while I listened politely. I wasn't leaving here with a cat. No way.

A few hours later, she was smiling gratefully at me as I signed a cheque for one hundred and twenty euros that I could ill afford. At my feet, a plaintive mewling came from a pet carrier as I wondered how it had all happened.

Merel had taken me down to the kitten section, 'just for a look'. I knew I should have resisted more but she had me firmly in her sights. My heart sank a little bit more with each step as we went down into the basement. Opening the door, she led me in to where another couple were cooing over a pen of tiny black kittens. Merel's basement had been kitted out with five state-of-the-art heated pens in which various litters of kittens slept, played or just miaowed piteously at anyone who stopped to look at them.

'Gosh, this is all very grand isn't it?' I exclaimed.

'Yes, we were very lucky to get a grant from a French charity.' She mentioned the name of a charity that I vaguely recognised as being run by some former French film star or such like. 'It has made it much easier for us to take in more kittens and deal with the sick ones. All the surfaces are washable...' I zoned out as she droned on about the facilities. I was, after all, only being polite.

'So, in this pen we have...' She rolled off six names, one for each kitten and all beginning with C. The alliteration confused me.

'Why do all their names start with the same letter?'

'Because it is the year of the Cs.'

'The Cs?' I was none the wiser.

'Every year in France, pet names begin with a different letter of the alphabet. This year it's C, next year will be D, the year after E and so on. The year of Z is always a challenge but by then I will have retired so it will be someone else's problem.'

'Right,' I said marvelling at how the French could continually manage to surprise me, 'and if I chose a name that didn't begin with a C?'

'Well, that would be very bad.'

I bent down and stuck my finger through the grille to rub the multitude of little pink noses that were pressed against it. They really were incredibly cute but I was window shopping, nothing else. As I stroked their noses, one kitten decided that the only way to be noticed was to stand out from the crowd and set about climbing up the grille mewling at me in a 'look at me, look at me' sort of way.

I smiled and tickled his tummy. 'This one is really cute.'

The words were barely out of my mouth before Merel had opened the pen door and swooped on the kitten, prising it quickly off the grille and placing it gently in my arms. The kitten miaowed hopefully at me. He was a little ball of grey and cream fluff with rather alarmingly crossed eyes. 'What's the matter with his eyes?'

'This is Cédric. He's part Siamese. They are often cross-eyed.'

I looked suspiciously at the other kittens, all of which seemed to have eyes resolutely pointing in the same direction. I held the little kitten up in front of me and looked him straight in the eyes. Cédric? Poor little bugger. He stared back at me, his head moving slightly from side to side as he tried to decide which me was the real one.

From that moment on I knew I was doomed. Doomed to cat-ownership despite my best intentions. The rather unfortunately named Cédric was coming home with me.

Chapter Twenty-eight

'Take this bloody cat would you, *chérie*?' Julien walked in with the now re-named Basil attached firmly to his thigh. I had held my breath and waited for fire and brimstone to rain down on my head when I went ahead and gave him a name that went against French custom, but so far there had been no repercussions.

'Come here, you naughty kitty,' I scolded as I prised his needle-sharp claws out of Julien's leg.

'*Putain de merde*,' he swore. 'Be careful!'

'Oh don't be such a baby. He's only a little kitten.' I gave Basil a quick kiss and put him down on the floor of the kitchen in front of his food bowl.

'Would you like me to rub it better for you?' I said archly, giving Julien an exaggerated pout.

'Later *chérie*. We have to go.'

Julien was taking me to a lunch in the village which was hosted by *la chasse*. I had gradually got used to the sound of gunfire each weekend and the almost weekly visit from a hunter looking for his lost dog.

As we pulled out of the drive, I noticed some movement next door. For a moment my heart skipped a beat. Maybe Tracey was back already, although I doubted that she could write and record a new album in less than a month. There was a lump in my throat when I saw it was strangers unpacking boxes. It looked like Tracey had moved on permanently. I felt Julien's hand on my cheek as I fought back tears and put my head to one side, pressing his hand against my face as a single tear broke ranks and ran down my face.

'You miss her, don't you?'

'More than I thought I would. I hadn't realised how much I relied on her.'

'You still have me.'

'I know,' I laid my head on his shoulder, 'but you're often so busy with the farm.'

'But what about all the other English?'

'They are all so much older than me.'

Julien smiled. 'What is that expression you used about the Club in Bussières? "God's Waiting Room".'

The *salle des fêtes* was like a warm embrace when I walked in from the damp cold of the day. Inside, everyone was decked out in their finest clothes, which for the most part meant a clean housecoat and wellies for the women and a shirt and trousers instead of the more usual camouflage clothes for the men. Wine was being served in plastic cups and bowls of crisps dotted the room. I had long since realised that the idea of the stylish Frenchwoman and gourmet food existed more in the minds of British fashionistas and food writers than in real life. *Haute couture* had barely managed to totter across the River Loire in its spike heels before it got swallowed up in a pair of sensible shoes and the sort of clothes that had been fashionable in England in the 1980s. It was a strange conundrum.

The *maire* greeted me brusquely. My liaison with one of his compatriots had seemingly done nothing to make me any more acceptable in his eyes. He was still a committed Anglophobe who tolerated the invasion of *Les Rosbifs*, or in fact anyone who wasn't French, as a necessary evil in his *commune*. I took it in my stride. Some of them did little to endear themselves to their new neighbours and I knew they fuelled a large and very unwelcome Black Economy.

I waved to Martine and Laure, who were at the other side of the room chatting with Monsieur Lenoël from the newsagent in Bussières. He was one of the *pompiers* who had taken me to hospital that fateful time and although he was nothing other than professional when we met, it still made me uneasy to think that he'd seen me half naked.

The room was set up with rows of long tables dressed in white paper tablecloths with sprigs of winter foliage in little white vases dotted along each one. Bottles of wine were grouped along each table, only red and *rosé* as usual, white wine was only for heathens in these parts. There was also the habitual single set of cutlery, the custom being to eat each course with the same knife and fork. When I had first arrived I was constantly having to retrieve my cutlery which I left on my plate as I had done since I was small. Julien thought this was a ridiculous waste; but I still preferred to eat each course with a clean set.

Giving me a cup of passable wine and with his hand on the small of my back, he led me to where Louis was holding court with a group of younger people from the village. It suddenly struck me how little I went out now Julien and I were in that place in a relationship where we were totally happy with just each other's company. We spent most nights together at Les Tuileries and during the day, while he was working on the farm, I busied myself looking for a job and preparing something delicious for our supper.

As we approached the group, the conversation dropped off. I fixed a smile on my face and Julien, if he had noticed, feigned indifference. I had met most of them before at the Bastille Day *fête* and found them as warm as a box of frozen kippers. I had put a lot of it down to the fact that I didn't really speak French then, and it was never easy fitting in with a group who had known each other practically since the delivery room. Today was going to be different. I could speak passable French for starters.

I tried to follow the conversation and was pleased to see that I understood more, but they spoke so fast that by the time I had formulated a comment they had moved on to something different. So I stood silently and listened, trying to show I at least understood what was being said. It was fairly depressing though and I could have kicked Julien for not bringing me into the conversation more.

When he told me that, as one of the organising *comité* he would have to sit on a separate table, I very nearly did kick him.

'The others will look after you,' he told me. I somehow doubted that. When the time came to sit down, I found myself virtually ignored and pushed to the end of their group next to a heavily made-up woman. She introduced herself as Pia and I opened the conversation by asking politely if she was from the area. The woman quickly pointed out she was Belgian not French in a way that left me in no doubt that I had made a *faux pas*. It was going to be a long lunch. On the positive side though, she spoke slow, clear French, rather than the relatively impenetrable local version and I breathed a quick sigh of relief that I would at least have someone to talk to who I had a fighting chance of understanding.

The first course arrived, *soupe de Gaston*, which was served in a huge, steaming tureen with a ladle so we could all help ourselves. It was made of white beans, wine and a bucketful of garlic, with thick slices of baguette floating in it. The heat and the copious amounts of garlic made my eyes smart. After three mouthfuls, Pia pulled a face. '*Pipi de chat!*' she announced, pouring the remainder back in the soup tureen. I had no trouble guessing what that meant. I looked around nervously to see if anyone else had heard while Pia poured herself more wine.

'So why did you move to France?' she asked

'Oh, you know. I just wanted a change of pace, to connect a bit more with nature.'

Oh God, I sound like one of those stupid programmes I used to watch, I thought.

'How about you?' It was a question I would regret asking.

'I moved here for my health. I have bad asthma,' she told me. 'Hate the bloody French though.'

I nearly spat out my soup. Our neighbours, thankfully, were all deep in conversation so it looked as if no one had heard.

By the time the second course, a salad of endive and walnuts, was placed in front of us, Pia was in full flow, alternately throwing more wine down her throat and continuing her diatribe against France. It seemed there was nothing about it she liked, except the climate in the summer. I couldn't quite understand how this wet, cold weather could be any good for her chest and clearly living in France was no good for her humour.

Next we ploughed through *pâté de sanglier*, followed by *pâté de chevreuil*. I didn't mind eating boar, it was just a type of pork after all, but I always felt uncomfortable eating deer. Images of Bambi kept appearing in my mind. Pia continued to moan.

'Look, they even make us eat off the same plate. They are so common here. Not like Belgium and England. We are so much more refined.'

I had kept quiet in the hope that it might discourage her from further comment, but by now, she was well into her second bottle of wine and it had well and truly oiled her vocal cords. So far, this was turning out to be the meal from hell. I looked hopefully across at Julien but he was engrossed in conversation with the *maire* and I couldn't quite get his attention.

The next course, *daube de sanglier*, wild boar in a rich red wine sauce, was placed in front of us. I could feel myself flagging. Not so Pia, who despite developing a serious list to one side, was still droning on. From the tenseness I noticed in our neighbours, I suspected that Pia's xenophobic rant had reached their ears. Feeling a tap on my shoulder, I turned round to see the welcome face of Martine.

'Would you like to take a little stroll to let our food settle?' she asked.

I would happily have agreed to a triathlon if it got me away from the mad Belgian.

'Come on, bring your coat. It's cold outside.'

'I'll just let Julien know.'

'Oh, don't worry about him. We'll be back before he even notices we are gone.'

Outside, the cold air was bracing and just what I needed to revive my flagging energy and spirits.

'Who *is* that woman?' I asked Martine as soon as we were outside.

'She's just *une dingue*. What is it you say? "Mad as a box of frogs". Her husband left her not long after she moved here and she blames France and the French rather than her own objectionable character for it.'

'She certainly has what we would call a chip on her shoulder.'

'I think it was a bit mean of the others to put you with her.'

'I expect they only did it so they wouldn't have to put up with me,' I sighed. 'Honestly Martine, I try so hard with them but they give nothing back. They hate me.'

Martine looked away and thought for a minute. 'It's not you they hate, I'm sure of that. It can be very difficult when they have all grown up together for a stranger to try and fit in. We all adore Julien and Louis but sometimes situations arise that mean…'

'Hey ladies, wait for me.'

I turned to see Julien running after us. 'Where are you going?'

'Martine and I were just going for a little walk between courses.'

Julien caught up with us and pulled me towards him, wrapping me up in a bear-like hug. I laughed and reached up to kiss him.

'I'm so sorry, *chérie*. I would much rather be sitting with you than with the *comité* but it's tradition.'

'You know what they say about traditions. They were made to be broken.'

'I thought that was rules.'

'Picky! Have you seen who I'm sitting next to? Bloody Pia, the mad Belgian with the runaway husband.'

Julien laughed. 'You poor thing.'

'Well, I'm going to head back and leave you love birds,' said Martine.

'Oh you don't have to. Walk with us for a bit,' I pleaded.

Martine looked at Julien and then at me. 'No, if you don't mind I'll head back.'

'Well, OK. See you later then.'

I watched her go, wondering why she had changed her mind so suddenly.

I slipped my arm though Julien's and we headed off in the direction of the little market square.

'What is that building?' I asked, pointing at an old ruin attached to the next building and then to the *mairie* or town hall.

'That's the old keep. This was originally a fortified castle with a church for the *comte* and *comtesse* in the middle and that's all that's left of it. It's why it's so big and grand for such a small village. The other little chapel, St Martin, on the edge of the village was for everyone else. It originally belonged to the Comte de Beauclerc. He built it for his wife but when she died in childbirth, he could not bear to stay here anymore so he just abandoned it and it fell into disrepair over the years. They used the stones to build the *mairie*.'

'What a sad story. This village has certainly had its share of tragedy, hasn't it?'

'Hmm. I suppose it has.'

We sat on the bench outside the *mairie* watching our breath condense in the cold air. Julien slipped his arm round me and kissed the top of my head. I leaned into him and wondered if it was possible to feel any happier than I did when I was with him. The stupid Belgian didn't matter anymore, nor did the offhand behaviour of Julien's friends. All that mattered was Julien. I was in love with him. I was absolutely sure.

As if he read my mind, his lips brushed my ear and he whispered, *'Je t'aime.'*

I turned to him and looked deep into his eyes. *'Moi non plus.'*

'Pardon?'

'Moi non plus,' I repeated, certain that was what they said in that old Serge Gainsbourg song, the one about coming and going between your kidneys. On second thoughts, maybe I was wrong to rely on that for the correct response to a declaration of love from a Frenchman.

'You neither?'

'Pardon?'

'That's what you said. Me neither.'

'But… in that song, you know, with that Jane Birkin woman…'

Julien roared with laughter. 'Serge Gainsbourg and Jane Birkin? We always said that the English never really understood that song.'

I could have kicked myself for ruining the moment but still, he'd said it hadn't he? He loved me.

'Je t'aime, Julien.'

He kissed me deeply, holding my face in his hands. 'I have never been so happy, *chérie*.'

'*Moi non plus,*' I smiled. He smiled back at me and enveloped me in his arms.

'Come on, we should get back. We still have another three courses of meat to get through.'

'Oh God, I don't think I can,' I said, but knowing that Julien loved me, I could get through anything. 'Will there be cheese?'

'Of course,' he replied, 'this is France.'

Chapter Twenty-nine

The flash of lightning lit up the bedroom and the crash of thunder that followed was enough to rattle the windows. I sat up quickly, roused from a deep sleep by the storm. I padded over to the window, still half asleep. The rain battering against it sounded as if someone was throwing handfuls of gravel and the wind was whipping the poplars in the garden into a frenzy. I had experienced some storms since my arrival in France but this was in a different league. The gusts of wind whistled under the roof tiles, blowing small clouds of dust through the wooden slatted ceiling. The big oak tree next to the house was creaking and groaning arthritically and I hoped that it would hold up. There was no hope of any more sleep until the storm passed so I went to the kitchen to make myself a cup of tea.

Huddled under a blanket on the sofa with Basil snuggled up on my lap, I sipped a mug of hot tea as flashes of lightning illuminated the room, casting spooky shadows in the corners. Hot embers still glowed in the wood burner so I threw on a few more logs to get it going again. I was halfway through my tea when the lights went out. It was nothing unusual for the electricity to go off during a storm; in fact, it often took little more than a strong wind to knock it out. I felt my way to the dresser and took some matches out of the drawer then lit the candles I had dotted around the room, with the kitten attacking my bare feet as I went. I hoped that the henhouse was surviving the onslaught outside.

The wood burner started to roar back to life as I settled down on the sofa listening to the wind rattling the windows. From my vantage point, I could see through the window out across the valley. Forks of lightning split the sky, crackling with pent-up electricity. The storm still seemed to be some way off and I wasn't normally worried about storms; however, this one was making me a bit nervous. The rain continued to batter the windows and the rolling booms of thunder became almost continuous. On my lap, Basil started to look around nervously, digging his little claws into me every time he heard a thunderclap.

'It's OK, *minet*. It will be over soon,' I told him.

From the bedroom, a steady dripping started and I went to investigate. Water was leaking through the ceiling in big brown droplets that were splashing onto the bed. I quickly pushed it out of the way and ran to the kitchen to get a bowl. By the time I came back, more leaks had appeared and the water was starting to trickle down the walls at the point where it met the roof.

'Oh shit!' I muttered as I headed back to the kitchen to get more bowls. Basil followed me, mewing loudly. I bent down and picked him up, snuggling him close to my chest.

'Poor kitty, you're frightened aren't you?' He purred like a little train and nestled into me. As I was putting him down gently on the sofa, a huge fork of lightning lit the room up like daylight, followed by a loud clap of thunder that made the ground shake. I jumped and Basil dug all twenty of his needle claws into me, making me shriek with pain.

'Jesus bloody Christ,' I said loudly, half at the kitten, half in fear.

From the window, I noticed a glow in the distance, which seemed to get bigger as I watched it.

'Oh no,' I said under my breath. The flickering and dancing lights were undoubtedly flames and I tried to visualise what was there, but the darkness and the storm had disorientated me. Was it a house or just a barn? Either way, it had taken a direct lightning strike. Over the noise of the storm, I could just make out the sounds of the *pompiers'* sirens and as I watched, faint blue lights could be seen making their way up the hillside towards the flames. I'm not a religious person but I found myself saying a quick prayer that no one had been hurt.

Suddenly, an overwhelming need to speak to Julien hit me. Normally he would have been here but he had had to go to a meeting in Bussières to do with farming subsidies or some other such tedious subject, so we had decided to meet up again the next day. When I picked up my mobile, I saw that there was no signal, so I tried the house phone but that was dead too. Around me, the wind got stronger and the cracks and thuds of branches being ripped from the trees got more frequent. The old tree by the house was groaning loudly but so far holding up to the gusts of wind. *Rafales*, I thought. The French word for gusts made them sound so harmless but there was nothing harmless about these.

I climbed back under the throw on the sofa and pulled Basil onto my lap. Sitting there in the candlelight with nothing else to do but listen to the storm raging around me was a humbling experience. In London, I was barely aware of the forces of nature, but here, on a remote hillside in rural France, Mother Nature was getting right in my face and I wasn't enjoying it one bit.

I pulled out my phone to check the signal again, just on the off chance that I had one. As I tried to compose a text to Julien, my hands were shaking enough to make typing difficult. I still had no signal, but at least my text would be sent as soon as I did.

Firing up my laptop that had been left on the coffee table earlier, I was relieved to see it still had some battery left, but of course,

I had no Internet connection. The storm had obviously knocked that out too. I had never felt as isolated as I did now. If Tracey were here, we would have sat together with a bottle of wine and laughed our way through it but with only the kitten for company, the dripping ceiling in the bedroom and the gusts of wind howling round the cottage and lifting the roof tiles, I felt very much alone.

I was awoken the next morning by Basil sitting on my chest meowing furiously for his breakfast. I had finally fallen asleep sometime after four as the storm had started to blow itself out.

'Just a minute, buddy,' I said to the kitten, untangling my stiff limbs and stretching out my neck. The sofa definitely wasn't designed for sleeping on and I suspected it wasn't really designed for sitting on either as it had never been particularly comfortable at the best of times.

Hauling myself up, I circled my hips and arched my back to get my stiff muscles working again. I looked out of the window on to a bright, sunny day with whitish-grey clouds scudding across the sky. Remembering the fire, I looked across the hillside to see if I could pinpoint the location. It wasn't difficult. Blue lights still flashed in the distance, but I could see that it was definitely a barn and not a house that had caught fire.

Breathing a sigh of relief, I slipped my feet into a pair of Crocs, put the kettle on and ventured out to see how we had fared in the storm. The garden was a mess of broken branches and any trees that still had leaves on them were now stripped bare. On the bank behind the house several trees had come down, but apart from that there didn't seem to be too much damage, maybe a loose tile here and there and a bit of mopping up to do inside. I made a mental note to call Madame Mollet to let her know.

The kettle seemed strangely quiet as I went back into the cottage and then I remembered that the power had gone down during the storm. I emptied the water into a saucepan and lit the gas cooker.

At least I could still cook even if I couldn't watch television, use my laptop or do any of the hundred and one other things that made my life bearable during these dull winter months. I picked up the phone, hoping against hope for a dial tone. There wasn't one. My last chance was my mobile but that was still showing no signal. Bloody hell, I thought, it's like being in one of those 'let's live like the Victorians' documentaries; but I wanted to live like a twenty-first century girl and being so completely cut off made me feel a bit twitchy. I resolved to drive into town later in the hope that they still had power and access to up-to-date gadgetry.

A while later, after a lukewarm shower and a piece of toast made over one of the gas rings, I set off in the car to see what was happening in Bussières. I didn't get very far. The road had turned into a small but fast-flowing river as water ran off the hills and down into the valley. Tentatively, I drove through, hoping it wasn't deeper than it looked. When I reached the bottom, the little river, which normally meandered lazily in the vague direction of the Atlantic Ocean, had been transformed into a raging torrent of muddy water stretching about 20 metres across. Les Tuileries was effectively cut off. Standing at the edge of the floods, Martine, Monsieur Brunel and Monsieur Marcel were huddled together deep in conversation gesticulating wildly at each other.

'*Bonjour messieurs, dames,*' I called, stopping and getting out of my car. I performed the ritual *bisous*.

'That was some storm last night. Is everyone all right?'

They looked anxiously at each other then shook their heads and looked forlornly at the floodwaters.

'There is no possibility of crossing,' said Martine, 'I think we are stranded until the water goes down again.'

'Is there any more rain forecast?' I asked.

'Maybe a bit but nothing like last night.'

'And is all your power out as well?'

'Yes, the power is off all the way along the valley past Bussières,' said Monsieur Marcel, 'and I don't think they will be repairing the telephone line any time soon.' He pointed downstream to where a wooden telegraph pole had sheared off just above the water level, trailing broken wires down the river like pondweed.

'Monsieur Marcel has a CB radio and has managed to contact the *gendarmerie*. They have told us to stay put for the moment. Apparently there were some serious accidents last night so they have a lot to do, and as no one here is hurt we are not a priority.' She put her arm round me and led me away from the others.

'But Madame Brunel's brother was killed last night. He was hit by some masonry that fell from the roof of the church. God knows what the stupid man was doing out in the storm.'

I thought back to the drunk on the bicycle that I had rescued from the middle of the road during the summer. 'Not Armand? Is that her brother?'

'Yes, and now she needs to get to her family but she can't. The *maire* is sending the municipal tractor to see if it can get across and pick her up.'

Almost on cue, we heard the tractor chugging down the hill from Rocamour. A small group of Madame Brunel's relatives had congregated on the far side of the floodwater and they stood back to let the tractor pass. The driver jumped down to look at the floodwaters, taking off his cap and scratching his head as he contemplated the likelihood of getting across.

After a few minutes of animated conversation with Madame Brunel's relatives who were probably telling him that it was just a bit of a puddle and a man of his aptitude with a tractor could surely get across and back with no problem, he shrugged his shoulders and climbed back into the cab of the tractor.

Revving the engine, he started gingerly towards the water. The first few metres were easy but as he got further towards the middle, the full force of the water crashed against his tractor and I could see it being nudged slightly sideways. I held my breath. On the far side, a small crowd had gathered to watch. Some were egging him on, others calling him back and saying he would kill himself and what was the point of that when Old Armand was already dead anyway.

Slowly he inched the tractor forward. The water battered against it as he steered into the flow to stop the tractor being pushed over into the river. Martine grabbed my arm and together we watched nervously. As he got past the middle, we let out a cheer, which was soon taken up by the others. He was going to do it!

'Hang on,' I said to Martine. 'I'd better go and move my car so he can get over the bridge.'

I ran back, feeling in my pocket for my keys then remembering I had left them in the car.

This wasn't something I normally did, not because I was worried someone would steal it; the car belonged in a scrap yard anyway, but because the central locking had a tendency to play up and lock unexpectedly. In my excitement, I had just jumped out of the car and forgotten them. As I lifted the handle, I heard a sickening clunk as the doors locked, leaving me on the outside and my keys, tantalisingly out of reach, on the inside.

'Oh shit, not now!' I muttered under my breath, trying the passenger doors. They were all firmly locked. I tried the boot but that was locked too.

'Hurry up,' shouted Martine.

I saw that the tractor was almost across the river now and the only thing standing in the way was my car.

'I can't, I've locked the bloody keys in it.'

'What?'

'The keys are locked in the car.'

Martine rushed over and tried all the doors.

'I've already done that.'

By now, the tractor had made it across to the cheers of the crowds on both sides.

'Can you move your car please?' the driver called out.

'I can't. The keys are locked inside.'

'*Putain,*' he shouted. 'I can't get round your car. Have you got a spare set?'

'Yes but they are up at the house.'

'Well you'd better get going then, hadn't you?' he said, not altogether kindly.

He called out to the others, 'The *anglaise* has locked her keys in the car.'

The cheers died out almost instantly to be replaced by a low murmur which I was quite sure included the words 'stupid Englishwoman' at least once in every other sentence.

'OK, I'll be back as soon as I can.'

I set off up the hill, my legs pounding the road. It was quite clear that my current level of fitness was not up to a 1.5-kilometre uphill sprint and before long, my muscles were burning.

'Gotta keep going, gotta keep going,' I chanted as I sprinted up the hill, feeling as if someone had poured neat acid into my lungs. As I reached the fat white pony in his field, he whinnied softly to me and trotted along the fence as far as he could.

'Thanks for your support, mate,' I called out breathlessly. 'Just wish I could still ride.'

I stopped as an idea started to form in my head. It was a pretty stupid idea but it was an emergency and with my legs on the verge of giving up completely, I had to take a bit of a risk. The little pony was wearing a head collar and I knew that Laure always kept a lead rope knotted around the gate. I also knew that a very young girl from the village rode him as I had seen her a few times so I reasoned that the pony must be quite quiet. Whether or not he was quiet enough for a novice rider, who hadn't been in the saddle for a good twenty years, and in fact, didn't even have a saddle to get onto at this point, remained to be seen.

I called the pony over. Fortunately, he trotted up to me, hopeful of a little titbit, and didn't protest when I grabbed his head collar and attached the lead rope. I led him out of his field then stood helplessly as I realised that I had the first obstacle to overcome. Getting on him. I tried to lift my leg over his back and hop up, but he was too big for that. Fortunately, an old tree stump nearby made for a good mounting block and I climbed on enthusiastically. It was all coming back to me. I clapped my legs against his sides probably a little bit harder than was necessary, making the pony jump and we set off at a fast trot with me bouncing around on his back and hanging on for grim death. The pony's back banged against my bottom, threatening to unseat me at every step. I gripped as hard as I could with my legs but the uphill run seemed to have rendered them almost paralysed and it was more by luck than any skill on my part that I stayed on him.

With the first obstacle overcome, it wasn't long before I came across the next one. Steering. With only one makeshift rein, rather than two, I wasn't entirely sure how to get him to turn in both directions. I would be fine until I got to the last turn into the hamlet, but then I would have to make him turn left with only a right rein. If he went straight on, we would be into a huge field with nothing but open space beyond. My body might never be found.

With the left-hand bend coming up, I started shouting 'left, left' at the pony, who showed no sign of comprehension whatsoever. '*Gauche, gauche,*' I shouted, reasoning that a French pony might only speak French. Clearly this one was Spanish.

I thought back to the cowboys in the spaghetti westerns my dad used to love. They just pulled the reins against the necks of their horses and leaned in whichever way they wanted to go. With the turn fast approaching, it was now or never. Holding on to a handful of its mane, I leaned towards the pony's left side, praying that he would turn.

'Oh you wonderful little thing,' I shouted, patting his neck wildly as he trotted round the bend like a professional cow pony. Just the drive to negotiate now and I was home and dry. The pony, however, had other ideas and despite my best leaning, carried on, straight past the drive and towards the track by the farm buildings at the end of the lane. What's more, he seemed to be picking up speed.

'Whoa, boy,' I shouted, but he didn't seem to understand that either. Clearly, he was on a route that he knew well and that was what accounted for his turning rather than anything I had done. He was now obviously at the place where he was allowed to canter and set off like a mini rocket across the ploughed field as I bumped around on his back feeling absolutely sure that childbearing was now out of the question. I pulled on the lead rope, hoping that would slow him down, but all I managed to do was pull him round in a circle so we were at least heading back the way we came. Whatever happened next, I was sure it would be painful. As we careered across the field towards the hedge, I thought for one horrible moment he was going to try and jump it. Certain death stared me in the face but at the last moment, the pony swerved, depositing me in an ungainly pile in the mud.

'Arrrgghh,' I groaned, taking a quick inventory of my limbs which all seemed to be working. The pony wandered over and nuzzled my face.

'Cheers, mate,' I said, grabbing the lead rope and pulling myself up, 'come on, this is an emergency.'

There was no point trying to get back on so I set off back to the cottage, dragging the pony behind me. Tying him up to a tree in the garden, I rushed in to grab my spare keys and in a moment of sheer brilliance, ran into the bedroom to grab a belt that would work well as another rein. I ran back outside and threaded it through the headcollar before using an upturned bucket to get back onto the pony.

I don't know who was more surprised to see me trotting down the hill, caked in mud, waving my car keys, but a little cheer rose from the crowd. I shoved the lead rope at Martine before jumping in my car and reversing out of the tractor's way.

As I walked the pony back up to his field, the tractor was coming down again with a very regal-looking Madame Brunel perched on the wheel rim in the cab. She nodded to me as she passed and I smiled gently at her. Maybe I was finally making some progress.

'Good boy. We did well,' I said as I patted the pony's neck and he whickered softly in agreement.

I could already feel the bruises starting to form on my bottom.

Chapter Thirty

'Still!' I moaned, crossly. For the fourth day running I had woken up to no power, which meant no hot shower, no recharging my mobile, no laptop, no phone and more worryingly, no sign of Julien. I got out of bed and caught sight of myself in the mirror. It was probably not such a bad thing that he hadn't seen me looking like this. My hair, unwashed now for four days, hung down in dank, greasy rats' tails and although I was washing in water I had boiled on the gas cooker, I had a sneaking suspicion that I smelled none too fresh either.

On the plus side though, I now had a long list of things I could do with a torch held under my chin; washing up, cooking pasta, feeding the kitten, making a nice frothy latte, at least until the batteries in my milk frother ran out; but on the downside, I had discovered that playing Monopoly with myself was no fun at all. I had found an old set in the bottom of a cupboard but by this stage, I had re-named it Monotony.

In the kitchen, I turned on the tap to fill a saucepan and make some coffee but it just gurgled and spat, spraying me with unpleasant-looking brown liquid.

'*Merde*! What next? No electricity and now no water.'

I was surprised by a loud knock on the door. For the past few days, everyone in the hamlet had stayed indoors, no doubt not wanting to be seen in their present unwashed state. On the doorstep, I found two men from the water company with packs of bottled water.

'The batteries on the pump from the reservoir have run out,' one explained, 'so we are delivering bottled water to everyone until the power is back on.'

'Oh, right, well... thanks. Any sign of it coming back on? It's been days now.'

The man apologised for the inconvenience. Apparently there were over a million people without power, and the French power company was drafting in engineers from Germany and the UK to help with the repair work. I asked if he thought the engineers would be starting work today.

'Well no, *mademoiselle*. Today is Sunday.'

Oh, of course, silly me. As if they would let a major incident like this interfere with their thirty-five hour week, I thought, irritated. Damned French employment law. You'd think a national emergency would be a bit more important. I thanked them for the water and shut the door a bit harder than was necessary.

As I watched them drive away, it suddenly occurred to me that if they had managed to get into the hamlet then the road must be passable. Julien would surely be around soon. I ran my hands through my greasy hair and sighed, wondering how I could manage to wash it. Quickly throwing on some clothes, I jumped into my car to drive down and check out the situation. Sure enough, the floodwaters had gone down dramatically. The valley was still flooded but it looked as if the road might be passable in the right vehicle, which wasn't, sadly, my aged *bagnole*. I turned round, feeling even more despondent, and headed back up to Les Tuileries.

As I turned into the drive, I saw Martine standing on my doorstep. I parked the car and got out, calling *'bonjour'* to my neighbour. As soon as Martine turned round, the look on her face told me that something was wrong. Very wrong.

I stopped mid-stride. 'What it is Martine? Is it Laure? Is everything OK?'

'Could we go inside? Please?'

'Well yes, of course. I'm sorry I look such a sight but four days without washing my hair...' I led Martine into the lounge.

She took my hand and led me to the sofa. Basil jumped up onto my lap and started kneading me with his little paws. My hand slipped down to stroke him.

'Please, Martine, what is it? You're making me nervous.'

'There's been an accident.'

I felt my blood run cold. 'What accident? Who? Not Julien?' I shook my head as if to rid myself of such a ridiculous idea. Martine watched me with tired, sad eyes.

'A fire. A barn was struck by lightning during the storm. He went to help...'

'No, stop. Don't say anything more. Please, not Julien. I couldn't stand it.' Huge tears spilled over and ran down my cheeks. I felt sick. 'Is he...?'

'No, he's not dead but he has been badly hurt. I'm so sorry.'

'No, it's not Julien. It can't be. How could you know anyway? The phone lines are down and there's no mobile signal. How could you possibly know? Anyway, it might be Louis, I mean, they are so difficult to tell apart.'

My voice was desperate as I twisted the sleeves of my jumper into tight knots. Even the kitten had fallen silent, sensing something wrong.

Martine pulled me towards her, wrapping her arms around me.

'I'm so sorry but it is Julien. Louis came over earlier to tell me. He couldn't face telling you himself.'

'I have to go to him, Martine. Where is he?'

'He's in the clinic in Villeneuve but I don't think you should go, not today at least.'

'I have to, Martine. I have to.' I could feel panic rising like a tsunami in the pit of my stomach. 'Please, Martine, will you take me?'

'Are you sure?'

'Yes please,' I whispered, my voice barely audible.

'OK, but you can't go looking like that. I have a generator arriving shortly. Come up to my house in half an hour and you can have a shower and clean yourself up. Will you be OK?'

I nodded numbly. Martine hugged me, then took my shoulders and looked hard at me.

'You must be brave, *ma biche*.'

I nodded again, unable to speak.

'I'll see you later, yes?'

As the door closed behind me, I slumped down on the sofa. My mind raced. Was he in pain? Was he conscious? I imagined the worst possible scenarios. Life without Julien. How could I survive? I had not realised until that moment how completely and totally I had fallen in love with him. Hot tears ran down my face relentlessly but I didn't even have the will to wipe them away. They dropped in my lap, wetting my clothes. Basil climbed back onto my lap, mewling to me but I couldn't even lift a hand to stroke him. My heartache was a physical pain but with it came a numbness that made even the slightest thing a titanic effort.

I had no idea how long I had been sitting there but suddenly the need to see Julien became so acute that it was all I could do to stop myself running up the road to Martine's. I went into the bedroom and grabbed some clean clothes and then ran as fast as I could all the way to Martine's.

Laure opened the door and stood back to let me in, her own eyes red-rimmed from crying. She touched my face gently. 'He will be fine. I know it. He is strong and he has much to live for.'

I tried to smile at her but my strength failed me. Martine came and took my arm, leading me to the bathroom and handed me a pile of towels that had been warming on the kitchen range.

'Take these. There is shampoo in the bathroom.'

I nodded and took them.

As the scalding water pounded my body, I washed my hair and scrubbed my body, removing the dirt of the past few days. I wanted to look perfect for Julien when I got to the hospital.

After the shower, I sat in front of the dressing table mirror in Martine's bedroom, as she gently combed out my hair then dried it while I sat there staring blindly ahead of me, crying silently.

Laure came in and started to speak but Martine shook her head and spoke to her softly in French. She turned and quietly left the room.

Finally dressed, Martine led me out to the car, opening the door and guiding me in. I had barely uttered a word since my arrival. She reached across and took my hand and I squeezed it, grateful for the human contact and only letting go when Martine had to change gear.

'I, I don't know how bad...' she stopped mid-sentence. After a few moments she spoke again.

'You must be brave. Whatever you have to face, you can get through it. You are a strong woman. You gave up your comfortable life to come and live in a country you barely knew. You left behind your friends and your family. You are resourceful. You can overcome this.'

I looked at her and smiled. 'Thank you, Martine. Thank you for being here.'

I looked ahead and the dark clouds of despair that had engulfed me earlier descended once again.

At the hospital Martine took charge, finding out where Julien was and leading me down the maze of corridors until we found him. Louis was standing in the waiting room, leaning against the wall, his head hanging. He looked up as we arrived.

'How is he, Louis?' I asked, my voice breaking. 'What happened?'

Louis looked exhausted. He ran his hands through his hair as tears welled up in his eyes. 'There was a fire in a barn on the farm next to us. We were trying to put it out but the roof collapsed. Julien was hit by a beam. He has some burns to his back, they are not serious, but he also has a head injury. He will live but...'

'Where is he?'

'He's in the room at the end,' he told me, pointing down the corridor.

'Thank God,' I said. It felt as if a curtain of despondency was being pulled aside to let some hope in. I went to pass Louis but he grabbed my arm.

'There's something I need to say...'

'Let me pass, Louis,' I said, twisting out of his grip.

'Please, wait a moment,' something in his voice made me stop, 'this is not the right time.'

'I have to see him, Louis, please don't try to stop me.' I walked towards the door of Julien's room, stopping to look through the window to prepare myself for what lay ahead. It was an image I would never forget. Jo, the girl I had met at line dancing, the one who had told me all about her fiancé, sat at Julien's bedside, holding his hand to her cheek. A sudden stillness descended on me. I paused for a moment then turned back, pushing past Louis and Martine who were blocking my way.

Martine raced after me. She caught up with me by the car.

'It all makes sense now,' I cried bitterly. Everything was falling into place. The way Louis treated me; the hostility of Julien's friends; his absences which he had told me were because of the harvest but which just so happened to coincide with Jo's visit. Maybe even Tracey's strange behaviour.

'So, his childhood sweetheart?'

'Don't.'

'Don't what exactly, Martine? Don't worry, there's plenty more fish in the sea? Don't torture yourself with the fact that the man you love is actually engaged to someone else and nobody told you?' An irrational anger was starting to replace the shock I had been feeling.

'Why didn't you tell me? I feel so stupid.'

Martine was silent.

Eventually she sighed, 'I tried to, many times, but you were not ready to listen. Anyway, Jo had been away for nearly three years. I didn't know how strong their relationship was. For all I knew, he planned to leave her and be with you. It was not my place to say. It was Julien's to be honest with you.'

'Ha! What would he know about honesty? I hope... I hope...'

'No you don't,' Martine put my hand on my arm. 'Come on. Let's go home.'

We travelled home in silence, Martine occasionally glancing anxiously at me. I stared straight ahead, eyes fixed on the road.

We turned into Les Tuileries and she stopped in front of the cottage. I got out of the car and, without a backward glance, ran to the front door, slamming it behind me. Inside, the tears that I had tried to keep at bay on the way home from the hospital started to fall. I leaned against the door, then slid down to sit on the floor, sobbing as if my heart would break. It was broken. I was sure of it.

Chapter Thirty-one

I stood in the Arrivals hall at the little airport. It was the first time I had been back to it since my own arrival eight months before. The naive young woman who had stepped off that plane in a pair of ridiculous heels was long gone, replaced by someone who was more down-to-earth, far less bothered by material possessions. I had swapped handbags for hens and could split logs like a lumberjack. I had the callouses on my hands to prove it. And my heart really had been broken.

Six weeks after that fateful day, Julien was out of hospital having made a remarkable recovery from his head injury. He had tried to contact me, leaving messages and texts asking if he could come over and talk to me, but I had ignored them. Eventually he had given up. I heard on the grapevine that Jo had been far from happy when the truth of Julien's relationship with me had come out, but had decided to stand by her man.

The loss of Julien was like a yawning gap in my life. I felt it like a raw, open wound in the fabric of my being, like a part of me was missing. I had loved him completely and without compromise. It was something I had never felt before and which I wondered if I would ever feel again. Even all these weeks later, the sense of loss was huge and overwhelming.

'Hey!' called a familiar voice. I looked up to see Charlotte waving madly from the passport queue. I smiled, more pleased to see her than I ever thought. I had missed my best friend and been so wrapped up in my new life that I had neglected the people in my old one. I wondered whether it was too late to try and rebuild those friendships.

After a few minutes she came flying through the doors from customs, flinging her arms round me and hugging me hard. She let me go and held me at arm's length, studying me closely.

'Well you look like shit, don't you?'

'Ah, thanks, I love you too.'

She hugged me again. 'God I've missed you.'

I felt my eyes start to mist over.

'I've missed you too. More than you'll ever know. It's so good to see you.'

I released her from my embrace. 'Come on, let's get going. I've got so much to tell you. I can't wait to show you Les Tuileries... I did mention about the toilet, didn't I?'

In no time we were pulling into the gravel drive.

'Well... what do you think?' I asked as we stopped outside the cottage.

Charlotte was quiet for a moment. 'It's a bit remote, isn't it?'

My heart sank. I had so wanted my best friend to see the beauty of the cottage and understand why I loved it so much here.

'Obviously you're not seeing it at its best. It's glorious in the summer. Come on, let's get inside.'

'Yes please, its bloody freezing! I thought the South of France would be warmer than this in winter.'

'South west,' I corrected, 'there's a world of difference.'

Charlotte unloaded her bags from the boot of the car while I unlocked the cottage.

'Ta dah!' I said, throwing the door wide open. 'Come on in.'

I did the guided tour of the cottage, studiously avoiding the bathroom facilities – there'd be enough time to face that little trauma. Sadly though, not quite as much time as I had hoped.

'I'm bursting for a pee. Is this the bathroom?' asked Charlotte, pushing open the only door that had remained closed during my tour of the estate. Won't be a minute.'

I went back to the lounge to wait for the explosion. I didn't have to wait long.

'Jesus bloody Christ, someone's nicked your toilet,' she called from the bathroom.

'No, that's it actually.'

'What, this hole in the ground?'

'Yep.'

'You cannot be serious. Come on, where's the real toilet?'

I winced. 'That really is it.'

Charlotte's shocked face appeared round the door. 'Seriously?'

'Seriously. On the plus side, I have thighs like steel.' I slapped them loudly by way of proof. To be honest, that was probably the only good thing about it.

'You can get thighs of steel at the gym. You don't need to squat to pee to do it. I mean, how do you... no, never mind.' Charlotte shook her head. 'Once more unto the breach, dear friends,' she sighed.

With her bags unpacked and a restorative cup of tea in front of her, Charlotte produced a small pile of celebrity magazines.

'Thought you might like these,' she said, 'so you know what's going on in the modern world.'

'Lottie, this is France, not Outer Mongolia.'

Since my arrival in France, not so much as a Kardashian had crossed my consciousness and I'd barely even turned on my laptop. The broadband around here was so slow that I was sure it must run on a rubber band and an old piece of chewing gum anyway. I started to leaf through them.

'Ooh, wait a minute,' I said, my attention suddenly caught by a headline. 'Stepney Songstress Storms States,' I read aloud.

'Isn't that your friend Tracey? The one who decked you in front of the paps?' Charlotte asked.

'Ex-friend. And thanks for the reminder. She dumped me and ran off to the States without so much as a goodbye.'

'That sucks. Did you fall out or what?'

'Well, I don't know really,' I sighed. 'It was all something and nothing, a silly argument over an over-enthusiastic cockerel, but I honestly thought she'd get over it and get back in touch.'

'Have you contacted her?'

'Yeah, I sent a few texts just after she left but no reply.' I skimmed the article. 'Wow, she's doing really well. I'm so pleased for her.'

'She's been all over the gossip columns at home. I've lost track of the number of gorgeous men she's been linked with, the lucky cow.'

'Really? Tell me all.'

'Well, she brought out a single which went straight to Number Two in the charts and there's a new album coming out in a few months apparently. She's really living it up in LA. If there's a premiere or party going on, she'll be there with some gorgeous hunk on her arm. Her current main squeeze is apparently Rowan Finch.'

I looked blankly at her.

'Rowan Finch. Oh come on, you must have heard of him, even in this backwater.'

'Unless he's the best mate of Johnny Hallyday or in the latest series of L'Ecole des Stars they probably won't have heard of him over here.'

It was her turn to look blank. 'Johnny who?'

I wagged a finger at her. 'Don't ever admit to not knowing Johnny Hallyday around these parts. He's a national treasure, even if he did try to become Belgian to avoid paying tax. He's France's Cliff Richard except without the religion and with increasingly young wives.'

Charlotte screwed up her face.

'So, Rowan Finch?' I asked.

'He's like the big noise in Hollywood at the moment. Drop-dead gorgeous, unmarried, straight and tipped for an Oscar for his last film.'

I smiled. 'Good one, Trace.'

'So,' asked Charlotte, 'what's she like? Give me all the dirt.'

'Nothing to give you really. She's just a very sweet, down-to-earth Essex girl with the same anxieties as the rest of us.'

'Yeah, with one of Hollywood's most eligible bachelors on her arm. Come on, there's got to be something. I can't go back to the girls at home with no scandal about her.'

'Honest, there's nothing. She was just Tracey from next door who'd had a brief brush with fame but who thought her singing career might well be over. I'm so glad it's gone well for her.'

'So will you get in touch again?' she asked.

'No, I don't think so. It was her who put the barriers up, so it's her who needs to take them down.'

'Well there's nothing lost in sending her a message to wish her well. It might break the ice.'

'Yeah, maybe,' I said wistfully. 'Come on, my neighbour Martine has invited us round for coffee. You can see inside a real French house.'

'With a real French toilet?'

'That,' I said pointing towards the bathroom, 'is a real French toilet. And you might want to change your shoes. I discovered fairly quickly that killer heels have no place in the country.'

'Get them away from me!' Charlotte squealed, hopping from one foot to another as we ran the gauntlet of Martine's chickens. My own chickens had treated her with studied indifference.

'Oh, for heaven's sake, Lottie, they won't hurt you.'

She squealed as one pecked her shoe, dropping her bag in shock. It landed squarely in a fresh pile of chicken poo.

'Oh my God, that's a Mulberry bag.' She picked it up carefully. 'Look at the state of it!'

I tried hard to stifle a giggle while Charlotte glared at me, wiping at her bag with a tissue.

The door opened and Martine's smiling face appeared round it. 'Come in, come in. Make yourself at home.'

She led us into the lounge where Laure stood shyly by the window, twiddling her hair between her fingers.

'*Salut*, Laure,' I said. '*Je te présente mon amie, Charlotte.*' I kissed Laure on both cheeks.

'Hi,' said Charlotte, waving at her. Laure stepped forward to kiss her but, to my embarrassment, Charlotte backed away leaving Laure looking confused.

'Lottie!' I hissed. Hurriedly, Charlotte stuck out her hand, which Laure took and shook politely. She muttered something that I couldn't quite make out then left the room.

'I'll just go and make some coffee,' said Martine quickly, following Laure out.

'Jesus, Lottie, that was really rude.'

'Look, no one goes in my personal space without my say so. And anyway she doesn't look that clean.'

I was horrified. 'What are you talking about? She's got some learning difficulties but she's certainly not dirty. I can't believe you just said that.'

Charlotte shrugged her shoulders and looked away. 'Sorry, but she's your friend, not mine. You might be used to all this, but I'm not.'

I shook my head, disappointed at her attitude but before we could talk further, Martine returned with a tray of steaming cups of coffee to find an uneasy truce between us.

As she set the tray down, she looked from Charlotte to me, not sure what had happened, but aware that something had.

She gave us each a cup of hot, black coffee. 'Sugar? Milk?'

'Yes please,' said Charlotte, taking the sugar bowl from Martine.

'So, Charlotte, you are here for a long weekend, I hear.'

'Yes, just a few days. I can't take too much time off work unfortunately. I work in the film industry, as assistant to a producer.'

'Really? That must be a lot of fun.'

'Yes, it is. I forgot to say,' she turned to me, 'that last job I did has been nominated for a BAFTA. How brilliant is that? I'll be off to the awards next February.'

'Wow, that's great. Well done.'

'Yes, *félicitations,* as we say in France.'

'Thanks,' Charlotte stared down at her cup, still sulking from our earlier *contretemps*. I could have kicked her!

'So,' I quickly interjected, trying to retrieve the situation, 'Martine used to dance at the Moulin Rouge, didn't you Martine?'

'Really,' said Charlotte half-heartedly, 'how exciting.'

'Yes, it was,' the older woman answered. 'Would you like to…'

'Oh, I've got a mobile signal, will you excuse me a minute, I have to go and check on my emails,' Charlotte interrupted, jumping up like a scalded cat.

She rushed out of the room into the garden, where Martine and I could see her talking animatedly on her phone.

I sat awkwardly, sipping my coffee. Every now and again, gales of laughter could be heard coming from the garden as Charlotte glanced over at the house. I had the uncomfortable feeling that she was laughing at us. I seethed inside, not wanting to let Martine see. How could she be so rude? Had I been like that before? So totally self-obsessed?

'She's not like you, is she?' Martine said.

'No, she's not. Not anymore at least,' I replied, leaving the comment hanging in the air.

'Don't worry. From what I've seen of her, I don't think she's the sort of girl who would understand the way we live in the country.'

'I know. I mean, who would turn up in the French countryside in a pair of heels?' I smiled.

Chapter Thirty-two

'Come on, lazybones, get up!' I jumped onto the bed next to Charlotte, shaking her shoulders gently.

'Whaaa? Wassamatter?'

'It's time to get up. Come on, or we'll miss the market.'

Charlotte sat up, rubbing at her eyes and running her hands through her thick, chestnut hair. 'What time is it?'

'It's seven-thirty. Time to shake a leg.'

'Seven-thirty? I'll bloody shake you. What are you doing waking me up so early when I'm on holiday?'

'Well if we don't get to the market by half-past eight all the croissants will be gone. You're in France now. You're having some delicious full-fat croissants for breakfast. None of your boiled grapefruit nonsense.'

'I happen to like grapefruit and, for your information I have never boiled it. Hmm, looks like you've been enjoying one too many croissants yourself.'

I sucked my stomach in. 'It's my French Winter Survival Suit. Just in case I get snowed in. I could survive on my own fat supplies for at least a week. You, on the other hand, would be dead within a day.' I pinched Charlotte's skinny arm. 'Anyway, come on, get moving.'

Forty minutes later, I was at the market with Charlotte trailing behind, still complaining about the fact that she hadn't had time to straighten her hair.

'Oh, for goodness sake, would you stop moaning for five minutes,' I told her firmly as I led her to my favourite fruit and vegetable stall. 'Look at it all, delicious and local.'

'Well, if you call Morocco local,' said Charlotte sniffily, pointing to the board hanging above the oranges, which clearly stated that they came from North Africa.

I rolled my eyes at her and went back to choosing some carrots.

'And it's all muddy. You'd never find it like that in Waitrose.'

'You'd never find it so fresh in Waitrose either. Look at these,' I said pointing to a pile of fresh, dewy lettuce. 'I actually know the lady who grows these. She lives a few miles away. They'll have been picked this morning.'

Charlotte looked unimpressed. I sighed, realising I was flogging a dead *cheval* and carried on with my shopping, ignoring her griping. God, did I use to be like this I wondered?

After an hour of dragging my increasingly irritated and irritating friend around, I gave in. 'Come on, let's go and get a coffee, then we can go home and demolish these croissants.'

'That's the best idea you've had in ages. I don't suppose there is a Starbucks near here?'

'I think its six hundred miles to the nearest one,' I said drily. 'Come on, I'll take you up to the café in the village.'

At the Café du Midi, Claire was busy working behind the bar.

'Oh, hello. I wasn't expecting to see you here today,' she said, looking from me to Charlotte.

'Hi Claire, no Noélia today?' I had quite fancied seeing her try to get the better of Charlotte. 'This is my friend, Charlotte. She's staying for a few days.'

'No, she's er, busy today. Hello, Charlotte, nice to meet you. What can I get you? Why don't you take that table at the back?'

'Actually I think we'll sit by the window so we can watch the world go by.'

Claire looked a bit uncomfortable, not her usual bubbly self, and she kept glancing anxiously towards the window.

'Are you waiting for someone? I asked her.

'No, no, it's fine really.'

I ordered a *grand crème* for Charlotte and a *petit café* for myself. The dreadful Muffy was there sitting at a table with a man I didn't recognise, but whose florid face marked him out as a drinker. They were swilling down the first of what were probably many glasses of red wine and barely bothered to acknowledge me, offering limp handshakes to Charlotte and a half-hearted *bisou* to me as we passed.

'He's cute,' Charlotte whispered to me as she caught sight of Jack through the door to the kitchen.

'And very married, you wouldn't stand a chance with him,' I whispered back.

'Maybe not, but it would be fun trying.' Charlotte thrust out her chest and winked at me.

'Don't even think about it,' I warned.

'So, what do you think of my little corner of France?' I said, changing the subject.

She thought for a moment. 'The thing is, this is all very lovely,' she swept her arm around, taking in the quaint café and the sleepy little village, 'but it's not really you, is it? I mean, you're a London girl. It's all very well playing at being a French peasant and all that, but at some point you've got to go back. You have no job, you say your savings are practically gone. If you are out of the market in the UK for too long you'll never get back in again.'

I worked hard to quell my rising annoyance with her. Charlotte and I had been friends for so long and had barely exchanged a cross word, but I was seeing her through new eyes. How had I not noticed her thoughtlessness? Had she always been so self-centred? Or was it just that I had changed since arriving here? I felt a lump in my throat as I realised that we may never again have the closeness we had once shared.

'Actually Lottie, that's where you are wrong. This is absolutely me. The new me. You know, when I look at you, all I see is how self-centred you are, how judgemental.'

'Judgemental?' Charlotte exploded. 'Me? Judgemental?'

'Keep your voice down, if you don't mind,' I chided her, seeing Muffy's head turn in our direction. 'Yes, judgemental. Look how you were with Martine and Laure yesterday. You treated Laure like she was something nasty you had just stepped in and you couldn't wait to leave. You spent the whole time – when you weren't on the phone that is – looking as if you had a bad smell under your nose. Don't think Martine didn't notice. I was mortified.'

I looked down at my cup of coffee, not meeting Charlotte's eyes. Behind the bar, Claire was bustling around noisily. We were the only people in the café so there was no way that she could have missed the argument. She threw me a sympathetic look.

Charlotte stared out of the window in silence while I quietly fumed. How dare she come over here and criticise my life and my friends? I felt tears stab at the back of my eyes. I had so been looking forward to her visit and so far it was a disaster.

She was the first to break the silence. 'Oh look, a wedding. I wonder who it is?'

I looked out of the window. Sure enough, at the *mairie*, a crowd had gathered, all dressed in their best threads, the men wearing buttonholes.

As we watched, the happy bride and groom appeared on the steps and I gasped. I felt sick and my head started to swim. Charlotte looked at me.

'Oh my God, it's him isn't it?' she said, reaching across to take my hand.

I nodded mutely as Julien leant to kiss his new bride to the cheers of the crowd. At the bar, Claire had stopped what she was doing and was watching me intently, a look of concern on her face. As we watched, the wedding party crossed the square and disappeared into the church for the blessing.

I had convinced myself I was over Julien d'Aubeville but the pain of his treachery was suddenly as raw and new as it had been months before. I noticed he was still limping from the injuries he had received in the fire though he looked every bit the happy groom. Next to him, Jo looked radiant. My grief hit me head on and I bit my lip, trying not to cry.

'Come on, darling,' said Charlotte, 'let's go while they are in the church.'

I shook my head. 'I have to stay,' I whispered.

'Don't torture yourself like this,' she said, 'please, let's just go.'

'No,' I snapped, 'I'm staying here.'

Quietly, Claire slipped a glass of brandy in front of me. 'For the shock. I'm sorry. I should have said something.'

I stared wordlessly at the door of the church through which they had disappeared.

'Thanks,' said Charlotte, realising that I was not going to reply.

Some time later, the bride and groom reappeared on the church steps to the renewed cheers of their guests. They were smiling and laughing for the photographer. Around them, their friends, the same ones who had ignored me for so long, jostled for position in the photographs. I caught sight of Noélia among the guests. Well, that explained a lot. It was the perfect tableau of a French country wedding. A rustic horse and cart, decorated with white ribbons was waiting to whisk them off to wherever they were having their wedding breakfast. Even the pale winter sun had come out to shine on them. The sudden peal of the church bells made me jump. Outside, the happy couple waved to their guests and climbed into their carriage.

I stood up quickly, knocking the chair over, and ran for the door, a maelstrom of emotions churning around inside my head. Charlotte lunged at me across the table but she wasn't quick enough.

'Don't,' she called out to me. I went out and stood on the terrace watching the cart as it turned round in the square, passing right by the café, with Julien sitting on the side nearest me. Jo, busy waving to her friends and family, didn't notice me standing there.

Charlotte appeared next to me and quietly slipped her hand into mine, squeezing it hard. I looked nervously at her. As the cart drew level, Julien looked across in our direction and started slightly when he saw us. I noticed that he did at least have the good grace to look embarrassed although he did try an awkward smile. I watched him, my head following the cart as it made its way past me. Julien shifted uncomfortably in his seat but within seconds he was gone and I was left standing there.

Charlotte put her arm around me. 'You OK?'

'Yes, thanks. I'm fine. Really I am. I just wanted him to acknowledge me.' I felt completely wrung out.

'Come on, let's go home,' said Charlotte, gently taking my arm.

Chapter Thirty-three

'Come on, darling, eat up.' Charlotte placed a plate of croissants in front of me then sat down and poured us both a mug of hot chocolate.

I said nothing but wrapped my hands around the mug and lifted it to my mouth, stopping to blow on it. I still felt shaken. Basil sat on my lap, purring loudly, wondering why I wasn't stroking him. Charlotte buttered a croissant and twisted the top off a jar of apricot jam she had found at the back of cupboard.

'Eww, what are you doing? Growing the cure for the common cold? You got any more jam?'

I shook my head.

She shrugged. 'Nothing for it then.' She spooned out a thick crust of fluffy, green mould and flicked it into the bin.

'It's fine underneath. Don't be such a wimp.'

'She speaks!' smiled Charlotte.

'Oh, ha ha. Come on, pass me the butter. You have to feed a broken heart don't you? Or is it a cold? Or a fever? Oh well, let's just feed all three.'

We ate in silence, both lost in our own thoughts; I thought about the events of the morning, aware that Charlotte was watching me surreptitiously, quietly concerned for me. Finally, she broke the silence.

'So what now?'

'What do you mean, what now?'

'Well, you can't stay here can you? Not now.'

'Why not?' I snapped.

She came round the table and sat down next to me, putting her arm round my shoulder.

'You gave it your best shot but this isn't living the dream, with your ex-boyfriend and his new wife just down the road. You'll be running into them all the time. Are you strong enough for that? And what happens when the cottage is sold? You need to be back at home where we can all take care of you, not stuck here in the middle of nowhere with a bunch of wine-soaked expats.'

I got up, picking up Basil and cuddling his soft, warm body to me and went to the window. From there I could look out over my beloved valley, not looking its best it was fair to say, but still beautiful to me. In spite of everything, I couldn't really imagine being anywhere else.

'Lottie, I know you don't understand but I love this place. I've changed so much since I moved here that I hardly recognise the person I was. I think I'm much more self-reliant, much less consumer-driven. I feel like I've got back in touch with the real me.'

'Oh stop, you're sounding like one of those dreadful self-help websites.'

'You can laugh, but honestly, I think I've realised how unimportant most of the crap in my old life was. Who needs hundreds of pairs of shoes and a diet of reality television and talent shows? Here I live in flip-flops in the summer and wellies in the winter and I have time to read now. I've even learnt a new language. Well, more or less. OK, the money is an issue, granted, but I've got my flat on the market. All I need is a buyer.'

'But your savings have nearly run out and you still don't have a proper job. How will you manage?' said Charlotte. 'I'm sorry but I just don't think you are being realistic.'

'Look, I have enough wood to get me through the winter so at least I can keep warm. That was at least one good thing Julien d'Aubeville did before he publicly humiliated me.'

'Yes, shame he couldn't have chopped it up for you.'

'I guess he thought he'd be around to do it for me. Anyway, he left his axe and if he tries to get it back I'll probably embed it in the back of his skull.'

'I'd bloody do that anyway if I were you.'

I turned to look at my friend. 'Come on, let's not argue. You're only here for a few days.'

I slipped my arm around Charlotte's shoulder, feeling rather less confident about the future than I was letting on to her.

'Have you ever noticed that woman in the café looks like a tortoise in a wig? What was her name? Buffy? Fluffy?'

I snorted. 'Muffy. Yeah, she does, doesn't she?' I hugged her. 'Love you, Lottie.'

'I love you too, but I'm worried about you.' There was a catch in her voice as she said it.

'You don't have to, really you don't,' I replied. 'I'm fine here. I'm going to sit the winter out then if nothing changes I promise you, I'll think about coming back. OK?'

'OK. Scout's honour?'

'Scouts? I never even made the Brownies,' I said, 'but yes, Scout's honour.' Charlotte didn't notice that I had my fingers crossed behind my back.

Two days later, we were standing in the queue for check-in at the airport laughing at an older English couple, all beige slacks and half-moon glasses, who were complaining loudly about the unfairness of the queuing system. They had joined a queue only to have their check-in agent disappear for a coffee break minutes before the desk was due to open.

'So how's this going to work then?' the woman demanded loudly to the one remaining check-in agent.

'I'll take one person from each queue,' she replied calmly.

'But that's not fair. We were here long before some of the people in the other queue and they'll check in before us.'

I rolled my eyes at Charlotte. 'Now do you see why I want to stay here?' I whispered. 'For heaven's sake, you're all getting the same flight. It's not going to leave anyone behind.'

A bit later, having checked Charlotte in, we sat in the waiting area flicking through the latest copy of *Hello!* which Charlotte had found in the airport shop. She had spotted Tracey on the cover and we were reading through the interview and looking at the photos of her in her new Malibu home.

'It looks amazing!' I sighed, admiring the opulent décor and the infinity pool surrounded by palm trees.

'Oh look,' Charlotte squealed, 'she mentions you. Well I suppose it's you.'

'Where?' I said, grabbing the magazine from her.

'Here, look. "Interviewer – You famously appeared in the tabloids fighting with another British woman outside your home in France. What was the real story behind that?" That's you isn't it?'

'Sadly, it is. What did she say?'

Charlotte read aloud. '"It was just a misunderstanding. We went on to become good friends. Interviewer – Are you still in contact with her? Tracey Tarrant – Sadly no." Sadly no, eh? You *should* get in touch with her.'

'Oh, I don't know,' I replied, 'she's moved on now. I doubt she'll ever even come back to France.'

'Well I think you should.' She paused to listen to an announcement. 'Oh, that's me. I've got to go.'

We stood up and flung our arms around each other, hugging each other tight.

'I'll miss you, Lottie,' I whispered into her ear.

'Me too. Take care, you.' Charlotte's eyes glistened with tears.

'Oh don't or you'll set me off. Go on, you don't want to miss your plane.'

I stood watching her go, waving until she disappeared from view, trying to ignore the lump in my throat. I was sad that she was going, not sad that she was going back to the life I had left behind. Despite all that had happened with Julien, I was still right where I wanted to be. I turned to leave but then stopped and thought for a moment.

'Nothing lost,' I told myself, then got out my phone and composed a text to Tracey.

> 'Hey Trace, remember me? Just reading about you in *Hello!* So glad it's all worked out for you. Would love to hear from you. X'

As I walked back to the car, my phone binged to tell me that I had a text. I grabbed it from my pocket, surprised that Tracey had got back to me so quickly, especially with the time difference, but it was from Charlotte.

> 'Guess what? Ground staff held the bolshie woman and husband back at the gate saying there was a problem with their passports then didn't let them on till last. There is a God! Xxx'

Chapter Thirty-four

'So this is the lounge. It's a lovely light room in the summer and it's great to be able to just step through the door and go into the pool when the weather's hot. Not that it's easy to imagine at the moment!' I laughed.

It was the first viewing I'd had in weeks. The rush of prospective buyers in the autumn had dwindled to nothing, which was probably just as well, because St Amans remained resolutely shrouded in heavy mist, often for days on end. The landscape was a wintry symphony in brown. Brown fields were presided over by bare brown trees. The house felt damp, the clothes in my cupboard felt damp, even my bed felt damp. It was a kind of raw, unloved cold that got right into your bones.

'Hmm,' said the morbidly obese American who was looking around the house. So far, she had said very little about anything, just walked around with a look on her face that barely concealed her lack of conviction. I had become quite adept at spotting which ones were genuine buyers and which ones were tyre-kickers. This particular one I had put firmly in the tyre-kicker category.

'So, what do you think? Is it what you are looking for?' I asked.

'Well,' answered the woman in a nasal East Coast drawl, 'it's real sweet but I need to speak to my husband and family about it. I don't know if they want to move to France yet.'

I resisted the urge to kick the woman myself for wasting my time.

She eventually left, promising to speak to her unsuspecting family and assuring me that she would be in touch with Madame Mollet soon. I advised Madame Mollet not to hold her breath.

I decided to head up to the café for a coffee and a chat with Claire and Stéphane. They were still trying to sell it and we had had a good laugh swapping notes on prospective buyers.

Getting into the car, which Julien had had the decency not to take back from me, I headed down the hill in the thick pea-souper. I had done this trip so many times that I thought I could probably do it with my eyes closed, which was just as well as I could barely see past the bonnet of the car. I wondered when the fog would lift. It had been hanging around for weeks now, with only the briefest of breaks. Having safely navigated my way up to the village and parked in the square, I made a point of not looking at the church. Julien's betrayal still hurt me.

Seeing no lights shining through the gloom from the café, I quietly cursed my luck. Out of season, opening hours were a bit of a lottery but usually they were open at lunchtime. As I approached, I could see that the café was definitely closed. The shutters were tightly locked and there were no lights on either upstairs in Claire and Stéphane's apartment or downstairs in the bar.

'They've gone,' called Claudine, who was shutting up her shop for lunch.

'Gone where?'

'To their family in the south.'

'Oh, how long for?'

'For good.'

'What?' I was stunned. I walked over to Claudine, kissing her on both cheeks. 'When?'

'They left yesterday. There were still no buyers for the café and they decided to cut their losses and go.'

'But I didn't even get a chance to say goodbye.'

'Well, they are quite private people and didn't want a lot of fuss. They have left all their furniture there until they find a buyer so I guess they will be back at some point to say goodbye.'

'I can't imagine the village without the café. It feels like it has lost its heart.'

'You had better go and tell that lot,' said Claudine, pointing to a little clutch of people who were milling around the closed café. Chummy and Rodders were there with a few other people who seemed to spend most days there.

'Better had. God knows what that little lot will do now.'

I walked across the square to the café, calling out a greeting to Chummy and Rodders.

'What's happening, eh? Any ideas?' asked Chummy, looking rather like a polar bear in a very politically incorrect fur coat and matching hat.

'Yes, the café has closed down. Stéphane and Claire have left to go and live with their family in the south.'

'What?'

'Yes, apparently it's closed until a new buyer can be found. Claudine just told me.'

A murmur of disbelief spread through the little group.

'But what about my lunch?' she demanded.

'Well, I guess you'll have to make your own.'

Rodders chortled. 'Chummy cook? My dear, she hasn't cooked anything herself since she made a bacon sandwich in 1978,' he wheezed.

'Sorry, I'm just the messenger,' I replied. I wouldn't put it past Chummy to ask me to cook her lunch for her.

With nothing else to do, I decided to head back to the cottage. If the *Météo* was to be believed, heavy snowfalls were on their way, and it was cold, really cold. The cottage was well insulated with foot-thick walls keeping the worst of the cold at bay, but it had no central heating. I had to keep the wood burner in the lounge going full blast which meant logs, and lots of them. I had an important date with my axe.

Later, as I struggled through the door with a basket laden with chopped logs, the phone began to ring.

I stamped the mud off my boots and went to answer it.

'Good, you're there,' boomed the not so dulcet tones of Chummy.

'Yes.' The woman had a real knack for stating the obvious. 'Hi Chummy, did you find somewhere to have lunch?'

'Yes, went to that new Moroccan place in town. Best *Couscous Royale* I've had in years. Anyway, meant to ask you earlier but forgot with all the kerfuffle over the café. I'm organising a little skiing party to the Pyrénées. Shall I count you in?'

'Well Chummy, I'm a bit strapped for cash...'

The older woman interrupted me. 'Don't worry about that. We've borrowed a chalet belonging to an old school friend of Rodders. No charge. He owes us a few favours. You can drive down with us. CeeCee is coming too so you won't just be stuck with the old fogies. She's got some spare kit so don't worry about that either.'

'Err...' I had never quite caught the skiing bug, although I'd been once, years ago with an old school friend and twisted my knee on the second day which had been the end of my skiing. And I also knew that the chances of me fitting into one of CeeCee's ski suits were small, unlike my backside.

'Marvellous. We're leaving on Friday at midday, back Sunday.'

'Well...' The line went dead. 'Well, that's that then,' I said to Basil, picking him up and stroking his soft, downy head, 'better see if Martine can feed you and the chooks.' I looked through the window at my hens standing by the back door like giant powder puffs with all their feathers fluffed up against the cold. I almost felt like letting them in but their ability to poo often and without prior warning made them very unsuitable for indoor living. Plenty of corn and extra straw would have to do.

Sitting pale-faced in the back of Rodders' car, my hands gripped the armrest on one side and the handle of the door on the other until my knuckles were white. Outside, a sheer drop fell away as far as I could see as we wound our way up the mountain road.

We had arrived late the previous night at our ski chalet in a little town in the foothills of the mountains. Before we left, I had heard talk of snow chains and winter tyres so when we arrived, having driven there on major roads with little sign of snow, I had thought it was just bluster.

Now, as we wound our way up the mountain, past all the signs saying that snow chains were compulsory and teams of *gendarmes* were checking that everyone complied, and with the chains making the car feel as if it was driving over cobbles, I was starting to feel slightly sick. The constant juddering as we drove on the chains was threatening to rattle my teeth out of my head. The others, all seasoned skiers, didn't seem bothered.

'You'd think they would put crash barriers up at the side of the road, wouldn't you?' I said in a shaky voice.

'Don't you worry, girl, we'll be fine,' Rodders replied. 'Feeling a little stressed are we?'

'No, no I'm fine.'

'She doesn't look it,' commented CeeCee, 'she's definitely a bit green.'

'Honestly, I'm fine,' I told her, tightening my grip on the door handle as the back of the car slid slightly round a corner.

'Come on girl, man up. Rodders has driven in far worse places than this. We're in the hands of an expert.'

'In any case,' continued Rodders, 'if we go over the edge, there's precious little point in hanging on to the door. We'll all be goners.'

Rodders grinned, gunning the engine to make the wheels spin. I smiled weakly.

'Thanks for that,' I said and went back to clinging on for dear life.

As we climbed higher, the snow deepened, until I became aware of skiers on the slopes at the side of the road. The deep ravines appeared to have gone, to be replaced by huge open snowfields. Despite my reservations, I was starting to feel quite excited about skiing again. And here it was, almost on my doorstep.

Rodders pulled into a car park near the bottom of the chair lift and we all bundled out of the car. The resort was tiny. Just a car park, a restaurant and a ski-hire shop, but the slopes looked perfect. Wide and treeless. Just how I wanted them.

CeeCee had lent me one of her old ski suits and, while in my London days I might have fitted easily into it, with my new fuller figure, I had to be shoehorned in and sitting down made my lips go slightly blue. It didn't help that it was a retina-burning lime green either. There was no chance of losing me in a white-out.

Rodders and Chummy had their own boots and skis so CeeCee and I stomped across the snow to the ski-hire shop to get ourselves kitted out.

'How much do you weigh, *mademoiselle*?' asked the handsome, shaggy-haired ski-bum in the shop. I blushed slightly. 'It is so we get the bindings on your skis right,' he continued. 'If they are not set up right, your boot may get stuck in your ski or else it will keep falling out.'

'Er, in kilos?'

'Yes, kilos.'

I did a quick calculation in my head then subtracted a few kilos. Quite a few. Was it my imagination or did he give me a disbelieving look?

'How are you getting on?' asked CeeCee, all legs and pert behind in a stunning, baby-pink ski suit. I felt like her frumpy older sister and unconsciously pulled in my stomach. Sorted out with our boots and skis we set off for the slopes.

'God, how are you supposed to carry these things?' I said struggling out of the hire shop with my skis. 'It's like juggling spaghetti.' They kept twisting out of my grip as I stumbled across the icy ground, my hard plastic boots threatening to slide out from under me at any moment.

'You'll get used to them,' she said unhelpfully. 'Come on, let's go and book you in at the Ski School.'

Despite its name, the Ski School turned out to be a little booth, built like a miniature Swiss chalet, and manned by a clone of the assistant in the ski shop. CeeCee flirted outrageously with him, leaving me feeling once again like the ugly sister. Determined not to be outdone this time, I tried fluttering my eyelashes at him but he just looked at me, slightly alarmed. He booked me onto a beginner's class and CeeCee into an intermediate one, then relieved me of twenty euros for an hour of skiing lessons and told me to be back in thirty minutes for the start of the lesson with Jean-Christophe, my ski instructor.

CeeCee wanted to get in some practice before her lesson, so we arranged to meet for lunch. She waved goodbye and headed off to the ski lift, while I planted my skis in the snow outside the café and went to find an outside table where I could watch the slopes and have a *grand crème* until my lesson started.

Tilting my head back to feel the warmth of the sun on my face, the sky was a perfect unbroken blue and the nip in the air contrasted with the feeling of the sun. It felt glorious. I was starting to understand how people could get so hooked on the mountains.

I sipped on my coffee as I watched the skiers coming down the run and after a few minutes, saw what could only be Chummy coming ponderously down the slope in long sweeping arcs. She reminded me of a battle cruiser negotiating an iceberg field. Behind her Rodders seemed to think he was in a James Bond film and was heading straight down the slope at a cracking pace and whooping loudly. As he got closer and closer, he seemed to pick up speed until I put my hands over my eyes, waiting for the sound of bone splintering as he hit something at the bottom.

'You all right, girl?'

I peeped out from behind my hands. 'Oh, Rodders, yes, I'm fine. You were going a bit fast weren't you? I thought you might break something.'

'Not me. Alpine ski rescue with the army in my younger days. Bit of a specialist if I say so myself. When's your lesson?'

'In a few minutes actually. I'd better get going.'

'It's like riding a bike,' he said heartily, clapping me on the back.

'Yes, well I've fallen off a good few of those in my time.'

'Well, have fun. Don't break anything. Has CeeCee made arrangements for lunch?'

'Yes, here at one.'

'Marvellous!'

He skated off towards the ski lift, ready for his second battle with the mountain.

I left the money for my coffee on the table and went to retrieve my skis. There were twice as many there now and it seemed that most of them had come from the same ski shop as they were identical. I walked up and down the line, looking at them all, before making an educated guess at which were my pair. Taking the coward's way out, I walked to the ski school, passing CeeCee setting off for her lesson with a gorgeous instructor in skin-tight ski pants. She waved and gave me a thumbs up sign.

Reporting at the ski school, I was told that my instructor had been delayed but would be there any minute. There didn't seem to be anyone else in my lesson. After a few minutes a loud, deep voice boomed out, *'Bonjour mademoiselle, j'arrive.'*

I turned to see a rather plump, middle-aged man whose ski pants were only marginally looser than my own. A rather pendulous belly hung over the top of them and his jacket barely did up round his girth. He shook my hand vigorously and babbled on at me in warp-speed French, his bushy moustache wobbling on his upper lip as he did so.

'I'm sorry, I didn't quite catch that,' I told him.

'Ah, *une anglaise.* Hello. I am Jean-Christophe. You can call me JC. How are you? I am very well.' He beamed at me, sounding like a comedy Frenchman.

'Me too. I'm really looking forward to this.'

'Only little English,' he said, shrugging his shoulders, palms turned upwards. It looked like my French skiing vocabulary was about to be sorely tested. He motioned at me to put on my skis. I placed them carefully in the snow in front of me before sliding the toe of my boot into the binding. As soon as I did so, it became apparent that I had the wrong skis. The bindings were way too loose.

'I don't think these are mine,' I told him in my best French. 'I must have taken someone else's from outside the restaurant. I'll just go back and have a look.'

It didn't take long to find my skis. A tall and very cross-looking man was swearing loudly as he tried to ram his feet into ski bindings that were clearly too small for his boots.

'Monsieur?' I said tapping him on the shoulder. He turned and glared at me. 'I think I took yours by mistake,' and held them out

to him. He looked at me briefly, snatched them and hurled them on the ground before thrusting his boots into the bindings and skiing off without so much as a backward glance.

'Parisian,' said JC, in much the say way as you would say 'mass murderer'.

I clicked my boots into their bindings then turned to JC. 'I'm ready.'

He led me to the bottom of the ski lift, skating on his skis like an ice skater while I followed behind as best I could, shuffling my skis along the ground. I watched carefully as the lift attendant helped each skier to place a T-shaped bar carefully behind their legs which dragged them slowly up to the top of the ski run.

Nervously, I followed JC to the head of the queue and waited for the next T-bar to come round.

'You go first, I will follow,' he told me. He whispered something to the attendant, which I took to mean that there was a complete skiing dunce coming up. The T-bar came round and the attendant passed it to me, helping me to get it in position. The bar was on a cable which in turn was attached to a long spring. It pulled taut until it could go no further then launched me up the slope.

I screamed as I took off on one leg and struggled to right myself. Behind me JC shouted instructions but I was so busy trying to stay upright that I couldn't hear what he said. By some miracle of gravity, I got my weight central, breathing a sigh of relief as I sat back against the bar. JC hadn't thought to tell me that it was only intended to pull me along, not take my weight. As I started to sit back on it, the cable got longer and longer until I was practically crouching.

'JC!' I screamed. 'What do I do?'

'Push down into your skis and stand up,' he called.

Despite months of using my Turkish toilet, my thighs weren't up to the job and slowly and very inelegantly, I rolled off the lift, ending up flat on my back in the snow, just as JC was dragged past me. A few metres further up, he let go of the T-bar and skied back down to me.

I lay in the snow and looked up at him, my thighs burning from the effort of trying to keep my balance.

'Hard work this skiing lark,' I said as he reached a hand down to help me up.

Having assured him I knew how to do a passable snowplough, I pushed my skis out into a V-shape to slow down my descent and set off for a second go at the drag lift.

This time, I was ready for it. I relaxed and let the T-bar pull me slowly up the mountain while JC shouted instructions from behind me. I even felt confident enough to have a look round at the scenery. The higher we got, the more stunning the scenery was. It opened out as far as I could see onto a white expanse of snow-capped mountains, dotted with colourful stick figures weaving down the *pistes*. Now, having mastered the 'getting on' bit, all I had to do was sort out the 'getting off'. Up ahead, I could see the end of the lift so I concentrated on what everyone else was doing. It didn't look too difficult. You got to the end, conveniently signposted, unhooked the T-bar from behind your legs and skied off, your sticks in your hand, onto the main run. All of which was fine if you could steer, ski without poles and keep your balance, none of which I was showing a particular aptitude for.

My stomach was in knots as the end of the lift approached. A conveniently placed sign told me when to let go and a small child on the T-bar in front of me safely negotiated the dismount. How difficult could it be? I braced myself for the moment and as I drew level with the sign, I unhooked the T-bar, pushed it away and made my way rather unsteadily onto the run.

'Bien fait,' called JC, congratulating me as he pulled up next to me in a spray of snow. 'Are you ready?'

'Ready as ever,' I replied nervously.

I felt my heart start to soar as I took in the view from the top of the run. Snow-capped mountains spread out as far as I could see. In places, clouds had attached themselves to the sides and hung like flags. It was like the top of an old-fashioned chocolate box. There was nothing like a bit of natural beauty to lift my spirits. A smile spread slowly across my face and for the first time in weeks, the heartache of 'The Julien Affair' as I now called it, was forgotten.

We set off in long, sweeping traverses across the run, with me following in JC's ski tracks. The run was wide and not too steep and mercifully free of trees. After a while, I started to relax and enjoy myself. I was happy just to mooch along slowly in a nice wide snowplough, leaving the youngsters to whizz down the slopes at breakneck speed even if it was a little disconcerting to be overtaken by a five-year old.

At the bottom, I felt exhilarated. The Queen of the Ski had conquered the slopes. I had never really been one for sport but this was so much fun. I loved the feel of the sun on my face contrasting with the snow all around me and the feeling that I was doing something healthy and outdoors. Letting my mind run away, I saw myself zipping down the black runs, skis together, legs working hard, jumping moguls, hair flying in the wind. I was also about 20 pounds lighter but enough of that.

'Well done,' said JC enthusiastically. 'You are a natural.'

I somehow doubted that but I smiled anyway. We set off up the slope again, this time managing to get on the drag lift first time. The run wasn't very long but with each descent I felt my confidence growing. The ski bug was starting to bite, which made a nice change from the mosquitoes.

The hour seemed to pass in minutes and just as I was really starting to get into it, the lesson was over and I was saying goodbye to JC with a promise to arrange another lesson soon. I took off my skis and headed to the café to meet the others, being careful to make a mental note of where I left them this time.

CeeCee was already there, sitting by an open fire, nibbling on a bread roll. 'I do wish they'd give you butter as well,' she moaned to me.

'Good morning's skiing?' I asked.

'Yes, not bad. No one very interesting in my group though. How about you?'

'No one in my group at all except me.'

'Well, you'll be an expert before long then.'

'Hmm, I don't know about that but I enjoyed it.'

'Do you fancy coming up with me this afternoon?'

'I don't know. Maybe. You're a lot better than me.'

'Hello girls,' boomed Chummy coming through the door like a whirlwind and stomping across the restaurant towards us. In her bright red ski suit she looked like an overripe tomato. Collapsing onto a chair, she stretched her chubby legs out in front of her.

'I'm parched. Get me a *vin chaud* will you CeeCee? You should try one,' she said to me, 'bit like mulled wine. Just the thing after a morning on the slopes.'

'Anyone else want one?' said CeeCee, getting up.

'Sounds lovely,' I replied, 'I'd definitely like to try one.'

A blast of cold air heralded the arrival of Rodders, ruddy-faced from the cold.

'*Vin chaud*, Dad?' asked CeeCee.

'Bloody marvellous. Just what the doctor ordered.'

He sat down next to me, patting my knee. 'Good skiing?'

'Well, more snowploughing than skiing,' I smiled.

'Never mind, you'll be schussing with the best of us soon.'

'No doubt,' I replied, wondering what schussing was.

'Right,' said Rodders, 'what's for lunch?'

He picked up the menu and looked through it. 'Looks like chips with everything. The choices are *steak haché* and chips, chicken and chips or omelette and chips, with a bit of lettuce on the side to make it healthy.'

I didn't really fancy anything but the others gave their orders to the waitress and we chatted about our respective mornings, sipping on the *vin chaud* until the food arrived.

'This stuff is really nice,' I said, pouring myself another glass of *vin chaud* from the big jug that CeeCee had put on the table.

'Steady on, girl, it's more potent than it looks,' said Rodders.

'Better get yourself some blotting paper,' said Chummy. Dutifully, I ordered a plate of chips, and picked at them as I felt the warmth of the hot wine flood my body. It made me feel all snug and cosy inside. I bent down to unclip my boots, pulling my feet out and wiggling my toes to get the circulation flowing again. Then I stretched them out in front of the fire and leant back in my chair, my glass of wine resting on my knee.

'Yes,' I announced to the table, 'I could get into this skiing business. Thanks so much for bringing me.'

'Our pleasure, dear,' said Chummy. 'You've not had an easy time of it recently,' her voice softened as she spoke.

I looked down and chewed on my bottom lip. 'No, I haven't, have I?' I looked up at Chummy as I spoke and smiled at her. A lot of people couldn't stand the woman but I knew that under that hard-nosed exterior, beat a heart of, well, maybe not gold, but certainly some sort of semi-precious metal.

'Anyway, that's all ancient history now. Onward and upwards, eh?' said Rodders.

'So, are you coming with me this afternoon?' asked CeeCee as we finished lunch.

'No, but thanks. I think I need to get a bit more practice with JC if he's free. Maybe tomorrow?'

Rodders paid the bill, refusing to take any money from me and they headed off to the slopes leaving me to finish the *vin chaud* and wait for the ski school to open again.

'See you back here at four then,' called CeeCee as she left.

I sat quietly, enjoying the relative peace of the café. Almost everyone had gone skiing for the afternoon and there was only me left and a young girl with a broken leg who clearly wasn't going anywhere.

I looked at my watch. Quarter to two. I downed the last of my drink and got up to go and find my skis.

As I clomped across the room, I felt a little bit light-headed. Probably just the heat of the fire, I thought to myself but the cold air that hit me as I stepped outside made me feel positively dizzy. Maybe skipping lunch wasn't such a good idea.

I located my skis and pushed my boots into them, forgetting as I did so to re-fasten the clips that I'd undone in the café. The moment I tried to ski away from the café I discovered that I had no control at all over my skis and with a thud, fell over backwards, winding myself. I lay for a moment, staring up at the blue sky, struggling for breath until a face suddenly blocked my view. It was an elderly French woman who looked far too old to be skiing. She looked down on me with concern.

'*Ça va?*' She asked.

'Yes, *oui*, I'm OK, *merci*,' I replied, mixing up my languages.

The woman reached out for my hand and helped me sit up. I put my head on my knees for a moment, slowly regaining my breath, then tried to stand up but with my boots still undone my skis just kept sliding out from beneath me. The woman, who was both small and very slight in build, tried her best to haul me up on to my feet. I was making a beached whale look positively graceful and after another struggle, I admitted defeat and sat back down.

'*Mademoiselle...*' a strong, tanned hand appeared and I looked up into a pair of stunning blue eyes.

Just my bloody luck, I thought. A gorgeous man appears on the scene and I'm floundering around in the snow like an ice-skating hippopotamus. I unconsciously sucked in my stomach again.

He bent down to fasten my boots, chatting as he did to the elderly lady. I didn't catch all that he said but he definitely mentioned novice skiers and I'm almost certain he said *régime*. I blushed scarlet, making a mental pact to cut out the croissants and start the diet, again.

Thanking them for their help, I skied off to the ski school to book in another lesson with JC.

He greeted me warmly with a big, loud kiss on each cheek and we set off, this time for the chair lift. At least I couldn't fall off that – I hoped. By the end of the lesson I was almost feeling confident. I had nearly mastered the parallel stop, though it was more out of self-preservation than anything else when I found myself heading, ever so slightly out of control, towards the queue for a lift. The looks on the faces of my fellow skiers, as they dived for safety in a torrent of French abuse, would be imprinted on my memory for a long time to come.

As the sun started to dip behind the mountains and the temperature dropped noticeably, a *chocolat chaud* in the café at the bottom was calling me. We did one last leisurely run back to the ski school and I bid goodbye to JC, promising to come back again. He skied off into the sunset, literally, and I kicked off my skis and headed into the café to wait for the others. I didn't have to wait long before CeeCee made her appearance in a whirlwind of pink ski suit and sunglasses.

'Hey there, did you have a good afternoon?'

'Great! I'm so glad I came. How about you?'

'Very good. You're not doing anything tonight are you?'

'Only thing planned is a hot bath, why?'

'I've organised a little bit of *après-ski* entertainment for us. It's about time you got back into circulation again. Can't be nursing that broken heart forever, you know.'

I smiled. 'You know, I think you are right. A good night out is just what I need.'

Chapter Thirty-five

'Urrggh,' I groaned as the sun fell across my face, waking me from a drink-induced sleep. The night out with CeeCee had been huge fun. Dinner then a nightclub, the first one I had been to since arriving in France.

Gradually, as the fog started to lift, snippets of the evening began to come back to me. I rather wished they wouldn't. I had turned into one of the people that my ultra-cool friends and I used to laugh at. The sort of people that would come up from the country and go a little bit mad, generally making fools of themselves, knocking back vast quantities of alcohol.

I had vague recollections of jiving with someone, I couldn't quite picture his face. My jiving was only slightly better than my line dancing and I could recall little other than being thrown around in ever more extravagant dance moves until I had started to feel sick.

CeeCee had got off with some tall, blonde god-like creature and made an early exit, leaving me dancing with a group of French students from Toulouse University. I felt practically old enough to be their mother but they were a good laugh, gently teasing me about my accent. One of them had tried to get me to go back to his chalet but I had declined, choosing instead to stay at the club and drink some more and bump and grind with all manner of strangers until the early hours.

I had staggered home, helped along by Kéving, one of the students. All the lovely French names there were and his parents called him Kéving. The French, I had found out, loved to give their children English names, but invariably they chose the names that the English had given up years ago. I had met several Brians and Kévins, but this was doubly tragic as his parents had clearly misheard the name and added a 'g' on the end. I had vague memories of him trying to kiss me and asking if he could come inside. What happened next was lost in the alcohol mist, but I was fairly sure that I had sent him on his way.

The door to the bathroom opened and Kéving walked out, dressed in a towel. I looked at him horrified. I hadn't, had I? Well the evidence was directly in front of me, so clearly, I had. He dropped his towel, standing stark naked in the middle of the room with a rather impressive erection.

'Oh my God, what are you doing?' I hissed at him, leaping out of bed to grab the towel and wrap it round him again. He looked understandably confused.

'How did you..? Oh never mind. I've got to get you out of here.'

I saw his clothes spread across the floor on the other side of the bedroom and hastily ran round, gathering them up in my arms before shoving them at him and turning him round, pushing him back into the bathroom.

'Get dressed,' I ordered him.

There was a knock at the door. 'Tea,' called Chummy, pushing it open without being asked.

I slammed the bathroom door, telling Kéving wordlessly not to make a sound.

'So how are you this morning?' Chummy asked, putting the tea down on the bedside table.

'Yes, I'm fine, good. How about you?'

'Yes, I'm fine too. Tired after the skiing but well rested. We plan to leave around midday today so we aren't too late home.'

'Great. Yes. OK.' I replied.

There was a bang in the bathroom and a muttered '*putain*'.

'What was that?' Chummy asked.

'Oh, nothing, probably just something falling over in the bathroom. I'm dreadfully untidy.'

I noticed a stray pair of men's blue boxers on the floor and pushed them under the bed with my foot.

'Well, breakfast is in twenty minutes then we'll pop you and CeeCee back to the ski shop to return your skis.'

'OK. I'll be ready.'

'You can come out now,' I whispered through the bathroom door to Kéving, having waited a few minutes after Chummy left to make sure the coast was clear.

He came out, fully dressed but minus his underwear, looking confused.

'Look, I don't know how this happened, but I'm a guest in their chalet so I shouldn't be bringing strange men back for sex.'

Clearly this was something that didn't figure in the French psyche. Kéving started to protest but I shut him up.

'Look, I've got to get you out of here without anyone seeing you.'

I opened the door a crack and peered through onto the landing. There was no sign of anyone. From downstairs, the sound of voices could be heard from the kitchen and I strained my ears to hear if everyone was there. I couldn't miss Chummy's voice, which could probably be heard in Spain and the low growl of Rodders' voice confirmed he was there too. CeeCee, if she had come home, would no doubt still be sleeping off the mother of all hangovers.

Kéving was standing looking dejected in the middle of the room, his boots in his hand.

I beckoned, motioning him to be quiet, then quickly led him out onto the landing. I stopped at the top of the stairs and listened again. Rodders and Chummy were still in the kitchen and from my room it was a straight run down the stairs to the front door. I tiptoed down, beckoning Kéving to follow me, wincing every time a stair creaked and at the bottom, held up my hand to stop him, and listened again. Chummy was reading out some hysterical story about immigrants from an English tabloid newspaper she had got her hands on. That would keep her occupied for hours.

I waved Kéving on again. We were nearly home and dry. I carefully pushed down on the handle of the door, praying it wasn't locked, but the planets were aligned. The door opened soundlessly and a rush of wintry air blew round my bare legs and I quickly pushed Kéving outside, still in his socks. He turned to say something to me but I put my hand across his mouth.

'Has someone left a bloody door open again?' boomed Chummy. I heard a chair being pushed back from the table and quickly shut the door on Kéving before bolting for the stairs again. I took them two at a time and had practically reached the top by the time Chummy hove into view. She looked up at me.

'Not dressed yet? Come on, lazybones. Can you call CeeCee for me?'

'Sorry, yes of course. I won't be a minute.'

Chummy returned to her 'state of the nation' discussion with Rodders in the kitchen leaving me to slump against the wall, heart pounding and breathing like a steam train. I composed myself then headed to CeeCee's bedroom to wake her up.

Later, with my stomach filled with bacon sandwiches and coffee, I went upstairs to finish packing. I wandered round the bedroom, retrieving make-up and toiletries from the bathroom and damp socks from the radiator and stuffing them carelessly into my holdall.

Downstairs, CeeCee was begrudgingly running round with the vacuum cleaner while Rodders tidied up the kitchen. Chummy had drawn the short straw and was on boot room and toilet duty.

Once Chummy was happy that the chalet was left as we had found it, CeeCee and I bundled our suitcases into the car while Rodders strapped the skis to the roof.

'I'll just do a quick whizz round to make sure we haven't forgotten anything,' said Chummy. 'I know what CeeCee is like.'

I settled myself in the back with a book for the journey, while Rodders tried to tune the radio into anything that wasn't white noise or crackle.

After a few minutes Chummy reappeared and turned to lock the front door. In her hand I caught a flash of blue fabric.

'Oh shit,' I said under my breath, remembering Kéving's boxers that I had left under the bed.

'What is it?' CeeCee asked me.

'Damning evidence.'

'Yours I think,' Chummy said, handing them to me.

'Look, I'm sorry, I can explain…' I stammered.

'Nothing to explain,' she replied, no hint of annoyance in her voice at the liberties her young guest had taken. 'You want to wear boy's pants, that's your business. Look pretty comfortable to me.'

CeeCee stifled a giggle and I kicked her hard.

'Right chaps, ready to go,' said Rodders, looking at everyone in the rear view mirror.

'Ready,' we said in unison.

I smiled at CeeCee and made a gesture of wiping my brow before settling back for the journey.

L'AMOUR ACTUALLY

As we started our slow descent of the mountain, I rested my head on the window and reflected on the past few days. I wasn't really the 'one night stand' type but surely the fact that I'd had one meant I was definitely moving on from Julien. I was certainly thinking less and less about him and when I did, the all-consuming pain I had felt a while ago seemed less acute. A weekend of skiing and a one night stand were no real cure for a broken heart, but they didn't seem to have done me any harm.

Chapter Thirty-six

'Shit, shit, shit,' I shouted to the empty barn flinging the axe so hard that it hit the far wall, throwing up a spray of stone chips.

I had spent the past two hours trying to split wood for the wood burner. It was like reinforced steel and the pile was depressingly small. On top of that, I had blisters on my palms. The snow had lain thick on the ground like a vast white overcoat for the past week and St Amans had been largely cut off as the temperature dipped to minus twelve during the day. Even with the wood burner running full blast 24/7, I had been sleeping in a coat and gloves. On the third day, the pumps running the water up to the hamlet had frozen and the taps had run dry. Today, thankfully, it felt noticeably warmer.

'This is supposed to be a bloody First World country,' I shouted again, stomping over to pick up the axe and attack the wood again, 'and here I am chopping wood and melting snow for water like some bloody medieval peasant.'

I lifted the axe over my head and swung it viciously at the log, hitting a knot in the wood so the axe vibrated painfully up my arms to my hands. In the cottage the phone rang and grateful for something else to do apart from chop wood, I rushed to answer it.

'Oh, Madame Mollet, how are you?' I said when I heard the estate agent's voice on the line. 'Do you have some more viewings lined up?'

'No, actually I have phoned to tell you that we have found a buyer for Les Tuileries.'

My stomach lurched. From what she had said, houses often took years to sell in France so I had never actually thought it would happen while I was still living there.

'A buyer? Well, um, that's good news for Monsieur Marin, I suppose. So what happens next? What sort of timescale are we looking at?'

'I have emailed you a letter giving you one months' notice of the termination of your tenancy agreement.'

'One month!' I felt my stomach hit the floor. 'I thought the agreement said three months?'

'I'm sorry, but if you read it again you will see that in the case of a sale of the property the landlord has the right to give only one month. I will bring a copy of the letter to you as soon as I can, but I wanted to make sure you knew as early as possible.'

I opened up my laptop and clicked on the email from Madame Mollet. It was there in black and white. I had one month to leave my beloved cottage and find somewhere else to live.

'Well, that's that then.'

'I'm sorry,' Madame Mollet said. 'You have been a good tenant.'

'Do you have anything else on your books that might suit me?'

'I'm afraid not. I don't really do that many rentals, just for some long-standing clients.'

'Right,' I said abruptly. I knew this day would eventually come, but now it had, it felt like a bereavement.

'Well, I must go. I will see you soon.'

'Right,' I replied.

'Goodbye, *mademoiselle*.'

'Goodbye.'

I sat down on the sofa. For once in my life, I had no idea what my next step would be. Should I stay in France? Could I stay in France? I had been clinging on by my fingertips for the last few months. Maybe it was a sign that I should give up this particular dream. The thing was, I really didn't want to. But then, what choice did I have? I had no money, my flat in London wasn't selling; I would shortly have no home, I had no job and my love life was in tatters. My life sounded like a second-rate country music song.

My phone beeped to signal the arrival of a text. It was from Charlotte.

'Living it up at the Baftas. Lots of people asking after you. Hope all is good en France. C xxx'

This time last year it would have been me there; glammed up, hair newly cut and highlighted, nails done. I looked at my hands. The blisters had started to bleed and my nails hadn't seen a manicure in months. My feet were clad in muddy wellies and the last time I had tried on a pair of my heels, my feet were too big for them, the end result of months in sandals and flip-flops. Country feet. Outside, I noticed that it had started to rain. At least it would clear the snow but it very much reflected my mood. I sat, staring into space, mentally arguing with myself about my next move. I had always been a fighter. A typical Capricorn, stubborn and unwilling to give in, but for once I felt totally defeated. Whichever way I looked at it, my French dream was surely over.

As the day rolled slowly on towards evening and the light started to fade, I knew that it was time to give up. I had given it my best shot, no one could argue with that. I had arrived in France as a naive London girl, slightly selfish and self-centred, and clearly with no idea what life in a foreign country involved. How far I had come. I now spoke passable French, I knew a fair bit about keeping chickens and had embraced a new culture. I had developed strong and hopefully lasting relationships with my neighbours and for the first time in my life, I felt as if I belonged in a community. It hadn't always been plain sailing and I had made lots of mistakes along the way.

I saw headlights coming down the drive. Probably Madame Mollet with the termination letter. With a heavy heart, I stood up and went to the door. No point in delaying the inevitable.

'*Bonjour*, Madame Mollet,' I said, opening the door. 'That was quick.'

A draught of cold air blew in.

'Bonjour, *mademoiselle*,' she held out a letter, 'your notice of termination.'

I took it wordlessly and shoved it in my pocket.

'Also, I hope you don't mind but I bought the new owner round. She wanted to have a look at the cottage.'

'Well, really you should have asked before. I mean, it's a bit of a mess.' I was faintly irritated by her presumptuousness.

'I'm sure she won't mind,' Madame Mollet said smiling. She stood back and the new owner stepped into the light from the open door.

'Surprise!'

'Tracey? Tracey bloody Tarrant? What the hell are you doing here?'

I didn't know whether to laugh or cry, but before I had a chance to do either, Tracey threw her arms around me, hugging me tightly. Then she stepped back, holding me at arm's length and looked at me.

'Bloody hell, you look pretty shabby. What's happened to you?'

Madame Mollet interrupted, 'If you don't mind, I have business to do in Bussières so I'll leave you to it.'

I led Tracey into the house and sat her down on the sofa.

'Well of all the people in the world, I never expected to see you again. I texted you, you know.'

'I know, I did get it but I was in the studio so I didn't have a chance to reply and then too much time had passed. You know how it is. I was too embarrassed to call you.'

'But not too embarrassed to make me homeless though?'

'Look, I've got so much to tell you.' Tracey looked round the room. 'God, this place would freeze the balls off a polar bear. Why don't you turn the heating on for God's sake?'

'Er, Tracey. Look around you. What's missing from this picture? Radiators maybe?'

'Glad to see that your sarcasm is still alive and kicking.'

'Just one of my many qualities.'

She stood up. 'Come on, grab your coat… oh, you're already wearing it. We're staying at a hotel in Villeneuve. I'll get you a room there and you can come and warm up. My shout. Then I can fill you in on what's happening.'

'We?' I asked.

'Oh shit. I've left him in the car. Hurry up, grab some overnight stuff, he's probably frozen to the steering wheel.'

'This is Nathan.'

'Hi Nathan,' I said, climbing into the back of the BMW four-wheel drive. In the half light I could barely make out his features but his deep, rich American voice, when he greeted me, was warm and friendly.

'So when are you going to tell me what's going on?' I asked as we purred along the road to Villeneuve.

'When you're cleaned up and wearing normal clothes. You look like a bleedin' bag lady. I had no idea you'd let yourself go so much after I left.'

I punched her on the shoulder.

'Ouch. That hurt.'

'No more or less than you deserve, just leaving like that.'

'Yeah, I'm sorry. The thing was, I knew what was going on. You know, with Julien.'

'You knew? How?'

'Remember the time we met his girlfriend, what was her name? Jo, that's it. It was at *la danse country*.' She said the last bit with a ridiculously exaggerated French accent.

'Yes,' I said, curiously.

'Well remember I went out for a fag while you were getting the licence thingies.' She turned to Nathan. 'Can you believe that you have to have a licence to line-dance in France? Imagine how well that would go down with the Good Old Boys back home!'

In the glow of the street lights, I saw his face crinkle into a smile.

'Yes, I remember,' I said.

'Well he was outside picking her up. He had no idea we were there. He nearly crapped his jeans when he saw me.'

'You saw him with her? And you didn't say anything?' I was stunned at the betrayal.

'I tried to, honestly, I really did…'

'Oh my God. The day when the hunting season started?'

'Yes, but I lost my nerve. So where did that leave me? I knew he was cheating on you, and on her, but I couldn't tell you. I felt awful. I couldn't be around you knowing what I did. Then the opportunity came up to go to LA and I jumped at it and I'm glad, otherwise I might not have met Nathan.'

He reached across and grabbed Tracey's hand, pulling it towards him and putting it in his lap.

At the hotel, Tracey checked me into a room while Nathan parked the car, then sent me upstairs to take a long bath and warm up.

'Nathan seems nice,' I said to Tracey. She smiled and made googly eyes at me.

'You really like him then?'

'Like? It's *l'amour* actually if you really want to know.'

'I'm really pleased for you, Trace.'

She smiled. 'It's so good to see you again,' and gave me a big hug. 'Right, better let you get sorted. See you down in the bar when you're ready.'

The room was sumptuous, not at all what I was expecting. From the outside, it was quite unassuming but inside it could rival the best London boutique hotels. I took off my clothes, stuffing them into a laundry bag I found in a drawer and wrapped myself in huge, fluffy bathrobe that was hanging behind the bathroom door. Pouring in a liberal amount of the *L'Occitane de Provence* bath foam that was on the side of the bath, I filled it to the brim with wonderful hot water. The smells were heavenly. I lay down on the bed while I waited for the bath to run, luxuriating in the deep, squashy mattress, so unlike the lumpy one at the cottage. I hadn't realised quite how much I had missed a decent bed.

When the bath was full, I slipped off the bathrobe and dipped my toes into the water. It was as hot as I could manage and as I climbed in and slid down, the heat enveloped me and started to thaw out the chill in my bones. It felt absolutely glorious. Ducking my head under the water, I pushed my hair back. I would wash it in a while. First, I just wanted to enjoy the sensation of lying in a bath for the first time since I had arrived in France.

Hair washed and conditioned, and body scrubbed to within an inch of its life, I climbed out, trying not to notice the dirty grey colour of the water. Tracey was right. I must have looked a sight. I caught my reflection in the mirror. One good thing about 'The Julien Business' and the hours spent chopping wood was that my croissant top had gone. Cleaned and polished, I didn't look too bad. I wrapped myself in a downy, white bath towel, winding another one round my head and went into the bedroom to sit down in front of the mirror. I looked hard at myself. I certainly wasn't a good advert for living the dream in France. My hair needed cutting, I had dark circles under my eyes and my hollow cheeks were just the wrong side of fashionable.

I tried hard not to think too much about why Tracey was making me homeless. It didn't add up. Sighing, I brushed out my hair – I'd find out soon enough no doubt.

I walked into the bar and looked around for Tracey and Nathan. They were deep in conversation, holding hands across the table in a quiet corner of the room. They were so obviously in love. I thought of Julien and the great times we had had and all the while he was cheating on me, and on Jo. I had always thought Louis was the one who couldn't be trusted but clearly I was wrong. So far I had proved to be a lousy judge of character.

I walked over to them and sat down. It was the first chance I'd had to see Nathan properly.

'Oh my God!' I said excitedly. 'You're Nathan from...'

He smiled and stopped me mid-sentence. 'And nobody needs to know.'

'What do you want to drink?' Tracey asked. 'Still on the *rosé*?'

'Forever.'

Tracey ordered a bottle then studied me carefully, brow slightly furrowed. 'I guess you are wondering what this is all about?'

'You could say that.'

'OK. Well here's the thing. My new album is doing really well over in the States and I've just signed a huge deal with a new record company and they've given me an advance that would make your eyes water. Might even buy you lunch in the café.'

'Well, you could if it wasn't closed. Stéphane and Claire left months ago,' I told her.

'Yeah, I heard. Anyway, I know we got off to a pretty rocky start...'

'You could say that.'

Tracey turned to Nathan, 'Did I tell you about it?'

'Yeah, you did. It was pretty full-on,' he replied.

Turning to me, she said, 'But you became a great friend and you helped me through a lot of shitty times with Warren and that. So I've bought it.'

'The cottage? Yes I know,' I answered, confused.

'Not the cottage, the café.'

'Sorry? You've bought the café?'

'Yep. You're looking at the new owner.'

I was puzzled. 'But you live in LA now. What do you want with a café in France?'

'Just think of it as an investment. Anyway, I've bought it and I'd like you to run it for me.'

I was stunned. I stared at her, chin in my lap.

'But I don't know the first thing about running a café.'

'That's why I've paid Stéphane and Claire to come back and help you for a few months.'

I was stunned, 'But where does the cottage fit in?'

'Staff accommodation. For my new manager.' Tracey smiled at me.

I stared at her, trying to fully comprehend what she was saying. 'But then why the notice? Why are you kicking me out of it?'

'So I can get it fixed up. You know, proper toilet, central heating. Can't have the management freezing to death in the winter. I've already spoken to Jack and he's really happy to come back and run the kitchen. It's going to be the first *rosé* bar and restaurant in the area. I'm calling it "La Vie en Rosé". The French probably won't get it but never mind.'

'But I don't know anything about *rosé*,' I stammered, completely flabbergasted at the turn of events.

'I seem to remember you know how to drink it though.' Tracey smiled at me. 'Look, are you up for it or what? I can afford to pay for whatever help you need to get you started. If you need to go on wine tasting courses and learn more about *rosé*, you can. Might even come on a few with you.'

I laughed. 'You know you are supposed to spit it out.'

'Pah! Spitting's for lightweights. We'll drink it and still be the last ones standing. Well?'

I flung my arms round her and squeezed her so hard that she had to cry out for me to stop. A million different thoughts were careering round in my brain. Just when I thought the dream was over, I'd been thrown the most unexpected lifeline. Not only that, but a friend I thought I'd lost was back in my life again, and for good now. Everything had finally fallen into place. It had been a long time coming but I had got there in the end.

'Tracey Tarrant, you are a bloody marvel. I'll even buy your new album.'

'Too right you will.'

'But I won't have to play it in the café will I?'

Tracey laughed and signalled to the waiter. 'A bottle of your finest champagne, *monsieur*. We're celebrating.'

Chapter Thirty-seven
Six Weeks Later

The sun shone down from a clear April sky. It was almost a year to the day since my arrival in France. I opened up the doors of the café and went outside to watch the little village slowly come to life. It was my favourite time of the day. I waved to Claudine, who was just putting out her sandwich board advertising today's specials. She had never left. Instead she had bought a franchise from a bigger supermarket chain and her once dingy store was now a bustling little monument to French gastronomy and local produce. It had taken a threat to sell the shop to developers to turn it into flats to make the good people of Rocamour realise how important their local shop was. Next to the supermarket, a new arrival in the village had opened a little gift shop. Valérie, the owner, called out *'bonjour'* as she unlocked her shop and I called back at her to come over for a coffee later.

I started to wipe down the new spotty oilcloths that adorned each table and arrange the little white jugs of wild flowers, putting the chairs straight as I went. Finally, it was the moment to unfurl the awning. I wound it down and slowly the words came into view. La Vie en Rosé. Tracey had been right. The locals didn't get it, assuming that it was just a misprint by the foreigners that now ran the café, but we didn't care. We had spent time trawling round the local vineyards sourcing wines for our stock. I wasn't an expert by any means but I knew what I liked and hopefully our guests would like them too.

'Morning,' said Jack, coming out of the kitchen wiping his hands on his apron. 'Here's the menu for today.'

I looked at it. 'It all sounds delicious, chef.' We were fully booked for lunch so it was going to be busy.

I swept the terrace, then, when I was finally happy that everything was in order, I stood back and looked around me with a growing sense of pride. The café was unrecognisable from the place it had been before. The old tables and interior had gone to be replaced by shiny bistro tables and lashings of Farrow and Ball paint, imported at vast expense from Paris. It was probably more of an English person's view of a French café but every time I went inside, I loved the way the light reflected around the room on the antique furniture that Tracey and I had sourced at various *brocantes* over the past few months. Tracey, despite her Essex roots (and my preconceptions), turned out to have a good eye for furniture.

My phone beeped and I took it out of my pocket. It was a text from Tracey.

> 'Lots of love and luck on your first day of trading. Trace and Nate xxxx'

I smiled and quickly texted back a thank you.

Basil rubbed around my legs and I picked him up and buried my face in his fur.

'It's just the two of us now.'

He purred and rubbed his head on my cheek. I looked around me. Everything was ready. Jack came out of the kitchen, beaming from ear to ear.

'Ready boss?' he asked, winking at me.

'I like the sound of that. And yes, I'm ready.'

'Right, we have twenty covers for lunch and another twenty booked for this evening.'

'Fabulous. Good old Chummy calling in the troops.' I think she had press-ganged everyone she knew into booking a table for our opening day.

Jack went back into the kitchen and I sat down at a table to take a quick breather before the lunchtime rush started. Stéphane and Claire were busy behind the bar and enjoying the prospect of helping me get the café up and running again. They had been absolute stars, cheerfully imparting their wealth of knowledge of the business, genuinely delighted that the café was going to stay open. Who'd have thought, when I had lunch here on my first day in France, that I would one day end up running it. I had set out on this journey full of hope, enthusiasm and a healthy dose of naivety. Now, a year later, I had found love and lost it, discovered strengths I didn't know I had and learned more about myself than I could possibly have dreamed of. Best of all, I had found my place in this little rural community that had stolen my heart.

'Hello, you,' called a voice I hadn't heard in a while. I waved to Sam and she waved back enthusiastically.

'Sam, how lovely!'

She kissed me on both cheeks and sat down, taking out a notebook and pen. She'd called me to suggest writing a review of the new café. Basil wound himself around her ankles, purring loudly. Bending down to stroke him, she smiled at me and said to him quietly, 'You're living dangerously. Don't you know her history?'

'Stop,' I chided her playfully. 'Seriously, I didn't think your boss would let you come today.'

'Nothing like a bit of notoriety to sell papers,' she said, laughing and picking up her pen. Right, *mademoiselle la patronne*, tell me your story.'

Acknowledgements

There are so many people I want to thank that this is going to sound more like an Oscar acceptance speech.

Firstly, I'd like to thank everyone at Summersdale and beyond, especially Jen, Abi, Abbie and Lucy for taking on this novice writer and leading me through the publishing journey with such enthusiasm and kindness. It has been a thoroughly enjoyable experience.

I'd also like to thank all my friends in the UK and France for all their support and encouragement and especially to Victoria Butcher who came up with the fabulous title. My children, to whom this book is dedicated, who put-up with half empty lunchboxes, un-ironed school uniforms and ready meals while I toiled over my laptop for what must have seemed like forever. I have to thank my parents, who encouraged me to start my blog in France, from which this book grew, and nagged me to write my experiences down, even if it was only meant to be for posterity. And I can't forget my lovely friend, neighbour and photographer extraordinaire, Christo Nicolle for the lovely publicity photos he took.

And finally, to everyone who buys or reads this book. If it makes you smile at least once I'll have done my job. Thank you.

About the Author

Melanie has loved writing since she was big enough to hold a pencil. The advent of the blog gave her an outlet for her creativity and somewhere to tell the rather plentiful funny stories about her life and the many adventures she has had. Parts of her blog about her life in France were reprinted in the 'Femail' section of the *Daily Mail* in 2009.

She is a serial mover, having now moved over twenty times in her life including spells in Bahrain, Ireland, Cyprus, Portugal and most recently, France, where she spent five years trying to understand the intricacies of the French bureaucratic system – and largely failing. After a career that included magazine publishing, Arts funding, celebrity PR, product placement and a brief stint as an air stewardess, she now lives in Wiltshire where she is an expert on the location of any cow in the county (and sheep and pigs too).

Melanie raises Orpington hens, has two amazing children, a lovely husband, a deaf cat with odd-coloured eyes, his very needy brother and the world's stupidest Lurcher puppy.

LUNCH IN PARIS
A Delicious Love Story, with Recipes

Elizabeth Bard

ISBN: 978 1 84953 154 2

Paperback   £8.99

*'This is amazing,' I said. 'You have to give me the recipe.'
'There is no recipe,' he said, smiling. 'I use whatever I have. It never
tastes the same way twice.'*

*I had no way of knowing, that first damp evening in Paris, how
this man, and his non-recipes, would change my life.*

Has a meal ever changed your life?

Part love story, part wine-splattered cookbook, *Lunch in Paris* is a
deliciously tart, forthright and funny story of falling in love with
a Frenchman and moving to the world's most romantic city – not
the Hollywood version, but the real Paris, a heady mix of blood
sausage, pains aux chocolats and irregular verbs.

From gutting her first fish (with a little help from Jane Austen) to
discovering the French version of Death by Chocolate, Elizabeth
Bard finds that learning to cook and building a new life have a
lot in common. Peppered with recipes, this mouth-watering love
story is the perfect treat for anyone who has ever suspected that
lunch in Paris could change their life.

*'Love, food and Paris – an irresistible combination… a witty,
readable and touching book that contains all the right ingredients'*
Helena Frith Powell, author of *Love in a Warm Climate*

TOUT SWEET
Hanging Up my High Heels for a New Life in France

Karen Wheeler

ISBN: 978 1 84024 761 9

Paperback   £8.99

In her mid-thirties, fashion editor Karen has it all: a handsome boyfriend, a fab flat in west London and an array of gorgeous shoes. But when Eric leaves, she hangs up her Manolos and waves goodbye to her glamorous city lifestyle to go it alone in a run-down house in rural Poitou-Charentes, central western France.

Acquiring a host of new friends and unsuitable suitors, she learns that true happiness can be found in the simplest of things – a bike ride through the countryside on a summer evening, or a kir or three in a neighbour's courtyard.

Perfect summer reading for anyone who dreams of chucking away their BlackBerry in favour of real blackberrying and downshifting to France.

'Tout sweet' is one of those rare books that you feel very sorry to finish because it was such a good read ! Immediately engaging, witty, full of extravagant,...   Patti Houisse

'The plot may be fairly familiar in the fish-out-of-water in France mould... but this take on it by a former fashion editor with the Mail on Sunday proves to be...
The Traveller in France, November 2009

Have you enjoyed this book?
If so, why not write a review on your favourite website?

If you're interested in finding out more about our books, find
us on Facebook at **Summersdale Publishers** and follow us on
Twitter at **@Summersdale**.

Thanks very much for buying this Summersdale book.
www.summersdale.com